STRAINS OF UTOPIA

STRAINS OF UTOPIA

GENDER, NOSTALGIA, AND HOLLYWOOD FILM MUSIC

Caryl Flinn

PRINCETON UNIVERSITY PRESS

PRINCETON, NEW JERSEY

COPYRIGHT © 1992 BY PRINCETON UNIVERSITY PRESS

PUBLISHED BY PRINCETON UNIVERSITY PRESS, 41 WILLIAM STREET,

PRINCETON, NEW JERSEY 08540

IN THE UNITED KINGDOM: PRINCETON UNIVERSITY PRESS, OXFORD

ALL RIGHTS RESERVED

LIBRARY OF CONGRESS CATALOGING-IN-PUBLICATION DATA

FLINN, CARYL.

STRAINS OF UTOPIA : GENDER, NOSTALGIA,

AND HOLLYWOOD FILM MUSIC / CARYL FLINN.

P.   CM.

INCLUDES BIBLIOGRAPHICAL REFERENCES AND INDEX.

ISBN 0-691-04801-0

—ISBN 0-691-00619-9 (pbk.)

1. MOTION PICTURE MUSIC—UNITED STATES—HISTORY AND CRITICISM.   I. TITLE.

ML2075.F55   1992   91-37867   CIP   MN

THIS BOOK HAS BEEN COMPOSED IN LINOTRON CALEDONIA

PRINCETON UNIVERSITY PRESS BOOKS ARE PRINTED ON ACID-FREE PAPER,

AND MEET THE GUIDELINES FOR PERMANENCE AND DURABILITY OF THE

COMMITTEE ON PRODUCTION GUIDELINES FOR BOOK LONGEVITY OF THE

COUNCIL ON LIBRARY RESOURCES

PRINTED IN THE UNITED STATES OF AMERICA

1   3   5   7   9   10   8   6   4   2

1   3   5   7   9   10   8   6   4   2

(Pbk.)

For Manuel Aybar

CONTENTS

ACKNOWLEDGMENTS

I WOULD LIKE to thank Rick Altman, Dudley Andrew, Daniel Cottom, Simon Frith, Sabine Gölz, Susan McClary, and Lauren Rabinovitz, all of whom offered close and careful readings of earlier drafts of this book. For their help as my ideas for individual chapters began to take shape, I would like to express my gratitude to Franklin Miller, Tania Modleski, Patrice Petro, Dana Polan, Geoff Waite, and Shari Zeck. Special thanks also go to Kaja Silverman for her long-time support. The personal and intellectual encouragement of these people has been helpful beyond measure.

I would also like to extend my appreciation to my many fine colleagues and students at the University of Florida, and to the English Department and the Division of Sponsored Research there for the support and release time that made writing portions of this book possible.

Thanks are also due to Jeff Johnson, Victor Vallo, and Robena Cornwell for their help with musicological research, and to Joanna Hitchcock, my editor at Princeton University Press, for her conscientious work and enthusiastic support.

Portions of this book appeared in previously published articles. For their permission to reprint, I would like to acknowledge *Cinema Journal* for "The Most Romantic Art of All: Music in the Classical Hollywood Cinema," 29, no. 4 (Summer 1990); *Canadian University Music Review* 10 no. 2, for "Male Nostalgia and Hollywood Film Music: The Terror of the Feminine"; and *Screen* for "The 'Problem' of Femininity in Theories of Film Music," 27, no. 6 (November–December 1986). Lyrics to *I'll Go Home with Bonnie Jean* (Alan Jay Lerner, Frederick Loewe). © 1947 Chappell & Co. (Renewed). All Rights reserved. Used by permission.

STRAINS OF UTOPIA

INTRODUCTION

A Deeply Nostalgic Strain

W HEN DMITRI TIOMKIN received the Academy Award for
the score of *The High and the Mighty* in 1955, he gave the
following broken acceptance speech: "Ladies and gentle-
men . . . I like to make some kind of appreciation to very important factor
which makes me successful and adds to quality of this town. I like to
thank Johannes Brahms, Johann Strauss, Richard Strauss, Richard Wagner. . . ."[1] There were peals of laughter. Perhaps the audience did not
understand just how much Tiomkin's words actually said about the impact
of classical music on the cinema and about Hollywood's debt to romanticism in particular (curiously, Tiomkin did not intend the joke).[2] Indeed,
his remarks sum up many years of studio scoring practices and honor a
composing style that, at the time of the 1955 Awards, was on its way out.
The nostalgic component of Tiomkin's words also points to a larger discursive tendency that, as this study explores, associates film music with the
idea of anteriority and idealized pasts.

The anecdote about Tiomkin circulates rather widely, in fact, although
it is usually read as little more than an insider's clever wink at Hollywood's
tendency to recycle music. And if common wisdom would have it, there
was not much to recycle in the first place. Film music has the rather curious distinction of being at the periphery of most people's concerns about
the cinema. In fact most studies of film music introduce themselves with
a comment on just how little has been done in the field. Music, the claim
is, has been ignored, its melodies, unheard[3] (one study in 1977 pro-
claimed it "a neglected art").[4] It is almost as if film music—to invoke the
past again—has to be absented before it can even be critically approached.

When I first began work on this book, I was tempted to make these
same claims and argue that film music had been egregiously "overlooked"
by scholars. After all, it has scarcely received the kind of critical attention
that genres like the Western have, nor has it sparked the level of animated
debate that film editing has over the years. Yet to call it neglected is, I
think, to overstate the case. True, one can count on a single hand the
number of scholars working on film music today, but this is a far cry from
calling the discourse silent. More important, it never was silent. As early
as the 1910s, there were primers, "how-tos" published for budding cinema
composers; in the 1920s, film music columns appeared in trade maga-
zines. During the studio era, practitioners and critics alike emphasized
the role music played in film; studios conveyed their interest by sinking

considerable money into their music departments, and, as early as 1934, Oscars were awarded for film scores. There are also the films them-selves—with scores that have always powerfully demonstrated to me that music is never really as "background" as some people might want to argue. These givens, such as they are, make it impossible for me to consider the field of film music as quiet or "neglected" as others have maintained

Yet at the same time it would be wrong to suggest that the literature of film music is without problems, for the work of a variety of commenta-tors—practitioners, popular critics, theorists, and scholars alike—has been limited by a number of methodological and conceptual problems. Most prominent among them is an aesthetic and formalist tendency that treats film music as a discrete, autonomous artefact. Scores are discussed outside of their cinematic context—in much the same way that music has been isolated from its social and historical setting within traditional musi-cology. By focusing on allegedly pure musical patterns and structures, this approach will often overlook how the score interacts with other facets of the cinema (concerns of narrative, editing, or genre, as well as the psycho-logical, social, and ideological factors of film consumption). It considers music simply as an art form.

The pitfalls of this approach are many. On one level, it reduces inter-pretation to a series of rudimentary analytical gestures: the formalist critic would not ask, for instance, how a rondo in a film score operates within the context of the film as a whole, nor consider the way it generates the mean-ings it does, but would assess it according to its adherence (or lack thereof) to conventional rondo form, checking for its "completeness," "correct-ness," and so on. When it is considered alongside other aspects of the film text, the score is put up for judgment: does it correspond, for instance, to the story's historical setting? Serial music would be considered inappro-priate, say, for a film such as *The Adventures of Robin Hood* (1938)—although Erich Korngold's actual score, composed in the style of late nine-teenth-century romanticism, has scarcely been attacked for committing the same infidelity (we will see why in a moment).[5] A highly evaluative critical enterprise, formalism has been concerned largely with the pre-sumed aesthetic successes or failures of musical form and structure.

Another aspect of film music scholarship against which this study is measured involves the efforts of critics to raise the status of their object of study, a feat typically achieved at the expense of the cinema more gener-ally. Here music and film are placed into categories of high and low art forms respectively, opposing "classical" art music to the mass-produced cinema, with the former receiving value only insofar as the latter is bereft of it (an argument with a certain self-defeating edge, to be sure). Critics have also felt compelled to "rescue" film music from its apperceived neglect or undervaluation by championing the creative abilities of individual composers who, like the directors with whom they collaborated, are usually approached as great auteurs (Bernard Herrmann, Alfred Hitchcock's long-time composer, often attracts this kind of criticism). Like the more properly formalist approach, the auteur-centered approach seldom considers film music beyond aesthetic criteria; also like the former it does not interrogate the mechanisms that enable music to create the effects it does so much as evaluate them.

Countercurrents to this trend do exist, and most have appeared over the last twenty years in the wake of the larger poststructuralist paradigm that has been reshaping the critical assumptions of earlier film studies. Claudia Gorbman's work perhaps best exemplifies this. Her book *Unheard Melodies* treats film music as a semiotic—as opposed to an aesthetic—phenomenon. In contrast to the formalist, Gorbman explores how the effects of non-diegetic music have become conventionalized, made unobtrusive and verisimilitudinous within narrative cinema. Gorbman concentrates chiefly on music's function in the film texts; she is somewhat less critical of the ways it has been positioned in theoretical discourse.

Scholars have only just begun to confront the relationship of film music to ideology. The problem here, as within musicology at large, is not a simple one. An obstacle plaguing them both involves the fact that music's current ideological function is, as we learned from the Frankfurt School, to generate the illusion of having none. Another problem for film studies in particular is the strong visual bias that surrounds the cinema generally. Film is, after all, widely understood as a primarily visual medium, an ontological misconception we uphold whenever we identify images without sound as a "moving picture" but do not for a soundtrack without images. (French composer Maurice Jaubert reminds us that "We do not go to cinema to hear music.")[6]

It is not surprising that this visual orientation has infiltrated film studies to the extent that it has (consider mise-en-scène criticism), or that it is been reflected in production procedures (during the studio era, film scores were rarely started until the picture had already been shot and edited). Contemporary theory, for its part, continues to emphasize cinema's visual component. Exemplary here is the work of Laura Mulvey and Raymond Bellour, who have argued that Hollywood narrative film and its patterns of consumption are based on scopophiliac and voyeuristic drives—structures of looking, as Bellour and Mulvey have so influentially asserted, that are believed to provide the very backbone of the classical cinema.

Recent work in film sound is beginning to expose the ideological factors behind this set of assumptions. Jean-Louis Comolli, for instance, has re-

ferred to the "ideology of the visual," which organizes so many components of our culture; scholars have continued after him to observe how this
ideology grants an epistemological privilege to sight at the expense of
hearing: to say "I see," after all, is to mean that one knows or understands,
whereas "I hear you" implies less a rational comprehension than an empathetic, emotional form of agreement.

Sound has thus come to function as sight's lesser counterpart, performing the role of an irrational, emotional "other" to the rational and episte-
mologically treasured visual term. Although film theory is increasingly
cognizant of this idea, it does not always move beyond it. Consider the
following insights by Mary Ann Doane:

> The ineffable, intangible quality of sound—its lack of the concreteness which
> is conducive to an ideology of empiricism—requires that it be placed on the
> side of the emotional or the intuitive. If the ideology of the visible demands
> that the [film] spectator understand the image as a truthful representation of
> reality, the ideology of the audible demands that there exist simultaneously
> a different truth and another order of reality for the subject to grasp.[7]

Doane rightly and succinctly observes that knowledge and sight have
been bifurcated from intuition and sound. Yet rather than rework this
arbitrarily and ideologically imposed division (to maintain instead, for
instance, that there exists a dialectic interaction between them), her
argument appeals to the very binary opposition it is unmasking. Sound
remains curiously "other."

It seems unlikely that the "different order of reality" Doane describes is
really *that* different or that it lies entirely beyond the scope of more traditional, visual, and rational understandings of the world. Are sound and
music in fact alien creatures? On the other hand, however, if we insist on
sound's *connection to* conventional representation, we need to acknowledge its different position in discourse from visual, linguistic, and other
more representational sign systems, for it would be naive to deny music
its distinctive features or to argue that it produces the same kinds of effects
that images do. In fact, sounds themselves work in a variety of ways. The
cinema soundtrack, for instance, has three main components, each of
which enjoys a different kind of relationship to the items raised in Doane's
observations. Sound effects are usually motivated by diegetic activity, and
dialogue is bound to a rational, ordered linguistic system. The two hardly
disrupt the representational ambitions of the classical cinema Doane describes. Music, particularly non-diegetic music, appears to stray furthest
from the "ideology of the visible" Comolli describes and promotes the
kind of epistemological unsteadiness Doane outlines. To begin with, its
source within the film's fictional world cannot be accounted for. It also
creates largely emotional effects and is distinctly nonverbal and nonrefer-
ential. Some have claimed that the representational and epistemological

alternative that music suggests undermines semiosis itself and have come to understand music as—to borrow a term from feminism—the "ruin of representation."

What makes music so "ruinous" or, more judiciously put, so untraditional? Semioticians like Eco, Jakobson, and others have commented that although music is a legitimate sign system, its meanings are extremely difficult to fix and ascribe. (Consider the problem of referentiality: does Claude Debussy's *La Mer* conjure forth oceanic ebbs and flows to an auditor unaware of its title?) Since music is not a denotative sign system, even its connotative associations are often little more than well-worn clichés (a piece in a minor mode is usually contemplative or "sad" to Western ears, particularly when performed slowly; brass instrumentation will often suggest heroic or regal action, and so forth). The problem facing film music scholars is how to talk concretely and specifically about the effects generated by a signifying system that is so abstract.

The ideological and semiotic issues raised by recent theory do not offer answers to this kind of question so much as reinforce the deep-rootedness of the problem. As I have already indicated, the idealized conception of music that considers it an autonomous art form enjoys a long, intricate history—one whose full range I cannot hope to cover in this brief work. A number of its supporting principles, however, can be traced back to nineteenth-century romanticism, a movement that emphatically separated music and musician from the world of mundane realities, and a movement that had a tremendous impact on the way Hollywood film music has been and continues to be conceptualized. Several points, which are pursued in more detail in the opening chapter, are worth introduction here. The first is romanticism's belief that music's immaterial nature lends it a transcendent, mystical quality, a point that then makes it quite difficult for music to speak to concrete realities. Even the more material structural features of music are believed to achieve much the same end. Because music depends on a relatively self-contained system of formal and mathematical relations, its existence was—and still is—considered more or less independent of the world as we know it. It is not believed to derive any influence from the social world nor to exert any upon it. Like all "great art" so construed, it takes its place outside of history where it is considered timeless, universal, functionless, operating beyond the marketplace and the standard social relations of consumption and production.[8] For traditional aestheticians and critics, of course, these are precisely the properties that enable music to be elevated above other, more representational (and especially visual) art forms; Walter Pater's famous dictum, "All Art constantly aspires to the condition of music" comes immediately to mind here.[9]

It should be directly stated that my own study does not share this romantic understanding of music. But for however misguided the idea that music enjoys an extracultural status may be, it would be equally mis-guided to discard it for its lack of theoretical, ideological, or political pro-priety. Nor will its influence be diminished by simply wishing it away, for romanticism has most decidedly shaped the way film music has been put into discourse. So, rather than abandoning this tradition, I will be examin-ing one of the main roles music has played within it—what I call its uto-pian function.

Film Music and the Promise of Utopia

In *La musique et l'ineffable*, Vladimir Jankélévitch writes that "music can take anything."[10] Jankélévitch's remark aptly expresses the widely held belief in the seemingly open-ended power of music. There is a long criti-cal tradition that supports his claim, a tradition that enforces the notion of music as a relaxed semiotic system capable of boundless effects and mean-ings. Music is almost magical: it entrances, seduces, and, in Congreve's famous phrase, "has charms to soothe a savage breast." It might incite a group to war or riot, or work like a narcotic and infantilize its listener. Or it might, like Proust's madeleine, produce absented pleasures through its sensual suggestiveness. Commonplace expressions like "wine, women, and song" suggest, moreover, that the delights of music are feminine ones: mother's lullaby soothes; the Sirens' lure seduces. Sometimes music is anything but sensual, as it was for Jean-Philippe Rameau in the eight-eenth-century or in the serial music of the twentieth when composition was commandeered by the principles of rationalism, order, and scientific calculation.

Indeed music is a lot of things, so many that one might conclude it is bereft of any imprint of its own or that it passively awaits meanings to be imposed upon it. As Eisler observes, music's abstract nature makes it par-ticularly susceptible to ideological encoding, and that it operates within different cultures as a sort of tabula rasa. From this he also—and rightly—discerns that music's functions do not emerge automatically or naturally but as a result of having been culturally assigned. It seems reasonable in this regard to expect a certain diversity to characterize music's different cultural inscriptions, especially given how it is widely understood to be so immaterial, unbounded, socially disinterested, and so on. One would think, in other words, that music could serve any number of functions and generate a wide array of meanings. But this is not the case.

In spite of the divergent claims made for music, many share the notion that it enjoys what Doane calls sound's "different" status, that it is, in other words, a phenomenon so abstract and otherworldly that it somehow remains immune to the influences of its immediate social, institutional, and discursive framework. It is as if music existed outside the base, material facts of culture. (These are the kinds of assumptions that have long been the bread and butter of Western musicology, a field that to this day has been slow to acknowledge the influence of culture, economics, and ideology on its object of study.)[11]

But this presumed transcendence does not suggest that music is finally as random or free-floating as critics might have it. Indeed, its abstract nature has not stopped commentators across a wide range of disciplines from coming to a rather striking consensus about its function. Music, they maintain, has the peculiar ability to ameliorate the social existence it allegedly overrides, and offers, in one form or another, the sense of something better. Music extends an impression of perfection and integrity in an otherwise imperfect, unintegrated world. This is the utopian function I believe has been assigned to music in general and to film music of the 1930s and 1940s in particular.

But how has this general utopian function taken shape? The impulse to divest music of mundane associations extends well beyond nineteenth-century romanticism, even though it was engaged with special force then. Today, we are still bombarded with the idea of music as a transcendent phenomenon. We find it in the conception of music as a "universal language" that overrides national and linguistic boundaries; or in Suzanne Langer's claim for it as "the total analogue of emotional life"[12]; or in certain pop cultural criticism that argues for the subversive, revolutionary power of forms like rock and roll. One notes the idea taking form as far back as Plato, who considers specific modes and instruments as sources of social and sexual unrest; in St. Augustine, who argues that rhythm both appeals to human senses and strives beyond them for higher, spiritual completion;[13] and in the medieval conception of music as the manifestation of a celestial harmony of the spheres.

As these examples illustrate, the utopian projections of music are construed differently according to their different critical and historical contexts. For the aesthetician, music's utopian function is derived from its presumed purity of form, for others through its allegedly authentic emotional expression. Still others appreciate the fullness of experience it purportedly offers its listeners or its ability to return them to better, allegedly more "perfect" times and memories. There are critics who connect music's utopia to its existence as a sign system. For them, music offers a radically alternative mode of signification—some go so far as to claim that musical forms actually threaten to undermine social order. (In his *Republic*, Plato responded to this by censuring the music he thought capable of producing these effects.) But whether encouraged or feared, music has been repeatedly and compulsively tied to the idea of some kind of social surfeit or excess.

The cinema is a generous host to this idea. One need only recall Marylee Hadley's patricidal mambo to the song "Temptation" in *Written on the Wind* (1956) or Fred Astaire's boisterous tapping that disrupts the stuffy reading lounge at the beginning of *Top Hat* (1935). In *The Lady Vanishes* (1938), a whistled melody conveys key espionage information, and Maurice Jarre's scores for films like *Ryan's Daughter* (1970), Weir's *The Year of Living Dangerously* (1983), and *Witness* (1985) romanticize the cultural "otherliness" of the films' Irish, Indochinese, and Amish worlds.

What sustains these connections between music and utopia? To begin with, there is music's non-representational component. I have already suggested how this feature has prompted critics to withdraw music from the realities of everyday life, an act that already sets the stage for a utopian scenario. Moreover, the idea of utopia is itself etymologically linked to the non-representable since it is a "no place," a society that cannot be put into representation (much less practice) but only described and alluded to, talked "about." In this way, music's abstract nature gains special resonance. Music also prompts the impression of utopia by being able to provoke such great degrees of affect in its listeners, an ability that, as I address in chapters three and four, is especially important in generating the feelings and impressions we associate with utopia.

This book examines how a group of diverse responses to film music have lent expression to its utopian components: industrial, practitional, aesthetic, psychoanalytic, and Marxist discourses alike uphold music's ability to conjure forth remote, impossibly lost utopias. I will be dividing these responses into two camps. The first, what I call the classical approach, had the greatest impact during the studio era and has remained the dominant theoretical and practitional approach to film music since the mid-1930s. The second, what I call the contemporary school, emerges from the work of recent critical theorists like Roland Barthes and Julia Kristeva (and, in a more complex fashion, Theodor Adorno). Both of these critical traditions uphold a utopian conception of music in the purist sense of the word—that is, as an impossible, plenitudinous, and nostalgic condition.

My own interest in the musical utopias of film departs from these accounts as well as from traditional uses of the word *utopia*. As it has been historically engaged, the term usually refers to a programmatic blueprint for an ideal society: think here of the work of Robert Owen, François Marie Charles Fourier, or Thomas More. (Owen and Fourier carefully outline how labor is to be organized in their utopias; More requires his to be geographically situated on an island—a detail that once again isolates utopia from the "real" world). My own use of the word is less indebted to this tradition than it is derived from Richard Dyer's recent essay "Entertainment and Utopia," which explores how the Hollywood musical gener-

ates the impressions and sensations of utopia to its spectators and auditors. Much of this, as I will be exploring in more detail in chapter four, is
derived from the abstract activity of music, what Dyer identifies as its
"non-representational signs."

It is the assumption of this study that utopian expression is by its nature
limited and incomplete since its borders are continually laid down and
demarcated by such forces as economics, history, and human subjectivity.
Utopian thought never fully "escapes" ideology but can only be expressed
through it, through what Ernst Bloch identifies as "traces," signs whose
meanings tentatively point to a "something better" that texts yield under
certain hermeneutic conditions. But the promise of utopia is nonetheless
there—my point is simply that it does not emerge from a radically other
or representationally obscured place, as conventional approaches to utopia—and music—would have it.

The aim of this study, then, is to consider the strain of utopia in relation
to the discursive, institutional, and subjective context of Hollywood film
music. In this spirit I will be focusing on the utopian function of film music
within a specific period, the mid-1930s and 1940s, and will concentrate
heavily upon the generic and spectatorial issues involved in shaping this
utopia. In chapter one I will show how the ideology of romanticism organized the classical discourse on Hollywood film composition during the
1930s and 1940s. This romantic model was collectively upheld by practitioners, theorists, and industrialists, but, as we shall see, proved so inap-
plicable to the actual historical conditions of studio work that its dystopic
dimensions virtually overshadowed its utopian ones. Chapters two and
three examine the two theoretical traditions that constitute the contemporary approach to film music: the former explores the work of Barthes and
Kristeva, paying special attention to the psychoanalytic theory on which
their ideas of musical utopias are based; the latter covers the work of
Adorno and other Marxists who understand music's utopian capacity as
one that potentially critiques relations under capitalism.

Chapter four reintroduces and develops the idea of partial utopias in
film music. After that, I go on to analyze the role of music in film genres
popular during Hollywood's classical era, most notably film noir and the
maternal melodrama, to examine how the theoretical utopias of film music
take residence in actual texts. Since these meanings, as I argue, are produced by certain conditions of reception and subjectivity, their different
strains need to be assessed as a consequence of the competing notions of
subjectivity engaged by the films and by critics like me who read them in
search of certain kinds of utopia.

A brief explanation of a few of my terms and methodological assumptions is in order. First, I will not be enforcing rigid distinctions between
diegetic and non-diegetic music. This is not to disregard the fact that the

two are separate phenomena (for it would certainly be naive to argue that non-diegetic music in a film like *Gone with the Wind* [1939] operates the same way as do the diegetic performances in *The Band Wagon* [1953]), nor is it to ignore the fact that most of the criticism surveyed here is more applicable to non-diegetic than to diegetic music, since the criticism tends to highlight the differences between music and diegesis or score and narrative. Yet, if one is to argue that music performs a variety of functions in the classical Hollywood film, as I believe it does, it is necessary to consider as many different levels of musical activity as possible, and for this reason I have chosen to consider diegetic and non-diegetic music together. In the same vein, I will also be referring to the contributions of other potentially "musical," auditory elements as well.

One thing this book is *not* is a musicological study in any strict sense of the word. I leave it for persons with more rigorous musical training than I have to perform close formal analyses of individual film scores. My chief interests lie instead in highlighting the ways in which music has operated in the critical discourse surrounding Hollywood film—and not just in the films "themselves."

I should also stress that my approach to film music does not attempt to be exhaustive, nor is it objective. For in order to counter the idea that music functions in singular, timeless ways, critics approaching the topic must acknowledge the critical, historical, and discursive contexts that shape their own writing. As difficult as it is to pinpoint these kinds of contextual factors, it is important work that needs to be done. For, until critics bring the forces of history and subjectivity to bear upon the study of film music, it will continue to strain from under the burden of its allegedly "pure" utopias.

ONE

THE NEW ROMANTICISM

HOLLYWOOD FILM COMPOSITION

IN THE 1930S AND 1940S

It is the expression of an honorable wish to reach back
from an unlovely present to the past, and therefrom
to reconstruct lost beauty.
(Richard Wagner)

Filmmaking is a composite art, a Wagnerian
Gesamtkunstwerk, and film music should
be written in this way.
(Miklós Rózsa)

DURING THE Hollywood studio era, film music was assigned a
remarkably stable set of functions. It was repeatedly and systematically used to enhance emotional moments in the story line,
and to establish moods and maintain continuity between scenes. A similar
uniformity was suggested by its style as well, since most scores were composed in a manner deeply influenced by late romantic composers like
Richard Wagner and Richard Strauss. Even the well-funded and carefully
stratified music departments indicate the secure position the filmscore
enjoyed within studio production more generally. It is scarcely coinciden-
tal that this period of overall stability is usually identified as the "golden
age" of Hollywood composition, a period that started in the mid-1930s and
endured until the studio system began to draw to a close in the early
1950s. The period also coincides with what scholars generally consider to
be Hollywood's "classical" era of film production. Not surprisingly, critics
have noted how Hollywood scoring techniques became routinized and
standardized at about the same time that the style of the classical film was
itself established and secured.[1]

Because film music can be discussed in terms of achieving a certain
aesthetic and industrial stability during this period, as I believe it should,
it is reasonable to expect that a number of other forces—economic, critical, ideological—helped to keep this stability in place. Indeed, the
amount of work required to maintain a stable, dominant conception of film
music makes it impossible for me to consider composing's golden age a
simple historical "fact" or accident. This is not to suggest that the relation-

ship of aesthetic and industrial production was one of parity or of simple cause and effect. Rather, it is to insist that the two were mutually involved and that film music must be considered from within this kind of institutional and historical framework. For, as I indicate in the Introduction, most film music criticism has remained largely unconcerned with music's place in social and institutional contexts, and so, like the object it studies, it cloaks itself in the illusion of apparent transcendence.

What stabilized film music's "place" was a critical and practitional dominant, one that I label the "classical" understanding of film music. Several factors justify this choice of terms: First and foremost historically, it refers to the classical Hollywood cinema that initially gave rise to this approach. Second, it suggests the force of its continuing influence, for although the classical conception of film music was first implemented within specific historical and institutional contours, its principles are still very much with us (and in fact my interest in its continuing legacy informs this entire work). I should add, however, that the idea of classical film music should not be confused with the classical era of music history since scores were influenced by late romanticism and *not* by the earlier classicism. And if my terminology refuses to make rigid distinctions between the concrete application of film music and the more abstract claims made for it in critical discourse, or if it appears to simplify the relationship between "theory and practice," it must be stressed that to trace two parallel and separate accounts of film music would presume—quite wrongly—that these histories are mutually independent. For it is precisely the *confluence* of institutional practices and critical discourse that demonstrates just how extensive the classical approach to film music has been.

But what does this classical conception of film music entail? Simply put, it maintains that the score supports the development of the film's story line, that it exists to reinforce the narrational information already provided by the image.[2] Music, in other words, is supposed to be subordinated to the presumably loftier ambitions of narrative and imaging and should not draw attention to itself on its own—something summed up in 1946 by critic Gerald Cockshott: "If incidental music is to be used in film, its rôle should be that of an unobtrusive servant."[3] Of course, other nonnarrative components of the classical cinema—performance style, cinematography, editing—are required to fulfill this subordinate function to narrative as well, but it seems to me that music's servitude is one enforced with special vigor. What is more, there are special rules for this servitude, rules that adhere to the principles of Richard Wagner and late musical romanticism.

Film music's link to Wagner goes back a long way, and it would be silly to argue that the classical conception of film music and its affiliation with Wagnerian principles emerged all at once in 1935. As early as 1911, *The*

Moving Picture World was claiming that "Every man or woman in charge of the motion picture theatre . . . is a disciple or follower of Richard Wagner"[4]; the year before, it predicted that "Just as Wagner fitted his music to the emotions, expressed by words in his operas, so in course of time, no doubt, the same thing will be done with regard to the moving picture."[5] By 1920, critics were openly drawing connections between the leitmotiv, musical parallelism, and the Hollywood film (one notes that "abstractions" like "Love, Home, Mother, and Virtue had their motifs as clearly assigned to them as did the heroes and heroines of Wagner himself").[6] A larger general interest in film scores was also taking hold before the advent of sound, when columns on film scoring emerged in periodicals such as the *Dramatic Mirror* and *Moving Picture World*, and in trade journals like *Metronome* and *Melody Magazine*. Composition primers began to be published and film music cue sheets circulated quite widely. Music publishing houses sprung up and in 1914, ASCAP, the American Society of Composers, Authors, and Publishers, was established as a clearinghouse to protect copyrighted works of creative workers (importantly, as we will soon see, ASCAP did not benefit the studio composer since it secured performance rights and compensation and did *not* establish copyright).

Hollywood producers were quick to learn the value of music in the silent era. They learned, for example, that it was far easier and cheaper for them to commission original musical works than it was to secure licenses on previously written compositions, since rising publishing houses maintained a near-monopoly on available music. Studios responded to this situation by sinking investments into their own music publishing houses (MGM, for instance, established its own recording label and encouraged what the press called "musical detectives" to be on the lookout for uncopyrighted material that could be appropriated); they also hired house composers. By the time sound was ushered in, film composition already enjoyed a somewhat comfortable place within the studio system.

One could say that this stability was even hinted at in the films themselves. As scholars of sound in the cinema are forever at pains to note, motion pictures never really were "silent" since most were accompanied by live ensembles, keyboard soloists, or small orchestras. The conventions that developed during this period were so influential that, as Charles Berg has observed, many of them were carried over into the sound era. Consider the "unending melody" (one of the growing allusions to Wagner springing up in film music criticism in the 1910s and 1920s): since the dramatic action portrayed on the silent screen was constantly being interrupted by intertitles, it was important for the film to establish continuity at other levels and silent film music, which rarely came to a full stop, did just that. Curiously, however, and despite Berg's contentions, the practice of continual accompaniment lasted well into early sound films, long after the apparent "need" for it vanished. Paramount, for example, the first studio to use non-diegetic music, featured uninterrupted accompaniment throughout the entire length of many of its early sound films; RKO, where Max Steiner worked in the early 1930s, produced films like *Bird of Paradise* (1932) with one hundred percent saturation scores. (This is not to say that all early sound films were saturated with non-diegetic music: consider Universal's 1930 hit *All Quiet on the Western Front* or United Artists' *Scarface* [1932], whose scores remain virtually silent once the opening title theme is finished.) Important here is that although background music was used intermittently by the mid-1930s, theorists and practitioners never fully abandoned its connection to the idea of film continuity—if anything, this function became even more lavishly asserted and naturalized. For Kurt London, a prominent film music scholar writing in 1936, music had a consistency and uniformity that the film image (which he characterized in terms of variability and change) ontologically lacked.[7]

"Silent" film music served other functions as well. Berg has compiled a list in fact: it smothered sounds that might distract filmgoers, such as the noise of passing traffic, coughs, and chatter among audience members or the loud sounds of the projectors (as we shall soon see, during the sound era this function of "covering up" for deficiencies of the film listening situation underwent a certain displacement); it also lent dramatic support to the film in order to amplify and highlight significant moments in the narrative—something that would go on to become film music's most significant role in the classical era.

One wonders how much of this archaeology of film music is predicated on hindsight (was music in the silent period merely a dress rehearsal, a necessary phase leading to a certain inevitable conclusion?); at the same time, and more importantly, it demonstrates that film music's soon-to-be-classic task of reinforcing visual and dramatic material did not emerge point-blank in 1935, that instead it developed over time and hence cannot be construed as a "natural" or automatic property of film music itself.

Indeed this function of uniting score to image appeared initially not to have been guaranteed at all, if a remark from American composer Frederick Converse is any indication. "At first," he complains, "music was employed to cover the uncouth noises of the machines projecting the pictures. There was no thought of its relevancy or irrelevancy to the drama being enacted upon the screen. It was just to distract attention from this unpleasant and unavoidable concomitant of the picture."[8] Converse's distress over the apparent lack of unity between music and drama will resurface as one of the leading concerns in the classical commentary on film music. It also shows how the "synthesis" of music and visual drama was erratically and unevenly achieved—and perceived.

It should also be noted that the increase in parallel relations between story and music intensified only with the advent of narrative film. While early cinema had relied heavily (both aesthetically and economically) on spectacle value,[9] the ascension of a predominantly narrative film by the 1900s saw with it, according to Berg, the growing "realization that the music should relate in some way to the stream of ongoing images."[10] Whereas Berg goes on to maintain that this marks cinema's rising "sophistication," I would argue that it reveals instead the growing impact of Wagnerian aesthetics on film. For, just as motion pictures seemed to be striving for a greater synthesis of their elements, so were critics beginning to naturalize or privilege this particular way of putting music to film. The idea has proved so tenacious that, sixty years later, critics like Berg succumb to it, considering it an index of alleged cinematic sophistication and propriety.

It is worth introducing—however briefly at this point—the ideological stakes involved in the notion that music's "parallel" relation to the image is not a consequence of an ontological predisposition but is a product of certain institutional and discursive conditions. Because music's relationship to the image is constructed, it is clear that it must be constructed and arbitrated *by* something—and one would assume that ideology provides such an arbitrating force. Such questions did not emerge *tout à coup* with poststructuralism, however; critics were beginning to pose them as early as 1915, the year, it must be remembered, that *The Birth of a Nation* was released: "Music lends insidious aid to emphasize the teaching of the screen, for the tom-tom beats from time to time to convince us that the colored man, well drest [*sic*] and educated though he may be, came from Africa. Why is not some Asiatic instrument used to remind us that the Aryan race came from the wrong side of the Caucasus?"[11] Not only do these remarks demonstrate how the ideology of race can affect scoring practices, they also show that the presumed norm around which this early film music was organized (the subject, if you will, upon which this musical discourse was based) was not universal, but decidedly white and masculine. It is through these kinds of implied subjects, as we shall see later on, that ideology has orchestrated some of its most forceful—and insidious—effects in music.

For as much as the silent and early sound era set the stage for the classical understanding of film music, it was not until the mid-1930s, however, that these practices and techniques settled into a more or less stable set of conventions. These conventions, as I have already indicated, found in Wagner's work not only a stylistic model but a theoretical one as well. Of his theoretical concepts, the central ones were his notions of the *Gesamtkunstwerk*, or total artwork, which would supposedly unite all other arts (lyric poetry, drama, dance, vocal and instrumental music, and so forth); the *unendliche Melodie*, or unending melody, which describes the score's role of giving continuity to the film, since background music is often used to disguise cuts that might disorient spectators and auditors; there is also the Wagnerian leitmotiv—a brief musical theme associated with a dramatic idea, place, situation, or character which has proven enormously influential on the Hollywood cinema. Its presence is easily detected in any number of classical scores. One need think only of Max Steiner's "Tara's Theme" in *Gone with the Wind,* or of *The Big Sleep* (1946), where another Steiner leitmotiv signals the lambent love of Philip Marlowe and Vivian Rutledge.

For critics of film music, these observations on Hollywood's debt to romanticism are hardly new. Yet romanticism has done far more than simply determine the compositional shape of Hollywood film scores. In addition to giving Hollywood a formal and stylistic model, it provided ideological directives as well—directives that influenced the classical understanding of film music even in nonaesthetic arenas such as the legal, institutional, and critical discourses of the time. In fact film music's long-standing association with romanticism has dramatically—and detrimentally—affected the way it has been constituted as an object of study. Even today, some of the most sophisticated scholars and theorists continue to uphold—however indirectly—a fundamentally romantic notion of music. But it was during the studio era that the conventions found their strongest support, and at a number of different levels. Not the least of these was institutional.

Film Music in the Classical Studio Era

During the period we are examining, 1935–1950, the Hollywood studio system was operating at its most efficient. It seems only logical that this golden age of film composition should coincide with a period of wider economic vitality and gain, and indeed the classical conception of film composing did find considerable support within the studio. The carefully stratified music department was structured much like a miniature version of the studio itself, with relatively self-contained resources and facilities. Typically it had its own executive offices, sound stages for production and postproduction recording, libraries, work rooms for composing, and so on. Efficiently run, by the mid-to-late 1930s it had an average weekly output of one and a half full-length scores (full-length scores ran for about 25 to 50 percent of the film's playing time or approximately forty minutes.)[12] Work tasks, like those in the studio at large, were highly compartmentalized: film composers, for instance, seldom oversaw the orchestration of their own pieces and frequently worked in isolation from one another, sometimes on the same assignment (during the preproduction of *Gone with the Wind,* David O. Selznick apparently hired Franz Waxman to write a backup score for the film in case Steiner's proved unsatisfactory). So pronounced was the division of labor that it was not uncommon for composers to turn over their basic melodic lines to other composers to be harmonized or developed. Composers came to be known for their own particular "specialty" of composition: at MGM, for instance, Miklós Rózsa was usually selected to score historical dramas (*Julius Caesar* [1953], *Quo Vadis* [1951]), and big-budget musicals were frequently entrusted to André Previn.[13]

As with the studio more generally, these specialized jobs were arranged hierarchically. Heading the music department was the music director, an employee valued at least as much for his entrepreneurial acumen as for his musical skills (the late Johnny Green at MGM, for instance, studied economics at Harvard).[14] He oversaw production schedules, budgets, and personnel matters within the department and often worked in conjunction with producers and other higher-ups to determine which composers would be selected for particular film assignments. A middleman of sorts, the music director was often called upon to translate the economic imperatives of the studio and the aesthetic ideas of the director into musical terms and instructions for composers, who were rarely part of production decisions (the few who did were more the exception than the rule, such as Bernard Herrmann). No matter how established or marketable these composers were, however, they seldom had final say over their work, something dramatized even by Herrmann, whose collaboration with Orson Welles was something less than rewarding in this regard.[15] Yet this is not to suggest that composers were at the bottom of the pecking order: below them were other, secondary composers, cue-sheet preparers, assorted copiers, and orchestrators.

The music department, like most of Hollywood after the late 1920s, was largely unionized: engineers, sound technicians, and musicians all had trade unions to protect their interests. But the composers did not, even though several nonunion organizations emerged over time to protect their rights, such as the Studio Composer's Association (formed in 1945) and the Composers and Lyricists Guild (1950). These groups were formed partly because ASCAP was unable to protect the film composer, whose work was legally not his own but belonged to the studio, which, having initially commissioned the score, was then given legal proprietorship of it.

Other aspects of the composers' working situation would also have made a union distinctly helpful. Not only were they barred from production decisions but, as numerous anecdotes convey, they were often at the mercy of superiors who knew precious little about music (Hugo Friedhofer recalls a producer once telling him, "Now, since this story is set in France, we should hear lots of French horns.").[16] Scores had to be produced quickly; David Raksin recounts that Otto Preminger gave him one weekend to write his now-classic theme song for *Laura* (1944).[17] As a matter of course, a Hollywood film would already be shot and edited before the composer even began working on its score; at this point he would carefully time the print so that his music could duplicate its pace, rhythms, and emotions.[18] If the film were behind schedule or over budget—a hardly uncommon occurrence—the composer's resources would be hampered even more. Given this standard production procedure, it might appear that the score was institutionally guaranteed to function as a simple auxiliary to the film's image, and in fact, in the estimation of one studio historian, postproduction was the studio film's "least important phase."[19]

The Contemporary Music Scene

Such a highly industrialized backdrop yields no immediate explanation for Hollywood's adaptation of a late nineteenth-century romantic composing style. In much the same way, there was little synchrony between the music being produced by the studios and that which was coming out of the United States more generally. Hollywood film music was distinctly out of step.

One could say that American music of the time was twice removed from romanticism since it was trying to move past the modernism that characterized the international music scene during the 1900s, 1910s, and 1920s; and modernism, in turn, was known for its rejection of romanticism, along with all of its supposed excesses of emotion and form. These excesses, such as they were, were generally associated with Wagner—although they arguably found their last gasp in Gustav Mahler.[20] At any rate, it was Wagner who was usually used to represent metonymically the perceived indulgences and eccentricities of romanticism. (This was abetted by the cults that sprang up around the composer at the end of the nineteenth century; after World War II, of course, condemnations of Wagner—for his official "association" with Hitler—became even more commonplace.) Yet well before the Nazis, Wagnerian music and romanticism were being blamed for some of the problems of the twentieth century. Ernest Newman went so far as to suggest that the grandiose forms of late romanticism (e.g., Mahler's Eighth Symphony, the well-named "Symphony for a Thousand," which premiered in 1910) and its so-called decadent sensibilities were permanently laid to rest by World War I.[21] For critics like him, the war effected a "cleansing" of Europe and the creation of a new era—much as Wagner and Nietzsche had envisioned decades earlier.

In order for modernism to expel Wagner in particular and romanticism in general it had to abandon some of the movement's fundamental principles. Among them were its highly sensual, expressive understanding of music, its affiliation of music with human emotion and immanence and with the idea of ineffability.[22] Modernism's neo-classical movement of the early twentieth century relied instead on a calculated, scientific conception of music, emerging in practices like Arnold Schönberg and Alban Berg's twelve-tone systems. Not surprisingly, early modernists were engaged in a great degree of technical experimentation, as if technology somehow enabled music to move beyond the subjective excesses of its romantic predecessor. This tendency was part of a larger antinaturalist, formalist trend that was leaving its mark on other arts at the time, such as the poetry of Mayakovsky, constructivism in painting, the theatre of Meyerhold, the cinema of Eisenstein, and so forth. But despite the tremendous musical experimentation of the era, and despite the fact that a few vernacular American forms were integrated into several modernist works (e.g., Stravinsky's "Ragtime" and "Piano Ragtime"), modernism remained by and large a European phenomenon.

By the 1930s and 1940s, however, Europe was witnessing a retreat from modernist and formalist experimentation (in Germany and Stalinist Russia, such retreats were of course politically mandated), and things were changing in the United States as well. American music of the 1930s and 1940s was marked by just that—Americanism. Composers were turning to indigenous resources and forms in search of a proper "American" musical heritage. This was the period of Aaron Copland's "Rodeo" (1942), "Billy the Kid" (1938), and "Appalachian Spring" (1943–1944) and Virgil Thomson's filmscores for *The Plow that Broke the Plains* (1936) and *The River* (1937). In general, American music of the time was trying to divest itself of foreign influences, something humorously exemplified in such patriotic songs of the subsequent war era as "Don't be an Absentee" or "Praise the Lord and Pass the Ammunition."[23]

It is tempting to link the growing nationalism of America to the country's own growing self-interestedness and isolationism, to associate it with a growing conservative trend. But it is not that simple. For, as Barbara Zuck has shown, music of the Left was characterized by these same kinds of American issues and concerns. Consider for example the work of composers Mark Blitzstein (*The Cradle Will Rock* [1937]), Aaron Copland, and Alex North (who would go on to score films like *A Streetcar Named Desire* and *Spartacus* [both 1951]). In 1931, the Workers Music League, affiliated with the American Communist party, emerged, and two years later Charles Seeger (father of Pete) helped establish the New York Composers Collective.[24] Such groups paid considerable attention to popular musical forms such as folksongs, blues, and workers' songs as examples of "authentic" American music. There was, however, considerable debate about what the "proper" American form should be. Although many lauded these popular American tunes, Seeger and other leftists observed how unremarkable and formally conservative they were. Conclusions could not be reached. Even in hindsight, the debate is not easily reconciled since all intense searches for identity—musical or otherwise—require a common point of departure just as they demand a sense of diversity and flexibility. In the end, it seems impossible and even foolish to expect any one musical form to accommodate or fully represent a single national identity.

One thing that emerges quite clearly from the musical activity of the 1930s and 1940s, however, is an emerging sense of utopia, an ideal organized around the notion that collective identity—be it national, political, or cultural—could somehow be materialized through music. Musically this was believed to be achieved in one of two ways: by expelling foreign influences, as we have already seen, or by paring down the formal complexity of a work. As Oscar Levant argues, "there came a gradual recession in the excesses of the music that was being written, an attraction to simplicity, a reverence for clarity as opposed to the former [i.e., modernist] adoration of complexity. . . . The simple life became an ideal in a composer's music as well as in his personal habits."[25] Levant's remarks acknowledge the economic conditions that helped prompt the need for simplicity. This was, after all, the Depression, and despite efforts like the WPA's Federal Music Project, federal support for music was low. Aaron Copland maintains much the same idea in arguing that Depression conditions helped clear the way for *Gebrauchmusik*, or functional music, to enter the American musical scene, an idea that had important ramifications for the cinema:

> In all the arts the Depression had aroused a wave of sympathy for and identification with the plight of the common man. In music this was combined with the heady wine of suddenly feeling ourselves—the composers, that is—needed as never before. Previously our works had been largely self-engendered: no one asked for them: we simply wrote them out of our own need. Now, suddenly, functional music was in demand as never before. Motion-picture and ballet companies, radio stations and schools, film and theater producers discovered us. The music appropriate for the different kinds of cooperative ventures undertaken by these people had to be simpler and more direct. There was a "market" especially for music evocative of the American scene—industrial backgrounds, landscapes of the Far West, and so forth.[26]

Clearly the machinery was in place to support music's return to America's so-called simpler forms. Yet, as Copland's remarks also suggest, this desire entailed more than an amorphous, unchained nostalgia for presumably purer times. The folksong, the Western song and others all worked to construct a very specific utopia, one which assumed the guise of an idealized rural or small-town past, the kind Leo Marx describes in *The Machine in the Garden*[27] (Copland's extremely popular "Rodeo" is exemplary in this regard). Ironically, however, the raiding of the past operating in pieces like Copland's "Rodeo" can also be found in European modernism—the movement against which all of this musical Americanism was defining itself.

Modernism may have rebelled against its immediate romantic predecessor, but its interest in the structures and rationalism of the even earlier classical movement kept it firmly indentured to the past. It also ensured that the old repertory of Bach, Mozart, Haydn, et al. appeared frequently in contemporary concert programs. So influential was this revival that critics said the period was ruled by the "principle of obedience" and a "cult of cleanliness." The interpretive quirks and innovations that Mahler had made famous as a conductor fewer than thirty years before were no longer tolerated. Instead, the new classicists consulted the composers themselves—dead though they were—for the final word in authenticity and interpretive strategies. As Wanda Landowska, the well-known keyboard player, quipped to a rival at the time, "You play Bach your way, I will play him his way."[28] (With equal panache, however, Landowska is also quoted as saying "If Rameau himself would rise from his grave to demand of me some changes in my interpretation of his *Dauphine*, I would answer 'You gave birth to it; it is beautiful. But now leave me alone with it. You have nothing more to say; go away!' ")[29] In the same way that American music was turning to its own indigenous forms, modernism too had based its utopian models on earlier movements. (Richard Taruskin has argued in fact that the interest in early music and the drive toward "authenticity" in performance is a function *of* modernism.)[30]

It seems clear that regardless of the violence with which they might attempt to break from the past, then, artistic movements rely on their predecessors for definition and motivation—even if only to define themselves against them (think of the relationship of modernism to romanticism; postmodernism to modernism). And yet the disphasures (critical, ideological, and aesthetic) that these kinds of quotations and debts involve are terribly striking, especially in the case of Hollywood and late romanticism. Nor has the idea escaped commentators: Alberto Cavalcanti once observed that classical film music was "fixed" at a stage that the contemporary musical scene had long since abandoned;[31] in a discussion of Erich Korngold, one of Hollywood's few composers who also had a strong reputation in the art music world, musicologist Richard Shead writes that, though "brilliant," Korngold's "music was frankly backward-looking, combining elements of Strauss, Puccini, and even Franz Léhar in a mixture that . . . was well away from the mainstreams of contemporary music."[32]

Hollywood's New Romanticism

Why would romanticism hold such strong appeal for Hollywood? Clearly it had run its course more generally. It was not simply because studio composers had emigrated from Europe, where, according to common wisdom, they had been influenced by the legacies of Wagner and Strauss, and not, apparently, by the more recent Schönberg and Stravinsky. What is more, and as we have already seen, Hollywood had been deploying romantic scoring techniques long before European fascism prompted the mass emigration. It seems to me that what finally explains the currency of romanticism in Hollywood has less to do with actual empirical history than with the appeals the movement offered to practitioners, in other words, with its utopian promise—an ahistorical promise that, contradictorily, was fundamentally rooted in history.

It is important to bear in mind that romanticism was a reaction against eighteenth-century classicism's emphasis on structure and rationality, just as the neo-classicism that followed romanticism would revive that emphasis. While preserving the general principles and forms of the classic era, such as tonality and the sonata allegro form, romanticism did not adhere to them as strictly. (Wagner offers the strongest case in point since his extensive use of modulation helped initiate the break from tonality.)

As most musicologists agree, romanticism's emphasis on large forms (symphonies, opera) reflect its interest in the concepts of grandiosity, universality, and totality (it is no accident, for instance, that Beethoven's Ninth Symphony marked a definitive early break from classicism). According to the nineteenth-century romantic sensibility, music's link to the universal was made possible by its abstract nature: its diminished referential abilities and its "indefiniteness" purportedly enabled it to express a spirit or natural force that, for Wagner, could unite humanity (see his concept of the "Folk" discussed below). Its sounds were something everyone could understand—and, apparently, understand in precisely the same way. In the 1830s, Longfellow wrote that "music is the universal language of mankind"; even today one commonly hears music referred to as an international language (a contemporary advertisement features André Previn, composer of one international language, promoting that of another, the American Express card). For Schopenhauer, whose influence on Wagner's later writings is well known, music's lack of mimeticism enabled it to express that which was distinct from other worldly phenomena or the "Will." Other arts could not lay claim to this, something E.T.A. Hoffmann made clear in his well-known remark that "Music is the most Romantic of all the arts—in fact, it might almost be said to be the sole *purely* Romantic one."[33]

In addition to its interest in the grandiose, the gigantic, and the universal, romanticism placed great stock on smaller, intimate forms such as *lieder*. The virtuoso performances popular during romanticism's heyday also focused people's attention on individual skills and accomplishment. Cults emerged around flamboyant performers like Paganini and Liszt, and the instruments they played, the violin and the piano, also became quite popular. Adorno would later associate the violin solo with the ascending ideology of individualism of late industrial capitalism, an ideology that, one should add, appears to have sustained itself into the silent era of the cinema when soloists who performed at theaters were frequently treated as stars with their own small cult followings.[34] American music more generally seemed reluctant to let go of this particular component of romanticism: conductors were still enjoying star status up until the mid-1930s when the trend began to diminish, and one need only consider the successful careers of Previn, Seiji Ozawa, and the late Leonard Bernstein to see that the idea is still very much with us.

The tension between romanticism's interest in the grand and the universal on the one hand and in the small and emotionally intimate on the other is usually articulated as an opposition between the international and the national or between the national and the individual. Wilfred Mellers, for example, divides his study on romantic music into two sections, "Introspection and Nationalism" and "Introspection and Isolationism."[35] In a discussion of Bayreuth, David Large and William Weber question whether the Wagnerian festival actually achieved the universalism it sought. "Although cosmopolitan in the sense that it catered to an international audience," they write, "Bayreuth was essentially inward-looking and Germanocentric: it meant to be a monument to the superiority of the German *Kultur*."[36]

The kind of tension in romantic music Mellers describes runs only skin deep, however. For, as his emphasis on the term *introspection* reveals, the movement's central contradiction is based on a dialectic that quite simply involves an exalted notion of the consciousness of a very singular, individual subject. In her recent study of the gigantic and the miniature, Susan Stewart notes how the romantic notion of the sublime relies on the combination of these two seemingly opposed ideas. Its concept of the grandiose and the gigantic, she argues, is borrowed from earlier, preindustrial cultures, which had cast the idea in terms of an expansiveness of nature and environmental landscape. Such vastness, Stewart goes on to say, is then coupled with romanticism's own "vastness of the individual world."[37] Here one need think only of Wagner's *The Ring*, where the possibility of change within an extremely expansive diegetic world rests exclusively on the shoulders of young Siegfried.

Romanticism's preoccupation with expansiveness and magnitude thus points to something else, something that is not universal or even national so much as it is personal. The idea does not stop with the individual characters that populate works like *The Ring*, but extends itself to the personality from whom this music is believed to issue. To put this another way, the "largeness" that preoccupies the movement is nothing more than an aggrandized notion of the human subject, the individual believed to be "behind" the music of romanticism. Viewed in this light, Bayreuth is less a festival that celebrates Wagner's music for its universality or even for its innate "Germanness," as Large and Weber maintain, but for the fact that it is, quite simply, Wagner's music.

How does Hollywood take up romanticism's investment in both the gigantic and the miniature? Its interest in large-scale musical forms is revealed in the rich, heavily orchestrated themes that accompany many opening credit sequences. Although brief, these pieces, often scored for small symphony orchestras, with strong brass and string parts, are characterized by their bold and often regal phrases (exemplary here are Korngold's themes for Warner Brothers films like *King's Row* [1941], *The Sea Hawk* [1940], and *The Adventures of Robin Hood*).

This is not to say, however, that Hollywood did not partake of romanticism's more intimate forms and techniques. This is evident through its use of the leitmotiv, the concept originally developed by Wagner as part of his "art-work of the future," the music drama. For both Wagner and Hollywood, the leitmotiv was primarily motivated by dramatic and not musical necessities, a fact that hints at the subservient relationship music ultimately serves to narrative. Curiously, Wagner, who insisted in his theoretical writings that music played a submissive, "feminine" relation to the drama, never relegated music to a lesser or passive role in his own compositions (one of the many contradictions between Wagner's theory and practice that have besieged critics since Nietzsche and Thomas Mann). Far from taking a back seat, the leitmotiv for Wagner helped music to produce meanings in two ways, first by anticipating them and second by retrospectively constructing them. The assumption here is that when the leitmotiv is first heard, the auditor experiences a vague emotional response that is only more fully understood later when the leitmotiv is repeated and readily associated with an object or theme.

Although Hollywood uses leitmotivs to designate significant places, situations, or dramatic themes, most are associated with specific characters. The central protagonists of *Mildred Pierce* (1945), for instance, are accompanied by their own motives, as are the characters of *The Best Years of Our Lives* (1946).[38] Now, given the general character-centeredness of the classical narrative cinema, this use of music is hardly surprising, for it is certainly reasonable to expect that just as characters' desires propel the drama, so would their traits shape the score.

More to the point, however, is the manner in which critics have responded to the leitmotiv in film. Their chief criticism has been that Hollywood tampered with its original function and did not use it as subtly as Wagnerian operas had (consider as one example the musically created wolf whistle that sounds each time the protagonist of D.O.A. [1949] catches sight of a beautiful woman). The common complaint is that Hollywood uses the device too frequently and with too heavy a hand; Eisler asked whether the leitmotiv was even appropriate to the film medium to begin with since cinema music lacks the long, uninterrupted periods of time necessary to develop it.[39] Adorno wrote that leitmotivs serve "the sole function . . . [of] announc[ing] heroes or situations so as to help the audience to orientate itself more easily," much like small advertisements for the film as a whole.[40] Thomas Mann, for his part, whose life-long obsession with Wagner was as profound and ambivalent as Nietzsche's, criticized the idea in an early essay in which he claimed that Wagner "was very German in his unfailingly brilliant grasp of the role of authority. The leitmotiv."[41]

It remains to be seen whether Hollywood's character-centered cinema violates romanticism's own interest in individualism, since one could easily extend any of the above criticisms of the leitmotiv in the Hollywood score to romantic music itself—just as Mann, Susan Stewart, and others have done. We turn now to this question, approaching the idea of "the individual" through an unseemly detour through "the universal."

Romantic Ideology and Authorship in Hollywood

Why would there be such overwhelming interest in universality during the late nineteenth century? The work of Jacques Attali is suggestive here. In his book Noise, a self-entitled "political economy of music," Attali insists on nothing short of the cultural imperialism behind the desire to transcend national differences through music. With an eye toward nineteenth-century history, he writes that the "will to construct a universal language operat[es] on the same scale as the exchanges made necessary by colonial expansion: music, a flexible code, was dreamed of as an instrument of world unification, the language of the mighty"[42] (it should be added that music was not the only area so considered at the time; 1887 marked the year that Esperanto—another supposedly "universal language"—was first introduced).

At the same time, romanticism's notion of the gigantic is sustained by the idea that expressive, universalizing artifacts or items (such as music) are derived from a privatized, subjective, and ultimately "authentic" base. I have already illustrated this in relation to Wagner's Bayreuth, but within the movement itself the emphasis is made dramatically clear through its heavily weighted notion of the "creative genius," something eagerly taken up by Wagner in his writings. Here the composer sidesteps his usual claims for music's universalism to stress the importance of the individual genius. Following a discussion of Beethoven's Ninth Symphony, he writes: "it was *by no means a mutual coöperation between art-hood and publicity, nay, not even a mutual coöperation of tone-artists themselves*, that carried through the titanic process we have here reviewed: but *simply a richly-gifted individual. . . .*"[43] Wagner's advocacy of the individual is rendered even more striking—in fact, ironic—since it is taken from his 1849 essay, "The Art-Work of the Future," written when the composer was still very much committed to leftist politics and socialism. The piece stridently condemns what it calls the "isolation of the single," be it on political, social, or aesthetic fronts; the true artist, that is, the creator of the "art-work of the future," like the artifact itself, is massified, fully integrated, and coherent: the "Folk." But such appeals toward collectivity spiral backward, however, for as Wagner himself reminds us, the Folk whose spirit generates the future artwork, is articulated by the "richly-gifted individual."

It was during the romantic era that the artist was first perceived in opposition to society. Wagner was one of many who argued that since "great art" strove for universality, it was necessarily out of step with its immediate social and historical context. The same was true for its creator. The ideal Wagnerian artist was someone who could transcend history—often by being "ahead of his time," always by creating "timeless" works—in order to reveal eternal truths to his listeners (although elsewhere Wagner maintains that the "art-work of the future" can be possible only under radically changed social conditions!). The subjection of the individual artist to the rules of time and place is, in Wagner's final estimation, "a tragedy"; the influence of historical context "detrimental" and "monstrous."[44]

From this Wagner extrapolated that the artist's audience—the "Folk," ironically enough—was an unenlightened and oftentimes antagonistic force, primarily because of the mercantilism which he felt had come to organize the basic patterns of aesthetic consumption and exchange. It is with great difficulty, in fact, that Wagner's artist releases his work into the public arena at all. He writes "that works whose genesis and composition lie entirely remote from this intention must be offered to 'the public' notwithstanding, is a daemonic fate deep-seated in the inner obligation to conceive such works, a fate which dooms the work to be surrendered in some sort by its creator to the world."[45]

Such romantic notions of authorship and creativity had a profound impact on Hollywood film scoring. Some studio composers believed, like Wagner, that there was a considerable gulf separating themselves and their work from their consuming audience. As Erich Korngold wrote, "I have often been asked whether in composing film music, I have to consider the public's taste and present understanding of music. I can answer that question calmly in the negative."[46] Korngold's calm disinterest turns into active disdain at the hands of George Antheil:

> [E]ven though symphony concerts were played at least once daily upon every radio network in the country, still Mr. Average Listener would probably rather turn his dial to Benny Goodman or Paul Whiteman unless a law be passed which compelled him to listen to a "good" symphony program for at least one hour a week.
>
> But he does not need a law to compel him to sit inside of his favorite movie theatre for three hours a week! He may not know that he is unconsciously being "emotionally conditioned" for better music.[47]

How did this rift between music producers and consumers first develop? Again Attali's work proves instructive. Arguing that music originally performed a communal, ritualistic function, Attali maintains that the patronage system changed this as early as the Renaissance. Relations of musical production and consumption changed even more dramatically with the French Revolution and the subsequent expansion of industrial capital. Particularly affected in this was the conception of the composer:

> When a class emerged whose power was based on commercial exchange and competition, . . . [t]he musician no longer sold himself to a lord: he would sell his labor to a number of clients. . . . Music became involved with money. The concert hall performance replaced the popular festival and the private concert at court. The attitude toward music changed profoundly . . . there was a gulf between the musicians and the audience . . . a perfect silence reigned in the concerts of the bourgeoisie . . . the silence greeting the musicians was what created music and gave it an autonomous existence. Instead of being a relation, it was no longer anything more than specialists competing in front of consumers. The great artist was born at the same time his work went on sale.[48]

More traditional music historians respond quite differently from Attali to the shifting social and economic structures of the nineteenth century, usually absorbing romanticism's values rather than putting them up for analysis. Alfred Einstein, for instance, argues in *Music in the Romantic Era* that the demise of the patronage system liberated the composer, who, in his words, became "an individual facing the world." So fully does Einstein endorse this view that he claims Beethoven was the first to extricate himself from being "in the service of the aristocracy; instead, he placed the aristocracy in his own service."[49] It is a telling coincidence that Einstein's "classic" work on romanticism was first published in the late

1940s—the same time that romantic tenets dominated Hollywood film music production.

Attali's analysis makes clear that romanticism's separation of "genius" from audience enforces capitalism's polarization of production from consumption. In fact, the movement's belief in transcendence and universalism suggests ways in which romanticism formed a utopian alternative to this advancing industrial capitalism, a utopia both based on and defined against some of capitalism's social and economic rigors. The same transcendent impulse can be said to characterize the classical discourse of studio film composition a century later.

But the number of film music critics and practitioners who have denied the influence of the industrial, material, and historical facts of their labor is in fact quite staggering. Erich Leinsdorf contends that "Music . . . is not a science, not a business, not a factory. It is an art, a means of expression—and you don't specialize."[50] Even more, the "expression" that film music allegedly engages involves the highly romantic notion of individuated creative production. When asked about the force of film music as an expression of patriotism during World War II, composer Gail Kubik says: "Music in the documentary film aids democracy to the extent that it is *creatively composed* music . . . it reflects the feelings of a free and unrestricted personality. I cannot believe that the democratic, the American concept of living is furthered by the writing of music dominated by any aesthetic values other than the composer's."[51] (I should stress here that not all composers or studio personnel shared this belief. Some, like Miklós Rózsa, publicly stressed the importance of teamwork in creating a film score, noting how individual expertise had to be shared within the studio system. Yet most leaned heavily on this romantic notion of individuated creative production.)

There were other ways in which music department personnel attempted to downplay—literally to romanticize—the realities of their own work situation. Some argued that composition was a form of high art and as such should not be (but usually was) bastardized by the film medium. Ironically, film music emerges as a "serious" art, but film itself somehow remains as nothing more than mass entertainment, an industrial product. Critics performed rhetorical somersaults in order to transform this industrial product into the document of personal expression, an artifact conceptualized by uniqueness and singularity—as Walter Benjamin claims, an "aura."[52] Such are the terms, of course, that give the artwork its cultural prestige and market value. The rhetoric of the film industry readily capitalized on this, suggesting that because the film score was artistic and unique, it was, hence, profitable. A recording director at Warner Brothers makes precisely this point in advising against the repeated use of film scores: "The score for each picture is written to suit the moods and tempos of the various scenes, and the music found suitable for one picture is seldom, if ever, later employed in another."[53]

It is unclear whether the remarks of this technician reflect actual studio practice, since other critics, like Roy Prendergast, maintain that Hollywood often recycled its scores (the films themselves suggest that the latter view is correct). In spite of their divergent historical accounts, however, both writers evaluate cinema music in quite the same way, deriving worth from the notion of singularity and uniqueness. As Prendergast states (although in contradiction to his earlier claim), "every film score, like a work of art from any other medium, is unique. It was, and still is, custom built and tailor-made for the picture."[54] In their eagerness to instill an aesthetic aura into film music, both camps imply that the repetition of a musical work diminishes its artistic and market value: to them, mechanical reproduction apparently cheapens film music and makes it vulgar.

Technology frequently becomes the whipping boy of those who are interested in upgrading the place of film composition. Rózsa once criticized the Academy of Motion Pictures Arts and Sciences for listing film scores under the heading "technical credits," complaining that it turned composers into "mere technicians."[55] In a similar vein, *Variety* featured an article entitled "Screen Musicals Killed Conductors, and Replaced Them with Engineers," claiming that this feat was "the direct result of technology." The same piece closes with a call for "music being performed as it is intended to be performed; with warmth, emotion from the heart and a personal conceptual involvement that makes music come alive."[56] Technology, it would appear, obstructs music's expressive capabilities: if it plays too large a part in the production of music, there is less of an available role for the individual "creator" to play. In fact, this idea, clearly a vestige of romanticism, circulates quite widely today. As Leonard Meyer explains in regard to atonal music's failure to become popular, "It seems probable that audiences object to the dissonance in this music, not because it is unpleasant, but because they believe that it is the product of calculation [i.e., a mechanistic intelligence] rather than an aesthetic affective contemplation [i.e., emotional, human intelligence]."[57] Ken Sutak, a student of film score copyright, puts the issue even more dramatically: "[Machine creators are] vastly more proficient than the individual author in stores of knowledge, calculation, abstract accuracy, and time requirements, but creators also vastly more deficient than the individual author in heart, passion, guts, and that precious wallop of unfettered individual imagination which allows beauty to be born apart from the machine and to be perceived through the conception of a single, fragile, human vision."[58]

This classical perception of film music, then, like that of romanticism, insists that it bear the marks of a subjectivity, the stamp of a human presence. This belief was not without some very real material consequences and effects which problematized the efforts of staff composers to secure better working conditions. One key issue involved authorship and copyright.

Romanticism and the Struggle for Copyright Control

In principle, copyright legislation has always existed to protect the works of individual creative laborers and to give them an incentive to produce more. Since its inception, it has been tied to the idea of creativity—more precisely, to a romantic, individualized notion of creativity and production. Copyright legislation first emerged after the French Revolution, coinciding roughly with the romantic era and its concomitant interest in individualism. This ideology finds its legal expression in an 1857 French copyright law that states: "The author of a work of the mind enjoys ownership rights over that work *by the simple fact that it was he who created it.*"[59]

For Hollywood composers who were contractually obliged to relinquish all rights of authorship to their work, however, this tradition meant little. The studio became the author of the material in the eyes of the law since commissioned film scores were considered "work for hire"; composers then were deprived of legal claim to their own music. (Although the Academy of Motion Picture Arts and Sciences established the Music Award for Scoring in 1934, for four years awards were given to the music department head and not to the actual composer.)[60] According to federal law, once the studios had acquired rights to a score, they were under no legal obligation to give credit, onscreen or otherwise, to the composers, even if it were later published, recorded, or otherwise reproduced. Composers had to request permission from their studios to conduct or otherwise publicly perform their work at a later date, often paying for the privilege. The contract also meant a significant loss in potential revenue for the composers since they could not reproduce or re-release their own music. This was no small problem since, in the 1940s, most composers' salaries were less than what the royalties from a hit song might have given them. It was up to producers at the time to decide whether to publish scores separately from their filmic releases in the form of songs, score sheets, or records, and the profits from this did not necessarily line the pockets of the composers.

Studio composers' efforts to better their situation met with poor results. I have indicated earlier that, they were never unionized and that, despite the existence of several associations that defended their interests (e.g., SCA, the Composers and Lyricists Guild), they did not enjoy the strong representation and support that other groups like the screenwriters had.

Although a variety of reasons help explain this, in the end, studio composers helped cripple their own case in the struggle for copyright control by adhering to an anachronistic conception of authorship.

Just as copyright is said to benefit the individual artist, so too is it said to benefit the public, simply by making creative works available to it. Yet copyright analysts often privilege the rights of the individual over those of the public sphere. In his 1976 work on film music copyright, Ken Sutak argues that the "public presentation" of a creative work always poses a "great threat" to its author, calling to mind Wagner's fear of "surrendering" one's music to the consuming masses. The "threat" to which Sutak refers is, in his words, the "theft of the author's creative discovery and loss of the author's control over the forms by which his creative discovery will be disseminated."[61] Defending the romantic conception of film music production, Sutak upholds the idea of a single, creative force in legal as well as aesthetic terms, placing the claims of the author over those of what he calls the "polluted creative atmosphere" of the public sphere.[62]

Unfortunately, lawyers during the classical era (and later) represented the interests of studio composers in much the same way. Leonard Zissu, general counsel for SCA, critiques contemporary copyright law for stripping composers of their status as "independent creators" and suggests that the marketplace is responsible. He writes: "Besides obliging the composer to render all manner of musical services which may be required, including conducting, this instrument [the composer's contract with the studio] virtually effaces the composer as an independent creator and, in the eyes of Anglo-Saxon law, relegates him to the rank of hired work or employee."[63] Curiously, in the early 1950s when composers tried to organize, the National Labor Relations Board (NLRB) considered them "independent contractors" and *not* "employees." As such, composers were not entitled to some of the basic rights of employees, such as wage floors, guaranteed work breaks, and so forth.

In his account of the struggles of the Composers and Lyricists Guild, composer Elmer Bernstein rejects the NLRB's idea of the film composer as "independent contractor." Yet his dissatisfaction with the term exceeds basic legal concerns. In situations of "work for hire," he argues, it is reasonable that employers should be able to consider themselves authors of the work, but, he adds, "must we not in fact call into question the whole concept of the use of terms like 'Employer and Employee' where 'art' is concerned?"[64]

By representing themselves as artists who transcended the usual relations of production and consumption, studio composers undermined their efforts to better these very relations. The copyright issue raises an interesting irony, because the inability of studio composers to defend their interests issues from their failure to conceptualize copyright and author-ship beyond the terms of individualized labor and romantic creativity—the very terms that, historically, have sustained copyright legislation.

The *Gesamtkunstwerk* and the Drive Toward Totality

Late romantic ideology shaped the classical discourse on film music in other ways as well. It is worth reconsidering here Wagner's interest in the *Gesamtkunstwerk* and Hollywood's own investment in unified, coherent texts, since both maintain that textual components should work toward the same dramatic ends. Forms and elements of a text should all be, in the end, mutually reinforcing. The difference between Wagner and classical film music commentators, however, comes from the fact that while for Wagner the unity of the music drama was achieved through the synthesis of its elements, with the total effect equaling more than the sum of its parts, classical film music critics and practitioners believed cinematic unity was attained through redundancy and overdetermination—not through a true synthesis of elements. To this end the film score was sup-posed to "repeat" the activity or mood of the film image and was not supposed to deviate from this nor draw attention to itself *qua* music.

Classically, the film score was obliged to embellish visual material, to reinforce meanings that were believed to have already been introduced visually. As Hugo Friedhofer advises, "the composer should regard the visual element as a *cantus firmus* accompanied by two counterpoints, i.e., dialogue and sound effects. It is his problem to invent a third counterpoint which will complement the texture already in existence."[65] Eisler, on the other hand, *laments* how film music was classically forced to serve what he identified as a "hyper-explicit" illustrative function.[66] A particularly ex-treme example of this is the practice of "mickey-mousing," a technique that, as the name suggests, appears frequently in animated films. In it, visual activity is accompanied by a complementary bar of music, the com-mon example featuring a descending musical scale "falling" as a character topples down a staircase on screen. Such an application of film music quite literally underscores visual and narrative meanings in simple and noncon-tradictory ways.

Critics starting with Rudolf Arnheim have come to label this relation-ship of image to music (or the soundtrack in general) as a "parallel" rela-tionship, as distinct from a "counterpoint" one. Claudia Gorbman has ob-served how each of these practitional and theoretical conceptions has dominated different periods, emerging as they have from particular aes-thetic and industrial milieux. The parallelist tradition Gorbman identifies with Hollywood film in the 1940s is, according to her, loosely affiliated with a realist aesthetic whereas the counterpoint school so important to filmmakers and theorists in Europe during the 1930s is based on the precepts of aesthetic formalism.[67]

Yet within the parallelist tradition, it is often difficult to ascertain just to *what* the film score is supposed to run parallel. Frequently discussants will conflate the idea of narrative with that of the image, the presumption being that cinema narrative and its visualization are so tightly intertwined as to prove virtually indistinguishable. But in spite of the terminological confusion, and despite the fact that music is usually described as running parallel to the film *image*, it seems to me more appropriate to understand it as being finally subjected to the demands of *narrative*. As one music educator advises in 1945: "Remember, the most important feature of any film is its story content. You paid your admission to be entertained by a story and not by a concert. No matter how distinguished the score, it is not successful unless it is secondary to the story being told on the screen. If you find that you are conscious of the music where drama is the thing, it means that the story has hit a new low or that the music is just plain terrible."[68]

Music's narrative function is frequently used by commentators to explain or justify its presence within a film. Herbert Stothart, musical director at MGM, recounts in 1941 how "We learned that a musical episode must be so presented as to motivate a detail of the plot, and must become so vital to the story that it cannot be dispensed with. The test today is—'If a song can be cut out of the musical, it doesn't belong in it.' "[69] (Interestingly, Stothart is not addressing the Hollywood film in general but the musical, a genre whose very structure and narrative are defined by the *presence* of song and of music.)

If music had to be integrated into the film as a whole, as Hollywood classicism required it to be, orchestration techniques needed to be devised to achieve this end. Max Steiner explains how the audience member should "be able to hear the entire combination of instruments behind the average dialogue," and that composers should avoid solos that are "striking" with very low or high timbres or with "sharp or strident effects." What is preferred? Instrumental color that, according to Steiner, enhances a meshed sound.[70] And although this drive for unity and coherence appears at odds with romanticism's ideology of the individual (and the solo instrument), it must be remembered that the ideal is preserved in other ways.

Even composers in foreign countries upheld the idea. Elisabeth Lutyens, one of the few female film composers working in Britain, writes, "The only film scores of mine or anyone else's, that I feel to be satisfactory are those that are the most completely identified and integrated with the film as a whole."[71] French composer Michel LeGrand echoes: "Music must be simple and perfectly incorporated into the entirety of the film."[72] For his part, Oscar Levant revises the idea of integration and unity with an anthropomorphic twist, "dressing," if you will, the film text in considerable cultural finery: "You never hear any discussion of a score as a *whole*. Instead the references are to 'main-title' music, 'montages,' 'inserts' [isolated musical segments used for dramatic emphasis], and so on, with no *recognition of the character* of the complete score. It is much as if one would discuss a suit in terms of its buttonholes, pleats, basting and lining, without once considering its suitability to the figure it adorned."[73] In this passage, Levant is the near-perfect romantic, neatly collapsing music onto the full, coherent subject believed to be underneath it.

Classical proponents become highly critical when film music gives the impression of working apart from the rest of the picture. Countless accounts raise the "problem" of film music's ability to distract its auditors. For some, the issue revolves around musical recognizability. As composer Jerry Goldsmith writes: "I think an audience should be aware of the music, like a beautiful piece of photography, a great costume or set. But if the music gets too complicated, too musical, it distracts from the drama."[74] Although one wonders exactly what "too musical" a composition might entail, Goldsmith's point is nonetheless clear: film music that draws attention to itself as music is unsuccessful and is no longer considered an integrated element of the film.

Miklós Rózsa recounts how important this lesson was for him to learn:

> When I finally came to do the music for *Thunder in the City* [1937] I made any number of novice's "howlers." In one scene an English family was taking tea outside on the lawn, all talking animatedly. This I underscored with an energetic scherzo for full orchestra. The director patiently explained to me that in order to allow the dialogue to be heard the music would need to be dubbed at such a low level that all we would hear would be a vague irritation of upper frequencies, principally the piccolo. So far from enhancing the scene the music would merely distract the audience. A pastoral oboe solo over a few strings or something of the sort was all that was needed. Well, I soon learned.[75]

Max Steiner discusses other ways to avoid film music that might distract its listener. Like many other composers and critics, he defends the common studio practice of using original music: the argument is that because existing material runs might be familiar to the audience, it runs the risk of drawing attention to itself, again, as music: ". . . while the American people are more musically minded than any other nation in the world, they are still not entirely familiar with all the old and new masters' works and would thereby be prone to 'guessing' and distraction."[76] The point is echoed by Ernest Lindgren in *The Art of the Film*: "The use of well-known music is . . . distracting, and has the additional disadvantage that it often has certain associations for the spectator which may conflict entirely with the associations the producer wishes to establish in his film. . . . The use of classical music for sound films is entirely to be deplored" . . .[77] That this position was not always upheld in actual film practice (consider Dvořák's "Humoresque" in the film of the same name) makes the matter all the more interesting. Even composers whose careers lasted beyond the demise of the classical era work to insist on its validity: Ernest Gold, who scored *Exodus* (1960) and *It's a Mad, Mad, Mad, Mad World* (1963), in addition to his earlier 1940s films, writes that "[Classical music] interferes. If you know the music, it draws more attention to itself than it should. . . . [And i]f you don't know the music, it doesn't support the picture because it wasn't written for the picture."[78]

Of course the question of appropriateness, applicability, and distraction presumes that the film auditor becomes distracted *from* something. It should be apparent by now that that something is narrative. The point, however, is seldom made explicitly, although it finds stunningly direct expression in a brief essay called "Jazz at the Movies":

> At the crudest level, one might say that the music is there simply to keep the audience from becoming distracted. And at a somewhat higher level, it is there to underline and perhaps complement mood, situation, and character. . . . If [the film composer] does not do his job well, he will be noticed, either because he does not contribute to dramatic effect well enough or because, one might say, he contributes too much—he distracts one from the drama and draws too much attention to himself. We would not underline a dramatic film with a Beethoven symphony because, no matter how good the film, the audience might end up listening to Beethoven. In short, good film music is a purely functional aspect of one kind of drama.[79]

For classical critics, it is really quite simple: bad cinema music is noticed; good scores are not. As one English critic in the 1940s argues, a noticeable score not only disrupts the listener but the film itself. "Today the soundtrack," he complains, "usurps more than its share of narration: sound, dialogue and the insidious orchestra weaken the practice of visual narrative."[80]

To help their argument, classical commentators frequently make references to the unconscious. Apparently, if music is made to be somehow "less" than rational, less than conscious, its subordination to narrative can be more fully guaranteed. Consider the following passage:

Music heard in the concert-hall differs fundamentally from music heard in films, because absolute music is apprehended *consciously*, film music *unconsciously*. In the course of the musical illustration of a film familiar or characteristic bars of music may have struck the filmgoer once or twice but otherwise he could hardly have told you, especially in an instance of well-made music, what he had really heard. Only at points where the music diverged from the picture, whether in its quality or meaning, was his concentration on the picture disturbed. Thus we reach the conclusion that good film music remained "unnoticed."[81]

Kurt London makes this point in his 1936 study, and it is echoed by many studio practitioners of the time as well. Roy Webb, RKO's chief composer from 1935 to 1952, maintains that "unless you want them to be aware of it for a particular reason, . . . you can hurt a picture a great deal by making audiences conscious of the music."[82] Music, it would seem, is best unheard—or as Eisler argued, in a curious twist of metaphors, unseen. (Eisler once remarked that film music in Hollywood largely performs a "vanishing function.")[83] It bears mentioning here that although the silencing of music characterizes the classical tradition of film music, it is by no means restricted to it. Even contemporary directors working outside of the United States adhere to classical percepts: Federico Fellini, whose innovative use of film form is well known, has referred to the score as "a marginal, secondary element that can hold first place only at rare moments;"[84] Michelangelo Antonioni writes that "The only way to accept music in films is for it to disappear as an autonomous expression in order to assume its role as one element in a general sensorial impression."[85]

By placing music into a passive, acquiescent relationship vis-à-vis the supposedly more important visual and narrative cinematic projects, classical accounts implicitly argue that its abstract, nonconnotative features make it impossible for music to generate meaning of its own. London states the matter quite plainly when he says that in film, music "must have its meaning" and that to "play music as an accompaniment to a text, without a definite justification of meaning, is one of the most criminal blunders possible in sound direction."[86] But the problem—indeed, the double bind—here is that film music, as it has been constructed in classical discourse, can *never* impart its own meaning since its existence within the text is always contingent upon the image track and narrative.

What is more, classicists frequently argue that the signifying capacities of film music—if it is granted any at all—are duplicitous, false, or unreliable. The assumption here is that scores dupe or seduce their listeners; consequently, they have come to be treated as an object of some scorn or derision, sometimes even by sympathetic critics. London, for example, states that when non-diegetic music "is employed to strain after effects which the film itself cannot induce, then it degrades the film and itself";[87] Irwin Bazelon labels Hollywood scores of the classic era "banal," stating that "film music was born illegitimately as a literal-practical child of necessity," and that in the end, "film music is *almost* composing, but not quite."[88] A 1946 BFI monograph on film music makes much the same claim, if in reverse, noting that the "*content* of English film music has risen most strikingly" since "serious composers" began working in the film industry (the piece cites native composers Vaughan-Williams, Bliss, and Walton as examples).[89]

Film composition met with at least as much derision in the United States, where it was far less common for native composers to be thought capable of ameliorating the status of the film score—despite the contributions of Copland, Virgil Thomson, et al. According to David Ewen, "For a long period . . . Hollywood did not have much use for good music." Instead of the "serious composer," there was "the Hollywood brand of composer," musicians who were "excellent" but "who made no pretense at artistic creation."[90] Ewen, who was writing in 1942, believed that the tides were finally beginning to turn since "Hollywood [had been] bold enough to avail itself of the use of good music" of composers like Korngold, Herrmann, and others.[91] His argument that Hollywood composers were adequate musicians but not "artists" is not surprising given the context of his discussion: the title of his book, *Music Comes to America*, clearly implies that music—or, more specifically, "good" art music, judging from the tome's focus on opera and symphonic works—has to be imported to American soil.

Such a perspective relies on the idea that unlike other musical forms, film music is intrinsically flawed or incomplete. Presumably this is due to its interaction with other cinematic elements—narrative, mise-en-scène, editing, and so forth. The very phrasing of the above comments is revealing in this regard, since film music ("illegitimate" and "degrading") is contrasted to "pure" and "autonomous" forms of music, suffering considerably in the comparison. As one Canadian composer remarks in 1965: "I don't believe that film music can have an existence beyond the audio-visual frame for which it was created. . . . Concert music is self-sufficient. It has no need for a complement. Film music, stripped of its visual support, no longer maintains its form and internal logic."[92] Certainly this is a far cry from the romantics who did not consider *lieder* or opera music to be tainted—even though these forms also worked in tandem with other textual elements.

To compare: whereas Hollywood classicism downplays the role of music, late nineteenth-century romanticism openly celebrates it. Yet both maintain that because of its abstract nature, music mounts a challenge to con-

ventional representation, epistemology, and narrative. With its investment in the ineffable and its suspicion of language, romanticism championed this notion, while Hollywood seemed to allow these challenges and
disruptions only to dismantle and contain them. This censure, of course,
was achieved by the demand that film texts absorb their scores, that they
be rendered "silent," unnoticeable, and indistinct from other more prominent—and, to be sure, narratively central—elements.

Yet, in the end, it is hard to consider the classical musical score to be as
passive and inactive as these claims would suggest. For at the same time
that the score conveys a sense of deficiency or lack to its classical proponents, so too does it also offer them the promise of making good this lack.
Indeed, one of film music's key roles in the classical paradigm is precisely
its capacity to compensate for the deficiencies of *other* textual elements.
This compensatory function reveals that music contributes much more to
the production of meaning in cinematic forms than is traditionally acknowledged. It also suggests that what ultimately preoccupies the classical tradition is not so much the representational deficiencies of film music
but the deficiencies and inadequacies of human subjectivity and the cinema more generally. The claims we have just covered regarding music's
alleged lack, in other words, disguise a concern over lacks of other kinds.
Music works to dispel those lacks in a variety of ways; specifically, by
granting an illusion of fullness and unity to the cinema, one that is engaged
at the level of the apparatus, the film text, and within the viewing and
listening situation.[93]

Music and the Restoration of Plenitude: The Cinematic Apparatus

Scholars and practitioners alike have tended to respond to the introduction of music—and sound more generally—into the cinema in one of two
ways: with great enthusiasm or deep regret. In either case, the event is
cast into a scenario of loss and restoration. Those who lament it highlight
the notions of absence, regression, and even death (one recalls Mary Pick-
ford's famous proclamation that the movies died once sound was born).
For them, as Rick Altman has observed, "the coming of sound represents
the return of the silent cinema's repressed," a repressed he links back to
a dialogue-heavy nineteenth-century theatre. This model, as Altman goes
on to argue, threatens the cinema because its emphasis on dialogue is
borne at the expense of other, nonverbal sounds.[94] In *A History of Narrative Film*, David Cook unwittingly upholds a similar idea, associating
sound cinema with earlier, supposedly less sophisticated textual practice.
He writes, "It is almost axiomatic to say that the movies ceased to move
when they began to talk, because between 1928 and 1931 they virtually
regressed to their infancy in terms of editing and camera movement."[95] To

be sure, Cook makes this point while discussing the ways in which early sound filmmaking was genuinely hindered by the cumbersome new sound technology—immobile camera units, microphones that were limited in range and overly sensitive to ambient sound, and so forth. Yet he remains nonetheless uncritical about the connection his argument draws between film sound and regression—a connection that even he admits has become perfunctory or "axiomatic." Rudolf Arnheim puts the case even more dramatically in his well-known essay, "A New Laocoön," where he addresses another kind of cinematic loss. For Arnheim, the advent of sound violates what he perceives as film's previously established ontological status, a status that, as he maintains, remains essentially visual.[96]

These concerns over the losses and regressions film sound brings to bear on the cinema are frequently tied to the issues of realism and verisimilitude. In other words, the introduction of recorded sound or music into the cinema is believed to have diminished the latter's ability to convey a sense of the real.[97] In a 1945 article taken from *The Musical Scene*, Virgil Thomson argues that unlike earlier kinds of music, twentieth-century music is not "made on the spot . . . [and therefore is] never wholly realistic" since reproduction reduces, among other things, its original dynamic range. He refers to contemporary music as "processed" music, comparing it to processed, canned foods that in his words, though sufficiently "nourishing," suffer for lack of "flavor."[98] Although Thomson's gastronomical metaphors provocatively raise the question of consumption, it is clear that his central concern, and that which he finds most regrettable about recorded music, is the loss of the phenomenally "real" component he attributes to live performance. For him, music itself is not so much the problem as is the fact of its transmission.

Unlike Thomson, commentators who welcomed the coming of sound insisted that film music partially restored a verisimilitudinous element to the cinema.[99] Traditionally, this compensation is accounted for visually since theorists have understood the camera's relation to pro-filmic objects as the means by which a phenomenal "real" (and with it a certain fusion of subject-object relations) is captured. Techniques like the long take, for instance, are claimed visually to depict phenomenal reality with a minimum of technological interference or mediation. The idea of verisimilitude, therefore, is promoted through the apparent reduction of distance between the *visual* signifiers of cinema and their referents.

Yet clearly the same drive encodes the sound track. The main issue here is that auditory verisimilitude, like its visual counterpart, is carefully constructed; it is, in other words, an illusion based on techniques, rules, and conventions with no actual or immediate connection to the real. Recently, film scholars have begun to consider how aural verisimilitude has been encoded in different periods (considering, for example, spatial depth cues, temporality, synchronization, and so forth).[100] Writing on music's contribution to this, Nancy Wood observes that "[In 1931,] non-diegetic music, would make a discrete entry within the individual scene . . . concealing potential temporal ambiguities in auditory space by its self-effacing presence. In the words of a transitional composer, 'tonal figuration' supplied by non-diegetic music 'fills the tonal spaces and annihilates the silences without attracting special attention to itself.' "[101] Members of the classical tradition, however, downplay the ways in which the sound-track negotiates and orchestrates the question of realism. One practitioner writes that, "The ultimate aim of the recording engineer is to secure such a degree of realism in recording and reproduction that the sound from the screen appears to be identical with the sound which originated during the photographing of the scene."[102]

Music performs a specific function in theoretically reequipping the apparatus with a sense of lost realism. One writer in the 1940s argues that "the desire to add realism to the active silent film resulted in the use of various devices in back of the screen" first, by producing sound effects, and later, through the addition of music.[103] Kurt London accounts for the development of non-diegetic music in a similar fashion. He argues that film music "was meant to serve as a compensation for the natural sounds [e.g., sound effects] which were [initially] absent," maintaining that the visual element alone could not sufficiently represent "life."[104] (London is careful to avoid claiming that music *guarantees* cinematic realism or that it is its automatic conduit, however.)

But just as music is classically said to enhance cinematic verisimilitude (or, in Virgil Thomson's case, to endanger it),[105] so too is it said to bestow "a human touch" upon the cinematic apparatus, something that the apparatus intrinsically "lacks" due to its technological basis. (As noted above, classical film composers have often considered the cinema's technical components to pose significant obstacles to them as "artists.") Non-diegetic music, although never directly bound to human forms on the screen, is connected to film characters by other means—most frequently through the use of the leitmotiv—yielding a sense of "human-ness" in this fashion. And, due to its widely understood connection—via late nineteenth-century romanticism—to emotional expression more generally, music has been associated all the more with the sense of human feeling. In these ways, music appears to offer the apparatus a means of rounding itself out, of adding a human dimension to its technological base, of imposing upon it the stamp of subjectivity. This idea is powerfully exemplified in the following passage by Charles Berg, the scholar of silent film music discussed earlier. "Unaccompanied film images," he writes, "were described in negative contexts as 'noiseless fleeting shadows,' 'cold and bare,' 'ghastly shadows,' 'lifeless and colourless,' 'unearthly and flat.' "[106] Whereas Berg identifies all of this as a discomforting "silence" of the early cinema, I think it even more convincingly testifies to the fundamental lack of human presence and liveliness critics associated with early cinema. Each of the words he selects describes death or some form of barren condition, and the "negative" critical contexts to which he refers point less to unfavorable judgment than to the idea of a nonanthropomorphic condition. Berg's argument moves closer to my own, however, as he goes on to observe how the addition of music into the cinema was *believed* to redress that lack and silence.

The central "silence" of the cinema before the advent of talking pictures usually refers to its lack of talk and of human speech. Non-diegetic music, which is rarely vocal, cannot directly stand in for speech but still it is constantly coupled with the idea of dialogue, as if critics saw in this the way to more closely align it with a human element. Silent film critics in particular seized upon this idea, using the two terms almost interchangeably. Max Winkler, active in the early film music publishing business in New York, puts the matter quite plainly: "On the silent screen," he writes, "music must take the place of the spoken word."[107]

The notion of substitution that is at the heart of the classical perspective of film music might help explain the failure of early efforts to accompany silent pictures with live human narration. Indeed there seems no other explanation since in Japan, for instance, the *benshis* who narrated films remained popular even after the development of sound, and in the United States, just prior to cinema's emergence, narrators usually accompanied magic lantern performances. One might expect that live vocal accompaniment would have been a large success in the American cinema but it was not, and by the mid-1910s it was largely a vanished phenomenon.

It was left for music to perform this more or less singular function of "filling out" the apparatus, of availing a sense of plenitude and unity that, as Walter Benjamin would remind us, is normally lost in mass industrialized production.[108] As a significant aside, however, it must be remembered that music restores these "lost" dimensions to the cinematic apparatus only at the same time it carries the threat of *denying* that completeness and of exposing the fundamental disunity of the apparatus, the separateness, for example, of sound and image tracks. Mary Ann Doane has stressed the importance of synchronous sound as a means by which classical film staves off that threat; in routine production procedure, the editor "marries" the sound track to the image track in order to domesticate sound's potentially disruptive effects.[109] Like Doane, though somewhat less critically, Bernard Herrmann has insisted that film music must be "wedded" to the screen. Curiously (especially in Doane's case) neither critic pursues the question of gender raised by his or her remarks very far. But it is nonetheless clear just which partner has the upper hand in this cinematic "marriage." Much like the mythological Echo who was consigned to repeat the words of others, so too, as Doane has noted in regard to synchronous sound editing, is the classical sound track stripped of any discursive authority or autonomy. Film music offers a particularly vivid example since more than other sounds, it is left to echo the image without, one assumes, telling us anything on its own.

Music and the Restoration of Plenitude: The Film Text

Just as music is classically thought to veil the lacks of the cinematic apparatus, so too is it believed to compensate for deficiencies within the film text. Earlier I suggested that due to its position within production procedure, film music performed what critics considered an auxiliary function and was little more than an afterthought. By now it should be clear that the Hollywood score also functioned to offer the film its final possibility of unification, of perfecting (and protecting) the illusion of cinematic wholeness and integrity. Classical commentators from industrial and nonindustrial backgrounds alike are constantly maintaining that music comes to the rescue of a film and corrects any errors that might have been incurred during production (such as mispaced or poorly acted scenes). In fact it was widely believed that these kinds of production problems could be easily solved by adding the appropriate scoring. Bernard Herrmann has said that while preparing his score for *Psycho* (1960), Hitchcock did not want any accompaniment for the famous shower scene, but that when the director was dissatisfied with what he believed to be the too slow pace of the scene, he asked Herrmann to write music that would speed it up.[110] Significantly, Herrmann stated elsewhere that Hitchcock "only finishes a picture 60 percent. I have to finish it for him."[111]

Accounts such as these are striking in their focus on the ideas of lack and compensation. A recent study of Max Steiner's early work at RKO, for example, claims that part of his job there was to compose music that would, in the author's words, fill in the "lacunae" of studio films going into foreign translation.[112] Herrmann, discussing cinema music in a general sense and not in terms of his collaboration with Hitchcock, maintains that its compensatory function is a result of a fundamental ontological deficiency of the cinema. He writes:

> The real reason for music is that a piece of film, by its nature, lacks a certain ability to convey emotional overtones. Many times in many films, dialogue may not give a clue to the feelings of a character. It's the music or the lighting or the camera movement. When a film is well-made, the music's function is to fuse a piece of film so that it has an inevitable beginning and end. When you cut a piece of film you can do it perhaps a dozen ways, but once you put music to it, that becomes the absolutely final way. Until recently, it was never considered a virtue for an audience to be aware of the cunning of the camera and the art of making seamless cuts. It was like a wonderful piece of

tailoring; you didn't see the stitches. But today all that has changed, and any mechanical or technical failure or ineptitude is considered "with it."[113]

Herrmann's passage raises a number of themes important to the classical approach—the drive to produce cohesive, "seamless" texts, the rejection of "cuts," the association of music with human emotion, and, to be sure, a discernible nostalgia for an original lost unity. Equally central are his somatic and sartorial metaphors, metaphors that recall Levant's discussion of film as a "suit." In fact, composers frequently referred to their work in terms of "dressing" the film text, of "curing" a weakened picture, or even of preparing the body of a corpse. As Manvell and Huntley write, "[t]he more banal the dialogue, the more the words can be made to seem dramatically significant if 'dressed' with a heavy musical backing. Used as an emotional prop, music can only too easily help the filmmaker disguise weak acting and weak dialogue."[114] Tony Thomas, for his part, writes, "Bernard Herrmann often said he feared producers calling on him in somewhat the same manner they called upon a mortician—to come in and try to fix up the body."[115] But the notion that music "rescues" or "doctors" the film text is most dramatically exemplified in the following passage by Irwin Bazelon: ". . . if the film-makers were unable to fulfill the dramatic requisites of their films—because of oversights, errors in cinematic judgment, or simple lack of talent—the composer could apply his witchcraft technique to soothe the sick film's ailments and, in some cases, completely cure it. In short, by doctoring the dramatic failures of the film, music could save the picture."[116]

The metaphors of lack and lacunae that organize these critical discussions reveal a deeper preoccupation with losses of other kinds, particularly when associated—as they so frequently are—with the human body. Doane persuasively theorizes that the classical Hollywood cinema constructs what she calls a "fantasmatic" body—constructed and enforced through strictly synchronized sound-image relationships—and that this body characterizes itself by the illusion of organic unity and a perceptual coherence within the film text which in turn is enjoyed by the listening and viewing subject.[117] In the following chapter, I will be discussing more fully how music has been asked to veil not only the fragmentation and lacks inscribed upon the "corpus" of the cinema but those inscribed upon the body of subjectivity.

Music and the Restoration of Plenitude: The Viewing and Listening Situation

The same wholeness and sense of totality that film music is believed to avail the cinematic text and apparatus are, in the words of classical commentators, extended to the act of film consumption as well. In fact, it is almost as if the first two are guaranteed by the latter. As one studio editor writes: "Picture and track, to a certain degree, have a composition of their own but when combined they form a new entity. Thus the track becomes not only an harmonious complement but an integral inseparable part of the picture as well. Picture and track are so closely fused together that each one functions through the other. There is no separation of *I see* in the image and *I hear* on the track. Instead, there is the *I feel, I experience*, through the grand total of picture and track combined."[118]

This account also suggests that the film score—though less indexical a signifying system than its visual counterpart—secures much the same illusory plenitude to its auditor that theorists have been arguing the image grants for the spectator.[119] Yet this is not an altogether new idea. Writing in 1945, Herrmann claims that film music not only propels the narrative and shapes its mood, but that it offers "the communicating link between the screen and the audience, reaching out and enveloping all into one single experience."[120] Similarly, Eisler has argued that music is a socializing "cement" that not only connects audience members to the film, but binds them to one another as well. Interestingly, this is precisely the effect Wagner wanted at Bayreuth, whose theater he designed so that the orchestra was lowered out of sight into the orchestral pit that is commonplace today. With this Wagner believed that audience members could more directly experience and participate in the music drama in front of them. One notes, however, that if the artwork extends the desired totality to its viewers and "engulfs" them in union with it, it is a fusion achieved at conspicuously individuated levels since the darkened theater allowed precious little to intrude on individual consumers' private communion with the artwork.

Unity and the Parallel vs. Counterpoint Debate

The advocates of the counterpoint school (Clair, Eisenstein, Honegger, Jaubert, et al.) merit a brief reintroduction at this point. Although not associated with Hollywood scoring, they nonetheless share a few of its interests in unity and in this way problematize the contention of Arnheim, Gorbman, and others that the two traditions are mutually exclusive. What links the traditions is precisely their interest *in* unity, although I hasten to add that this link is by no means immediately apparent. The counterpoint tradition, as the name suggests, upholds that music should be used in contrast to the image and should try to dispel any illusion of unity. In so doing, music would then expose—and exploit—cinema's basic heterogeneity, not conceal or deny it as under parallelism. The disunified text, proponents contend, makes film consumption more active, and the "critical distance" it allegedly promotes is valued more highly than the passivity and immersion they believe characterize auditor-text relations under parallelism.

The similarities between the two schools begin to surface in Eisler's critique of Eisenstein's theory of musical counterpoint.[121] Now to be sure, Eisenstein's promotion of the score as an element in dialectical "collision" with other cinematic elements has given the counterpoint tradition its greatest exposure and popularity. Yet, as Eisler observes, Eisenstein's films and his theoretical work adopt some of the conventional approaches to film music by establishing equivalences ("parallelisms") between the score and other film elements. On the one hand this is simply a terminological matter: for instance, Eisenstein's well-known advocacy of "rhythm" in film editing and music is limited by the differences that might be involved in the ideas of cinematic and of musical rhythm (one wonders how rhythm in the cinema can be satisfactorily defined in the first place); one might also question what Eisenstein means when he speaks enigmatically of cinema's "inner sounds." On the other hand, and perhaps more significantly, Eisenstein's film practice reveals some unquestionably "parallel" relations between score and image. An especially striking example is found in Prokofiev's score for *Alexander Nevsky* (1938). Here the written score aurally duplicates the formal composition of the image, with single, sustained notes appearing on the staff at roughly the same places where solitary characters appear on the screen.[122] In light of Eisenstein's interest in revising Hollywood practice, it comes as something of a shock that he praises the ability of Prokofiev to produce what he calls exact "musical equivalents."

It is all the more striking that Hanns Eisler, the outspoken critic of parallelism, fails to address similar kinds of inconsistencies in his own work. Repeatedly he states that music should work within and not against cinema's essentially composite structure (it can achieve this, he argues, by formally exploiting the idea of suspense and interruption). Yet at the same time, he maintains that music works to synthesize and to unify the film text: "There must be *some* correspondence—however indirect or antithetical—between music and image," he writes; ". . . structural unity must be preserved even when the music is used as a contrast."[123] In fairness to Eisler (and to Eisenstein), it should be stressed that the *means* by which they argue textual unity is achieved depart significantly from that of the Hollywood model. Whereas Eisler speaks to a structural unity and Eisenstein (at least in his early writings) to a collisional synthesis of elements, classical proponents understand unity as something naturally promoted by the text. Still, and despite this difference, what appear to be opposing schools find common ground in the drive for unity itself, a fact that demonstrates both the force and the range of the classical tradition.

Romanticism Redux

It has, of course, become something of a cliché to compare "the" cinematic art form of the twentieth century to the nineteenth-century *Gesamtkunstwerk*. But it remains a critical comparison to be made nevertheless since the similarities between Hollywood's interest in a unified product and Wagner's desire for synthesis within the total artwork are at least as intricate as they are plentiful.

Yet, lest we make too much of the "parallels" between late romanticism and classical theory, it should be acknowledged that differences do distinguish them, differences that are largely evaluative in nature. Whereas romanticism esteems music for its distinction from language, its lack of mimeticism, and its irrationality, believing that these features enable it to express important spiritual resonances hidden from the phenomenal world, Hollywood classicism tends to dismiss music for these same non-representational features, treating it as a minor, somewhat expendable element of the narrative text, something that, in the words of Jeffrey Embler, "doesn't tax the mind."[124] But in spite of these differences both in response and approach, Hollywood and late romanticism together construct music as a fundamentally emotional, irrational, and human phenomenon. And, of course, both camps subscribe—albeit in different ways—to its ability to generate a sense of plenitude and unity.

For classical Hollywood, this unity was offered at the sites of film apparatus, text, and reception. At the heart of this assumption rests a profound sense of—and uneasiness with—the lacks on which apparatus, text, and reception are each based. For instance, although the film score may work at the last minute to remedy production problems and to create the impression of a complete, totalized cinematic experience (e.g., *Psycho*), its own patterns of development remain highly fragmented and inconclusive. Interspersed among dialogue and other sounds (not to mention the activity of nonauditory elements), non-diegetic film music rarely appears in sustained forms and structures, and its themes are continually engaged in a tension between progression and interruption, exposition and silence. In other words, the sense of completion and synthesis that music allegedly promotes is not derived from the musical forms themselves but from their interaction with other cinematic elements, or more precisely, *from the claims that classical criticism has made* about this interplay. In short, it is an effect produced by a vast array of supporting discourses and technologies.

It must also be remembered that classicism's search for unity is a deeply nostalgic enterprise, with the film score treated as if it were able to restore an original quality or essence currently lacking—be it within the text, the apparatus, or the moment of consumption. The nature of that nostalgia will warrant further consideration, especially insofar as it evokes the idea of a lost humanity, as we have already seen in the belief that film music restored a human touch to the technological apparatus. Indeed the classical approach displays an almost obsessive concern with establishing the presence of some kind of human agency, and a number of discourses come together in enforcing this concern. Film critics have argued that music should inject a human element into the text; lawyers commonly represented studio composers as individual artists and not as collective labor. The overarching interest in the expression of an individual force again indicates the presence of late romantic ideology whose specter, in fact, has been hovering over all of these observations.

One may provisionally conclude that the investment in nineteenth-century romanticism during the film scoring era of the 1930s and 1940s reflects a wider ideological nostalgia of the time (although, as I have already mentioned, American music outside of Hollywood turned to other sources for its models). For the highly industrialized cinema, the romantic movement seemed to provide an escape from then current deficiencies, both real and perceived. Problems such as an alienating work milieu and division of labor would probably have appeared all the more alienating to workers whose backgrounds had trained them to believe that music was not a business, but an art. The high esteem in which romanticism held individual creativity and aesthetic production would doubtlessly be deeply alluring to the studio practitioner, a laborer whose own skills were rarely so highly acclaimed.

It is important to remember, however, that the social, economic, and discursive power of the nineteenth-century subject in actuality was not very strong. Marked by increased separation between producers, products, and consumers and by growing commodification in general, the period yielded not an omniscient subject but the conception of an omniscient one. In other words, the subject of the time was *believed* to wield social and economic power, just as he was assumed to enjoy forms of discursive control, of being able to express himself though music or other art forms. The larger utopian contours involved in this notion are outlined by Carl Dahlhaus in his study *Between Romanticism and Modernism*: "[late nineteenth-century romanticism] was romantic in an unromantic age, dominated by positivism and realism. Music, *the* romantic art, had become 'untimely' in general terms, though by no means unimportant; on the contrary, its very dissociation from the prevailing spirit of the age enabled it to fulfill a spiritual, cultural, and ideological function of a magnitude which can hardly be exaggerated: it stood for an alternative world."[125]

Although this chapter has concentrated on the practitioners and theorists of classical film music who looked backward to late nineteenth-century romanticism as a source of restored plenitude and unity, it must be recalled that romanticism itself also turned to earlier periods for models of integrity and strength. For Wagner and Nietzsche, ancient Greece provided this model; the Hellenic culture was "romanticized" and given tremendous coherence. (According to Wagner, the *Gesamtkunstwerk* arose naturally from the need of its people and culture; moreover, he claimed that the aesthetic integrity of the "total art-work" was testimony to the natural unity of its culture more generally and could only have emerged from the supposedly harmonious culture of ancient Greece.)[126] Like Hollywood's interest in romanticism, romanticism's own interest in Hellenic totality can be understood in terms of a desire to exceed contemporary experience, to get beyond the sense of social, economic, and subjective fragmentation or impotence. That this idealization finds its locus in bygone periods remains an ongoing question.

In the cinema, music repeatedly bears the burden of these nostalgic enterprises. It is the one element that critics consider indispensable in uniting the film into a coherent, mutually reinforcing text—or conversely, as that which most radically threatens to undermine it. It has functioned as a sort of conduit to connect listeners—and commentators—to an idealized past, offering them the promise of a retrieval of lost utopian coherence. But, because it is tied to anterior moments, music is obliged to operate as an outside term, an elsewhere removed from contemporary social relations and from the production of meaning, an idea that poses serious obstacles to anyone concerned about the way film music generates the effects it actually does.

In many ways the classical formulations of film music have set the stage for more recent speculations on subjectivity, representation, textuality, and music more generally. This current theoretical trend largely champions the nonrepresentational, abstract capacity of music that the classical tradition tried to efface. Yet like the classical understanding of film music, it also upholds the belief that music generates meaning as an effect of lack and that it remains more or less outside of signifying practices as we know them. Furthermore, this newer critical tradition, like its predecessor, aligns music with the idea of lost plenitude and prior states, a move that continues to limit our ability to examine the ways in which music functions in different texts, in different listening situations, and to different kinds of subjects.

TWO

THE MAN BEHIND THE MUSE

MUSIC AND THE LOST MATERNAL OBJECT

It is . . . only insofar as it refers to culture that the musical
form . . . confronts the individual with what formed
him, what fashioned his sensibility, with everything
that is consequently anterior to him, all he has
always known, and all that transcends him. This
experience confronts his fleeting, imperfect, unfinished
individuality with permanence, with completeness
and with ontological plenitude.
(*Gilbert Rouget*, Music and Trance)

So let us again listen to the *Stabat Mater,* and the music,
all the music . . . it swallows up the goddesses and
removes their necessity.
(*Julia Kristeva*, "Stabat Mater")

T HE LITERATURE surrounding classical film music is by no means
unique in claiming that music promotes the sense of completion
and unity. Insofar as the text "itself" is concerned, it is important to
remember that the model of the cohesive, integrated artwork has, with
differing degrees of emphasis, dominated Western aesthetics since Plato
and Aristotle.[1] In recent history, as the previous chapter has shown, it was
taken up with particular zeal by late nineteenth-century romanticism,
which subsequently bequeathed it to the classical Hollywood cinema.
But, since the demise of the studio era, the paradigm has shifted somewhat and the critical desire for unity has been replaced by an overriding
interest in fragmentation. Having survived modernism and postmodernism's efforts to destabilize coherence and totality on various fronts, critical
theory in the late twentieth century holds the notion of unity in deep
suspicion, aligning it with a humanist ideology that would have art conceal
the very real fragmentation and contradictions of the world around it.

These same debates over aesthetic unity and fragmentation have been
waged throughout the history of film criticism, although they gained special momentum during the 1970s when they were engaged with Marxism
(specifically, Althusserian theory) and psychoanalysis (Lacanian) to form

what some have retrospectively called the *Screen* school. Unity, according to this perspective (indeed, if the approach itself can be considered unified), outfits the cinema with a mistaken sense of stability at both ideological and formal levels; the goal of contemporary film theory, it was asserted, was to crack such an illusion of wholeness. By promoting interpretive and creative practices that exposed moments of textual "rupture" and "excess," proponents believed that spectators became critically distanced—alienated in the Brechtian sense of the word—and thus moved to challenge the politics of representation, be it through the works of classical masters like Sirk or experimental practitioners like Godard. The critique of unity thus not only involved films per se but their viewers and listeners who, like the classical text itself, were believed to be under a spell of false coherence, extended an illusion of power and integrity that in actuality eluded them.

The recent interest in distanciation and disunity has not been without its share of problems, and one would be hard pressed even to call it a dominant tendency anymore. To begin with, one might question the near perfunctory association of unity with ideological conservatism (consider early Soviet Marxism's interest in unity and totality, for example) or examine ways, as feminists have, in which empathetic, nondistanciated modes of textual consumption can engender equally active, informed readings. But even more striking is the fact that at the same time that these critics were doing theoretical battle with the idea of coherence, some gestured in its direction, subtly bemoaning its loss rather than cheering its demise. This tendency is especially marked where music is involved. Psychoanalysis, for example, gives music a key role in restoring a sense of lost plenitude to the subject, availing what Claudia Gorbman has called a "temporary, benign regression."[2] Marxist theory asserts much the same thing, with the assumption being that music offers a lost unity at levels of aesthetic production and consumption and within social relations more generally.

It is extremely ironic, but tellingly so, I think, that music should function in such a "unifying" way for a criticism that otherwise calls for decentered, destabilized subject positions and advocates disunifying, avant-garde textual practices as a means of changing standard consumption patterns. Like its classical Hollywood counterpart, this contemporary position upholds the idea that music has the potential of making good lacks and deficiencies and of restoring a lost, idealized plenitude to its listening subjects.

Significant differences do exist between these two theoretical frames however, not the least of which is historical. For the most part, the classical paradigm dominated during the 1930s, 1940s, and early 1950s, whereas the contemporary tradition has only emerged since the 1970s.

The classical approach, as I have already argued, considers film music a potentially disruptive and disunifying element, one to be contained and quieted within conventional film practice or managed within theoretical discourse. Music has been constituted in much the same way by contemporary theorists, although they openly champion its unsettling potential. Even its definition has been modified, as we will see in the discussion of Barthes and Kristeva below, with music and the musical now coming to designate an amorphous semiotic realm where the materiality of sounds, rhythm, and movement overpowers language's referentiality. This is where heteroglossia would reign and where subjectivity itself—as an effect of meaning—is thrown into question. In this framework, music functions much like the "different order" of reality and knowledge that Doane described and offers a utopian alternative through its capacity to undermine conventional symbolic practices and forms of subjectivity. It is thus worth a venture into contemporary theory not only to demonstrate the tenacity of music's nostalgic strain in critical debates but to expose the extent to which subjectivity is implicated in them as well. For it is difficult to understand the utopian landscape of Hollywood film music in the 1930s and 1940s without it.

Music, the Body, and the Psychoanalytic Subject

Psychoanalysis has made much of the place of the musical within the early history of the subject, for whom it is linked to a pre-Oedipal, pre-linguistic condition. Sound in general is considered quite important here. Theorists argue that the infant enters the auditory realm before it has access to visually encoded information, asserting that the child can distinguish its mother's voice from other voices before it is able to distinguish her visually. Guy Rosolato, for example, contends that the association between music and the maternal establishes itself before the subject is even born, when it is literally immersed in the sounds, rhythms, and voices of the mother's body. After birth, the primary identifications of the subject are forged first with the maternal voice and later with the paternal. Didier Anzieu, for his part, refers to an "audiophonic" system of communication that emerges directly out of the body (he indicates the oral cavity as one such site) in a link between infant and parents.[3] Indeed the auditory realm is a crucial shaping force in early subjectivity. Lacan, who has been widely read for his work on vision and the image in the formation of the subject, includes the desire to hear as one of subjectivity's four main sexual drives, although he never directly explores how sounds, music, and rhythm might function as *objets petit a*, objects fetishised for the plenitude they represent for the subject, and for the suggestion they bring of bygone wholeness.[4] Yet other psychoanalytic critics have referred to the musical process as the means by which original plenitude and the lost maternal object are restored.[5] Rosolato argues that the infant's first attempts to talk not only demonstrate the mastery of its speech organs but also play out "a reprise, an hallucinatory evocation of the sonorous features of the maternal object," in a sort of auditory restaging of the fort-da game.[6] He also argues that the pleasures produced by musical harmony respond to the subject's nostalgia for its original fusion with the mother, and that music continually plays out the imaginary scenario of separation and reunion between subject and mother (a scenario that of course depends upon the rigors of tonal music).

Although Rosolato contends that the maternal term is pivotal to music, he argues that the sounds of the voice are not solely under its domain. For him, the voice involves an oscillation between two poles, those of "body and language" since it is defined on the one hand by its pure materiality and an open-ended, heteroglossic signification (as Barthes will argue in reference to what he calls the "grain" of the voice) and on the other hand by its involvement in a system organized by a "scheme of potential double articulation." In other words, the voice for Rosolato never fully escapes structuration, although it never fully yields to it either. It is precisely the voice's movement between "body and language," Rosolato eloquently argues, that produces the pleasure of hearing.[7]

Rosolato's careful theoretical formulations absolve sound of the predominantly imaginary function it will serve at the hands of Barthes and Kristeva. (Although like them he is not completely immune to romanticizing music's effects: he writes that the developing fetus inhabits a "sonorous womb . . . a music of the spheres.")[8] In confronting the problem of "reducing music to a regression," he argues that music, like sounds and the voice more generally, are best theorized along the lines of fantasm, "whose very structure implies a permanence and an insistence of the recall to the origin. The voice, then, provides a somatic exercise of early images. . . . "[9] What Rosolato is stressing here is that as a primordial fantasm, one that endures throughout subjectivity, sounds have a certain regressive nature, but sounds and music per se do not: they merely put into play a series of fantasies of lost representations. He makes much the same claim in other works, stating that music does not bind itself to lost objects, but that musical *repetition* (one of the few nonvocal elements of music he considers) does: "Repetition postulates an anteriority that recreates itself. It thus leads to the fantasm of origins: reencountering a lost object (the mother, her time, the dead father, ancestors), or with one of its traits—sound, the voice. Throughout this return, it is the movement of the drive itself that is reproduced since it works to reestablish an anterior state."[10]

Rosolato's focus on anteriority introduces us to the larger preoccupation of psychoanalysis which associates sound with a temporally and spatially remote site, an enclosed place. Music supposedly summons forth an anteriority within the history of the subject or within the interiority of that subject's body. This latter point has dramatically influenced recent film scholarship, a discourse that has paid careful attention to the bodily "source" of music and other film sounds. It is worth recalling Doane's argument on how synchronous sound equips classical film with the sense of a unified, sensorially coherent body. The gestures, voices, and images of this body appear to emanate from an individual source, promoting the illusion of "presence-in-itself" and a particularly mighty and unified human subject for its listener. The voice, as Doane goes on to note, fulfills an important role in creating this illusion: "The addition of sound to the cinema introduces the possibility of re-presenting a fuller (and organically unified) body, and of confirming the status of speech as an individual property right."[11] Yet, although Doane does not herself address this, clearly the notion of fantasmatic unity is offered to a specifically male subject, the subject typically associated with the production of discourse and expression. And as Kaja Silverman has persuasively demonstrated, even the *disembodied* voice, when masculine—as it is so frequently in conventional documentary narration—is given tremendous discursive privilege, unlike the feminine body, which is repeatedly obliged to "contain" music, sounds, and the voice. In an analysis of *Psycho*, for example, Michel Chion observes how the voice of Mrs. Bates restricts itself to speaking from within the ghostly house, as well as from "within" the supposed body of Norman's mother.[12] Silverman pushes his line of argument even further, suggesting that what Chion observes in *Psycho* is emblematic of narrative cinema at large, namely that the female voice is compulsively confined to a woman's body and in this way (ironically, because of the attendant illusion of unity) becomes stripped of discursive authority and coherence.[13] Here, of course, even in her death the woman is rendered mad.

The belief that music articulates some kind of interior condition or provides it its bodily expression finds recent historical roots in romantic and expressionist movements. But romanticism, it should be stressed, like the classical account of film music that followed it, is much more concerned with souls than with bodies, be they male or female. As van Helmoltz wrote, "Music directly paints the movement of the soul,"[14] and most classical commentators followed his lead, arguing that composers and auditors were placed in a direct, unmediated relationship with music, squarely experiencing its presumed raw emotionalism. Roger Tallon, for instance, states that music "is almost directly plugged into the psyche";[15] Suzanne Langer argued that the forms and structures of music duplicate the "forms of human feeling" and that, again, "music is a total analogue of emotive life."[16] For Julia Kristeva and Roland Barthes, it is less the feelings so much as the body itself they believe is expressed through the often "subversive" practice of music and poetic language. Yet their position still shares with the (what they would call conservative) conventional one a fundamental belief in music's ability to summon forth interior and anterior states. This notion of anteriority—and its subsequent feminization—poses considerable problems in the work of Barthes and Kristeva. We turn first to Barthes, whose elaboration of *significance* is riddled with nostalgia for the maternal body.

Music and Subversion in Representation

Barthes's essay "The Third Meaning" (1970) perhaps best exemplifies the metaphorical ways in which music has been used in recent criticism.[17] In this well-known piece, Barthes zeroes in on the meanings and effects that traditional semiotics do not explore and privileges instances where these effects emerge, stressing moments of textual rupture and disunity. Such moments for him oppose conventional signification, which he divides into two layers: a primary, denotative level that simply communicates information and a secondary, "symbolic" level that conveys wider cultural connotations. To these layers of meanings—which are to an extent already determined for readers and viewers ahead of time—Barthes adds a third, one given special status. Although Barthes maintains on the one hand that the third level exploits language's inherent polysemy, he also argues that it exceeds—and, in a sense, opposes—language. Uninvolved with referentiality, he claims, meanings here roam unfixed: this is the realm of what he calls the "pure signifier." Barthes applies this notion to several stills from Eisenstein films, focusing on the texture and materiality of certain images, especially those depicting a woman's face and scarf.[18] Curiously, although Barthes here selects visual objects to exemplify this semiotic mode, he insists that music and sound are most crucial to it, a point he develops two years later in "The Grain of the Voice."[19]

In "Grain," Barthes explores what he calls the "space in which the significations germinate 'from within the language and in its very materiality,'" what he labels the "grain" of vocal music.[20] In many ways this idea of the "grain" coincides with his earlier notion of the "third sense" since both operate at the level of *significance* (signifying), the realm of the signifier that, for Barthes, eschews communication and referentiality in favor of non-representational play involving texture, color, gesture, and rhythms. These effects, he maintains, lie beyond the grasp of conventional semantics, syntax, and semiotics. Like Kristeva's account of semiotic excess, Barthes's acknowledges the importance of practices that trouble standard expression: puns, the carnivalesque, madness, and a textual erotics that, according to him, interfere with interpretation and cause it to "skid."

Stressing the somatic component of the third meaning, Barthes goes on to illustrate how the grain "speaks" and resonates in the body through the example of the bass voice.[21] Importantly, however, in this move to align semiotic excess with a bodily erotics, Barthes's prior claims for the heteroglossia and utter free play of signifiance are considerably abridged. Now these representational excesses are bound to a somatic base. He writes, "in music, a field of *signifying* and not a system of signs, the referent is unforgettable, for here the referent is the body." Although he maintains that this referral transgresses standard semiotic practice ("the body passes into music without any relay but the signifier. This passage—this transgression—makes music a madness"), it nonetheless limits the range of music's meanings and affects.[22]

Much the same move is made by Gilles Deleuze and Félix Guattari in *A Thousand Plateaus*, where they initially posit music as resistance in the form of a "body without organs," and hence, one would assume, without gender.[23] For them, a key component of this resistance is music's imperviousness to memory (a somewhat striking claim in light of music's profoundly temporal nature): "The musician is in the best position to say 'I hate the faculty of memories, I hate memories.' And that is because he or she affirms the power of becoming."[24] In spite of the use of masculine and feminine pronouns in Brian Massumi's careful translation, and in spite of the appeals made to "organless" bodies, gender is far from absent in this discussion. To begin with, memory is masculinized in no uncertain terms ("Man constitutes himself as a gigantic memory")[25] and "becoming," to which memory is opposed, becomes feminine. So forcefully is this polarity sustained that "woman" functions as a sort of sieve through which all other nonmasculine others are processed—women, children, blacks, Jews, and, more astonishingly still, "animals, plants and molecules": "It is perhaps the special situation of women in relation to the man-standard that accounts for the fact that becomings, being minoritarian always pass through a becoming-woman." Man, in marked contrast to this, knows no such process: "There is no becoming-man because man is the molar entity par excellence."[26] Here the allusions to Kristeva's subject-in-process are obvious (as is its feminization), but even more striking is how Deleuze and Guattari's initial attempt to unisexualize resistance returns to a fundamentally binarist, sexed way of thinking, one that constitutes excess as always-already feminine—presumably due to the fact that the forces it exceeds are patriarchal. Their argument, in other words, sustains the very gendered structures it purports to transcend.[27]

Music's semiotic function becomes somewhat restricted in Deleuze and Guattari's accounts, just as it does in Barthes's. What first appears to be a surfeit of signification, an excessive rupture on the "body" of the text, points instead to a particular localization of meaning, no matter how untraditionally that locus may be constructed.[28]

For Julia Kristeva, music is an important component of the poetic language she argues opposes more conventional representational practices. Like Barthes's notion of the third meaning, Kristeva conceives of this realm as a form of semiotic excess. Its practice, she claims, unsettles language as we know it: " . . . there is within poetic language (and therefore, although in a less pronounced manner, within any language), a *heterogeneousness* to meaning and signification. . . . [T]his heterogeneousness to signification operates through, despite, and in excess of it and produces in poetic language 'musical' but also nonsense effects that destroy not only accepted beliefs and significations, but, in radical experiments, syntax itself."[29] Kristeva makes it clear in this quotation that the poetic exists in all representational forms, if only as a latent force. *All* language, in other words, contains aspects of the poetic. Yet her metaphors of "poetry" and "music" are far from innocent, and they are not without theoretical consequences: consider how she (and Barthes) maintains that their fullest practice is found in specifically aesthetic forms like novels and poetry and not in the practice of everyday language. Moreover, and more pressing to the study of the Hollywood cinema, Kristeva and Barthes both turn to canonized artworks to exemplify the idea of "revolutionary" poetic practice: Barthes uses Schubert and Eisenstein; Kristeva, Mallarmé and Céline. Their emphasis on high art leads one to wonder what place, if any, the realm of the musical or the poetic might enjoy in the more banal classical film. (Barthes remarks at one point how rarely one finds the third meaning operating in film at all!) The trouble here is that by insisting on the essentially aesthetic nature of semiotic excess, Barthes and Kristeva place it beyond the perimeters of ordinary language and thus establish the two as mutually distinct. This, of course, considerably weakens their efforts to conceptualize the poetic in that which might be considered dialectical terms. Certainly the poetic cannot function as a truly oppositional force if it is to remain completely outside of signification.

To address this problem, both theorists insist that the poetic exerts a great deal of influence over standard language and that the excesses of the former provide language with its very foundation. For Barthes, the "grain of the voice" gives language its material basis; for Kristeva, the *chora* (a term she borrows from Plato's *Timaeus*) refers to a receptacle which houses the subject before its entry into language and whose activity continually impinges upon it (consider the two columns in separate typeface of Kristeva's "Stabat Mater").

Yet here Kristeva's notion of the *chora* warrants deeper scrutiny. Inhabited as it is by gestures, rhythms, sounds, and movements offered through the maternal body, the *chora* exists prior to naming, prior to language, prior to the father. Much as in Barthes's idea of *signifiance*, difference is negated here; meaning is made similarly impossible and erotics are random and free-floating. The *chora* is closely aligned with Kristeva's well-known concept of the semiotic, and in fact she often uses the two terms interchangeably.

The *chora* is a pre-Oedipal, imaginary place in which the infant cannot distinguish self from mother, subject from object, nor splits of any other kind. For the subject it offers a place of self-fulfilled plenitude, a utopian moment within its early history. Yet while the *chora* is first and foremost a spatial construct,[30] it also suggests a temporal one. In fact it might best be conceived as a space dramatically marked by time, inhabited by the ghosts of goods already past.

Kristeva is careful to downplay the idealized dimension of the *chora* and its relation to early subjectivity, however, maintaining that only after the subject has entered the symbolic can this site begin to gain meaning or be theorized at all.[31] Yet, at the same time, and because its utopian dimensions can only be gauged retroactively, the pre-Oedipal *chora* exists as a theoretical projection which, though attractive as an alternative for representational practice and subjectivity, ultimately remains an irretrievably lost utopia. In this way its traces that Kristeva believes to be mapped out within certain textual practices do not so much open up new conceptions of subjectivity or representation as they point to an already established model of utopian origins.

Kristeva's account becomes even more troubling when she places femininity and music into this radically elsewhere, lost place. (This problem also infiltrates Barthes's account of *signifiance* and the third sense, as I will develop in a moment.) The maternal is in fact the most indispensable female element of the *chora*. As Kristeva argues, in traditional subjectivity and symbolic operations more generally, this element normally is repressed: "Language as symbolic function constitutes itself at the cost of repressing instinctual drive and continuous relation to the mother. On the contrary, the unsettled and questionable subject of poetic language (for whom the word is never uniquely sign) maintains itself at the cost of reactivating this repressed instinctual maternal element."[32] Closely involved in this activity is music, which Kristeva defines as "intonation and rhythm which play only a subordinate role in everyday communication but here [i.e., in poetic language] constitute the essential element of enunciation and lead us directly to the otherwise silent place of the subject."[33]

Again echoing Barthes, Kristeva maintains that music's relatively abstract qualities permit a greater play of signification, a greater flexibility of meaning and a greater mobility of subject positioning. As part of poetic language, music and the *chora* help to unsettle patriarchal symbolic structures and traditional modes of subject formation.

At first, the connection of music to the *chora* appears an important and even necessary strategy since Kristeva, like other female French theorists (notably Irigaray and Cixous), believes that music's connection to the maternal register poses a significant challenge to the visual orientation of more traditional, patriarchal systems of representation. She casts music's "excess," in other words, to explicitly political ends. Cixous, for instance, openly embraces the idea of a feminine utopia and proclaims music to be an integral component of this and of the *écriture féminine* that helps articulate it. But Kristeva departs dramatically from a strictly feminist apprehension of music and, like Barthes, problematizes its association with notions of the feminine and the maternal. For them the feminization of music proves little more than a veil for a more profound "undoing" of the female subject.[34] If music is woman, she works primarily to cloak and adorn the male artist who remains the primary force beneath her.

The Lost Maternal Object

I have already noted the irony in Barthes's selection of still images to illustrate the dynamic, musical dimensions of his notion of *signifiance* in "The Third Meaning." But even more revealing is the fact that the one photograph which prompts the most discussion is that of an elderly peasant woman, a woman whose face creates a maternal presence in no uncertain terms. Barthes was later to demonstrate the profundity of his desire for that maternal image in *Camera Lucida*, where he also shows the difficulty of that desire (here, his eagerness to be reunited with his mother simultaneously acknowledges the facts of her recent death and their actual separation). What *Camera Lucida* bears out is that the maternal for Barthes finally cannot be represented at all: the photograph of his mother around which the entire book revolves is never printed. It would seem that, for him, although the maternal can be partially revived as semiotic excess in "poetic" moments in works by artists like Eisenstein, she never accedes to full symbolic representation.

It should come as no surprise that music plays a large role for Barthes in his scenario of lost objects and personal utopias. In "Music, Voice, Language" (1977), he explores music in the somewhat metaphoric "poetic" sense of the word by examining the recordings of Charles Panzéra, an obscure French singer, in order to demonstrate the physicality, the "grain," if you will, of musical meaning.[35] Since any number of vocalists might have stood up to Barthes's scrutiny, his selection of the little-known Panzéra merits some attention. He offers a few provocative details: First, we learn that Panzéra had once been Barthes's music instructor—a remark that suggestively calls to mind the mother's role in introducing music and sounds to her child and comforting him with them. Yet it is not enough to say that this vocalist cuts a maternal figure to Barthes; more to the point is the fact that he stands in for a lost and *absented* mother. Significantly, Panzéra stopped recording at about the time long-playing records were being developed—and so only a few "imperfect" 78 r.p.m. recordings of his work remain, according to Barthes. His voice thus represents a pleasure that for Barthes is bound to the past. Here the discussion is overcome with nostalgia—although it arguably motivated the entire hermeneutical venture from the beginning, or else Barthes would have selected a different vocalist. In fact his yearning for the maternal extends well beyond this lecture: one need only recall that the death of his mother prompted him to undertake *Camera Lucida*. Moreover, by never reproducing her picture, *Camera Lucida* makes the maternal element all the more "scarce," definitively beyond grasp.

These concerns continue in the notion of *jouissance* that plays such a critical role in Barthes's, and Kristeva's, notion of textual excess. It emphasizes what they believe is the corporal, material component of their "revolution of poetic language," and they insist on its erotic and auditory dimensions. "Every relation to a voice," as Barthes writes, "is necessarily erotic, and this is why it is in the voice that music's difference is so apparent.")[36] The physically disruptive force of music did not emerge *tout à coup* with the contemporary French notion of *jouissance*, however, but has roots within the aesthetic ideology of romanticism. Consider the discussion of the sublime by J. G. Sulzer, writing in 1771:

> The term sublime is generally applied to whatever in its way is much greater and more powerful than might have been expected; for this reason, the sublime arouses our astonishment and admiration. We enjoy those things which are simply good and beautiful in nature; they are pleasurable or edifying; they create an impression that is tranquil enough for us to enjoy without disturbance. The sublime, however, works on us with hammer blows; it seizes us and irresistibly overwhelms us.[37]

Here the beautiful and the sublime work much like Barthes's well-known distinction between *plaisir* and *jouissance*; note how the sublime, like *jouissance*, threatens the very boundaries of textuality and subjectivity ("work[ing] on us with hammer blows") whereas beauty, like pleasure, is something safe, predictable and established. The distinction becomes even more apparent in a comparison Gustav Mahler makes between Brahms's "Variations on a Theme by Haydn" with Beethoven's. Mahler describes the latter as "[c]arried away by his own soaring imagination and flights of fancy, Beethoven is incapable of sticking to the details of the theme . . . [whereas] Brahms's variations are like an enchanted stream, with banks so sure that its waters never overflow, even in the sharpest bends." Elsewhere, as Leonard Meyer has noted, Mahler makes his preferences and criticisms explicit. "Brahms is not concerned with breaking all bonds and rising above the grief and life of this earth to soar up into the heights of other, freer and more radiant spheres. . . . [H]e remains imprisoned in this world and this life, and never attains the view from the summit."[38]

The idea of "difference" to which Barthes alludes ("it is in the voice that music's difference is so apparent") raises the issue of sexual difference within his work on music since the role of the maternal is so crucial to it. At the same time, and more contradictorily, Barthes's conception of music *dispels* the idea of difference for the listener, reassuring him (and I do mean *him*) of his own wholeness and integrity. It is here that the theoretical fixing of music to the body secures a sense of unity to the body of the listening subject as well, not unlike the one advocated in the classical conception of film music. In a short piece entitled "The Romantic Song," for instance, Barthes argues that romantic *lieder* assure their auditors of an extraordinary, "fantasmatic" bodily unity.[39] He begins by praising the art song for loosening the gender identities to which Western music normally adheres (in a fascinating analysis he designates the traditional four vocal ranges as "Oedipal triumphs" with established places for father, mother, daughter, and son) insofar as a *lied* may be performed by either masculine or feminine voices. This relaxing of sex roles leads Barthes once again to proclaim what he considers to be a "unisexuality" emerging from the *lied*, something he heralds as its "revolutionary" component. Upon closer inspection, however, this allegedly gender-neutral erotics fails to conceal what Barthes claims to be music's feminine function.

In the essay on romantic *lieder* just mentioned, Barthes stresses the importance of the tessitura, which, he claims, reassures the body of its fantasmatic unity since it can be comfortably produced *by* the singing body.[40] He goes on to note that "it is always the affect of the lost, abandoned subject that the romantic song sings,"[41] an observation which immediately launches him into a discussion of Schubert's mother, who died just before the composer wrote "Gretchen at the Spinning Wheel." For Barthes this piece "utters the tumult of [her] absence, the hallucination of the return."[42] In the end, the random, unsexed freedom Barthes initially claimed that the *lieder* offered is gained through a specifically female element.

So important is the maternal to Barthes that he claims that the "grain" is "the materiality of the body speaking its mother tongue: perhaps the letter; almost certainly what I have called *signifying* [*signifiance*]."[43] Its effects are similarly mother-like and nurturing: "music has an image-repertoire whose function is to reassure, to constitute the subject, who hears it (would this be because music is dangerous—an old Platonic notion? Leading to ecstasy, to loss, as many examples from ethnography and popular culture would tend to show?)."[44] The last phrase begins to suggest the limits of the ecstatic conception of music and that in a very real sense, a powerful specter of loss and inaccessibility hovers over it. Kristeva acknowledges this directly in her notion of the *chora*:

> Rhythm, a sequence of linked instants, is immanent to the *chora* prior to any signified consciousness: henceforth, *chora* and rhythm, space and time coexist. Laughter is the evidence that the instant *took place*; the space that supports it signifies time. Located elsewhere, distant, permissive, always already past: such is the *chora* that the mother is called upon to produce with her child so that a semiotic disposition might exist. In the same way, later, after the acquisition of language, the child's laughter is one of a past event: because a prohibition has existed it can be overcome and relegated to the past—thus a weakened and masterable replica represents it from then on.[45]

Like the "grain" of the voice, the maternal *chora*—with its comforting sounds and rhythms—becomes the site to which music's restorative abilities are tied. But coinciding with its ability to reconstitute the maternal and to simulate the primordial pleasure of the subject's unity with her, music simultaneously reminds the subject of its present separation from her. In other words, music contains both the notion of reunion and the reminder of an eternally lost union. As Barthes's comment on "Gretchen at the Spinning Wheel" suggests, music leads its auditor to loss as much as it does to gain.

Just as Kristeva and Barthes argue that poetic language threatens to disrupt conventional language, so too do they suggest that the latent maternal element threatens subjectivity with its full emergence. In fact, the *Camera Lucida* example very nearly suggests that the image of woman can only represent death. Yet what is the precise nature of this subjectivity under siege? How is it constituted? What explains the ambivalence toward the maternal in Barthes and Kristeva? Kristeva's case in particular raises several special issues here.

It is easily contended that Kristeva's celebration of the radical "otherness" of the semiotic *chora* rests on the supposed fact of its negative virtues and, although she is at pains to demonstrate that "negation" (an element of the semiotic that refers only to absence) differs from "negative" (an evaluative term produced by symbolic processes), she does not entirely elude the latter, evaluative connotations. In other words, Kristeva frequently aligns the semiotic *chora* with negative, regressive values and functions; as Kaja Silverman astutely notes, for example, Kristeva projects the pre-linguistic, imaginary condition of the infant *onto* the body of the mother. The alleged radicality of the maternal *chora* for Kristeva, as for Barthes, ultimately emerges from its association with mortality and loss: "The mother's body . . . mediates the symbolic law organizing social relations and becomes the ordering principle of the semiotic *chora*, which is on the path of destruction, aggressivity, and death."[46]

Along with Silverman, Paul Smith and others have noted how Kristeva has retreated considerably from her initial assertion of the disruptive, transgressive nature of the feminized *chora*. Smith has commented on her growing theoretical investment in the notion of individuality,[47] and Silverman places great weight on Kristeva's remark "I yearn for the Law," a statement that appears, astoundingly enough, in the presumably semiotic portion of "Stabat Mater"'s double-columned typography. In *Powers of Horror*, Kristeva links the unnameable maternal element to abjection, transforming it into, among other things, a seat of fundamental horror.[48] At the risk of stating the obvious, Kristeva's construction of the feminine sex as an object of repulsion hardly departs from more mainstream accounts of femininity, and her recent work does not seem to challenge this dominant tradition so much as to recapitulate it.[49]

It finally appears that Kristeva's maternal *chora* is less a site of resistance or *significance* than one that itself must be resisted. "[Language] must swallow [the Phallic Mother], eat her, dissolve her, set her up like a boundary of the process where 'I' with 'she'—the 'other,' 'the mother'—becomes lost. . . . Know the mother, first take her place, thoroughly investigate her jouissance and, without releasing her, go beyond her."[50] In other accounts, Kristeva abandons the maternal (for its symbolic limitations and liabilities) in terms more brutal still—she writes of the necessity to overpower and vanquish the mother—surprising commentary once again from one who initially championed it for its alternative semiotic abilities.

In the end, Kristeva's scheme makes it impossible to put the generative, maternal component of the *chora* into discourse. She writes: " . . . as long as there is language-symbolism-paternity, there will never be any other way to represent, to objectify, and to explain this unsettling of the symbolic stratum, this nature/culture threshold, this instilling the subjectless biological program into the very body of a symbolizing subject, this event called motherhood."[51] Clearly this passage speaks to the oft-told unrepresentability of the feminine term within a patriarchal symbolic economy. Yet in a deeply baffling move, Kristeva goes on to argue that the feminine cannot put itself into untraditional, poetic language either, which leads one to question seriously the subversive force of the feminine at all. (In an interesting footnote, Kristeva writes "as for what situates the mother in symbolic space, we find the phallus again," referring approvingly to Lacan's notorious claim that the maternal can exist only insofar as it exists under the name of the father—an argument which, otherwise put, maintains that that which exceeds the father cannot be theoretically accounted for or even addressed.)[52]

How then can the maternal be articulated? Who, if anyone, speaks for it? Feminists have been disappointed by Kristeva's answer. The poetic—that which evokes the feminized *chora*—is promoted by texts she selects from male writers: recall her examples of Sollers, Mallarmé, de Sade, and Céline, all of whom, according to her, speak "the mother's tongue." (Kristeva is particularly struck by the feminine pseudonyms that Céline and Lautréamont both adopted and considers them acts which reject the name-of-the-father.) It is thus the male artist and *not* the mother who finally puts the semiotic into play, a point the following passage makes abundantly clear: "The very existence of aesthetic practice makes clear that the Mother as subject is a delusion. . . . [T]he artist lodges into language, and through his identification with the mother . . . he bears witness to what the unconscious (through the screen of the mother) records of those clashes that occur between the biological and social programs of the species."[53]

While Kristeva's debt to Richard Wagner is by no means explicit in this passage, it is worth noting how both oblige the artist to conquer his feminized, musical object. For Kristeva, he "bears witness" to it; for Wagner, he bears its fruit. Wagner writes, for example, that art is the result of an explicitly sexual union between "Man" and "Nature": it is "an immediate vital act, the perfect reconcilement of Science with Life, the laurel-wreath which the vanquished, redeemed by her defeat, reaches in joyous homage to her acknowledged victor."[54] Throughout his work, the composer's anxiety over what he terms the "gap" between male science and feminine life is in fact highly apparent. In "The Artwork of the Future," Wagner insists, "The true, creative, artistic craving proceeds from fulness [sic], not from void,"[55] and it would seem that even the concept of the *Gesamtkunstwerk* itself works to veil over these lacks and fissures at a more general level. Wagner is intent on asserting that the artist, individuated though he may be, speaks for a unified group or brethren ("[t]his love of man to man").[56] Fear of the feminine begins to become apparent: "Music's organism [can] never bear the true, living Melody, except it first be fecundated by the Poet's Thought. Music is the bearing woman, the Poet the begetter."[57] The parallels to Kristeva are obvious: what Wagner is arguing is that music puts "life" back into poetry but is incapable of generating it on its own. So fully is this accomplished that like Kristeva, he seems to forget the feminine element on which this achievement is initially based. (It is of course remarkable that Wagner gives music a passive function in the first place since it knows no such timidity in his own compositions. Perhaps this indicates an even greater investment on the part of the composer to keep music in its place.)

Barthes too writes the female subject out of his theoretical scenario of *signifiance*, although the terms of her dismissal are milder here than they are in either Wagner's or Kristeva's accounts. As we have already seen, Barthes stresses the maternal nature of music's comforts, yet in a curious slight of hand he goes on to erect these feminine pleasures upon a distinctly masculine corpus. For him, the male body literally comes to embody music's utopian element, an element initially theorized as feminine (recall here that his example of the voice's "grain," the human bass, comes from a masculine source). Like Kristeva, Barthes selects illustrations of the third, "maternal" meaning from the work of exclusively male authors and performers. Consider the "feminized" male figures that Barthes evokes in his work—the castrato on which his analysis of Balzac's "Sarrasine" is based in S/Z and the "maternal" Charles Panzéra. But Barthes pushes the issue even further. He describes Panzéra's voice as *"secured, animated by a quasi-metallic strength of desire: it is a 'raised' voice— aufgeregt (a Schumannian word)—or even better: an erected voice—a voice which gets an erection."*[58] In an essay devoted to Schumann's work, Barthes extends the metaphor with unabashed explicitness: "The third variation . . . is not 'animated' (*molto animato*): it is 'raised' (*aufgeregt*), lifted up, stretched out, erected; one might also say—but this will be the same thing—that it progresses through a series of tiny revulsions, as if, at each incision, something were coming undone, were turning back, were being severed, as if all the music were entering the sudden wave of the swallowing throat."[59]

Through the metaphor of fellatio, his homage to the male sex, Barthes no longer lays claim to the idea that music (here, romantic music) provokes a free-floating, unisexual mode of audition. Nor is it feminine. The pleasures to which *signifiance* give rise are decidedly male pleasures. What is more, like Kristeva, who finally places maternal productivity into male hands, Barthes appears to be disinterested even in the generative capacity of the female body, bestowing this quality onto the male sex, an organ which springs to life as it gives life.[60]

It should be stressed that the turning away from the maternal term in contemporary criticism is scarcely unique to Barthes or Kristeva. In psychoanalytic accounts in particular, the nostalgia for the mother-child reunion is as laced with the sense of dread as it is with desire and idealization.[61] In his discussion of repetition in Western music, Dominique Avron demonstrates the ambivalence of psychoanalysis to the mother and the extent to which she is ultimately considered a scorned object. He argues that repetition in music plays out the fundamental pleasures of sameness and uniformity which prevail in the imaginary. Yet into this he introjects a dystopic element, maintaining that it is the death drive that motivates the desire for sameness: "suffering," he is led to say, "is the motor behind all musical production."[62] Drawing a somewhat astonishing analogy between repetition in music with the idea of negation in representation more generally, Avron implicitly asserts that each functions as the absent, meaningless base, the "other" which bestows significance onto its opposing term. Avron explicitly extends his ambivalence toward the maternal fantasy by claiming that music functions as a good object (in the Kleinian sense) that the subject readily introjects, but one that also bears the threat of castration for him and must therefore be repelled. He repeats this feat theoretically, claiming there to be a menace within the heart of music and then elsewhere disavowing this observation: he argues that music's disinterest in referentiality, except in "mixed forms" like opera and cinema, makes it impossible for it to provoke reactions of fear ("only the image can do this"), but at the same time he believes that music carries the ability to launch feelings of anxiety. This alleged anxiousness in fact has led other psychoanalytic critics to discuss music as *unheimlich*, a force that invokes the familiar idea of an absented original space (or "home," as the German tells us), returning the male subject repeatedly back upon the threat of feminine castration.[63]

But the turn against the maternal body reaches its most excessive elaboration in a short 1927 essay by Georg Groddeck entitled "Music and the Unconscious."[64] Groddeck begins this piece by discussing music in terms of the space it constructs. First and foremost to him music is an empty, meaningless, and chaotic space (a lacking *chora*?) whose enclosure and containment can only be realized through the addition of the phallic, "key" signature. Furthermore, Groddeck argues, the introduction of the male term engenders meaning upon the previously anarchic, feminized space since the key signature provides the center around which the tonal material of the piece is organized. Yet he does not stop here, going on to observe that within musical notation, musical space is represented on a staff of five lines and four spaces. Together, this equals nine—the period of human gestation, according to his calculations. Notes, he continues, incredibly enough, are the product, the offspring, of the aforementioned coupling.

Groddeck's preoccupation with the metaphors of reproduction enables him to bestow upon music a sense of extraordinary plenitude. Yet he makes quite clear that this plenitude is activated only by the male term, whose insertion rescues the feminine, musical term from lack and meaninglessness. It would seem that here too male desire is firmly in control. Furthermore, Groddeck's short narrativization of musical coupling, with its inexorable conclusion of reproduction, calls to mind the narrativization of woman in psychoanalytic theory (and, to be sure, in culture at large), where her "biological destiny" is to serve a passive, childbearing function. It becomes clear that Groddeck's demarcation of music, like the routine landscaping of the female body, compels each to function as empty discursive spaces waiting to be organized and made meaningful by male desire. The feminine pleasures and plenitude repeatedly aligned with music serve, in the end, to reassure and protect the male subject from the sense of lack that not only defines him but that threatens to resurface in musical texts—even though this resurfacing may take the superficially desirable form of excess.

The reimmersion with the maternal body that music allegedly activates is, in the end, a by-product of masculine fears and fantasies, part of a nostalgic scenario that continually restages problems of mastery, lack, and the loss of plenitude. The feminization of utopia requires the female term to operate as the source of plenitude and unity for this subject, although at the same time, she is rejected for the goods she holds over him. Woman—and her "music"—are transformed into an empty theoretical space, a discursively meaningless body.

We can see how Kristeva's and Barthes's interest in semiotic excess strains in two different directions. On the one hand they promote the disruptions and fissures within standard language and subjectivity. Yet on the other they help reinforce unified fields for a surprisingly traditional subject. Both Barthes's fantasy of a sexually random textual erotics and Kristeva's notion of nonpatriarchal identities-in-progress end up dissolving into prescriptions for a male-identified, masculine subject. What is more, their work grants discursive privilege to the masculine at the expense of the feminine, since the latter term is introduced only, finally, to be excluded.

That the maternal body initially plays host to discursive excess is ironic since this body is also made to bear the more profound inscription of lack. Like Wagner before them, Barthes and Kristeva maintain that it cannot even articulate the semiotic meanings it is supposed to produce—only the male artist seems capable of this task. (In a different context, Vladimir Jankélévitch makes much the same claim when he writes that "It's not the voice of the Sirens that is musical but the chant of Orpheus.")[65] The female body contains excess but cannot actively produce effects of or on its own. Discourse remains forever external to woman and, by extension, music— so integral in this maternal semiotic register—becomes lost within an imaginary "no-place" and theoretically is precluded from generating meaning, be it of the third kind or not. Both become tied to a regressive condition that is activated either as a utopian or dystopian fantasy for the male subject. And the ambivalence of the male subject in regard to this "excessive" maternal element repeatedly weaves its way into psychoanalysis, although its nostalgic dimensions are certainly evident in other spheres as well. (Janice Doane and Devon Hodges have observed its impact on recent literary criticism, for example.)[66]

Despite its allegedly feminine status then, music works chiefly to abet and uphold the male subject (or artist) in his quest for plenitude and discursive mastery. Ironically, this same position insists that woman and music function outside of patriarchal inscription and standard symbolic forms—a claim made patently absurd given the extent to which the ideology of gender governs the entire argument. But whether its proponent is feminist or misogynist, the position ultimately consigns woman to theoretical obscurity—not to mention a genuine powerlessness at social and discursive fronts. And while music may momentarily recapture the anteriority woman represents, her actual presence, as Kristeva puts it in the quote at the beginning of this chapter, is no longer necessary.

THREE

MUSICAL UTOPIAS IN MARXISM AND

CULTURAL CRITICISM

> The disintegration of the fragments sheds light on the
> fragmentariness of the whole.
> (*Theodor Adorno*)

> When people hear good music, it makes them homesick for
> something they never had, and never will have.
> (*Edgar Watson Howe*)

LIKE THEIR poststructuralist counterparts, Marxist music scholars and cultural critics often believe music's untraditional, "excessive" effects challenge the ways perception and aesthetic consumption conventionally operate. And whereas Barthes and Kristeva take music into the realm of subjectivity to do this—only finally to disengage it effectively from its social or historical context—Marxists insist upon music's entanglement *with* the facts of history, culture, and ideology. The allure of this latter position comes from its refusal both to cast music's "subversive," alternative effects into predominantly subjective or metaphorical phenomena. By considering music as a relatively concrete object of study (consider, for instance, the growing interest surrounding popular and mass-produced music in leftist criticism), the cultural critic is less likely than someone like Barthes or Kristeva to treat it as an abstract condition.

Yet this is not to suggest that Marxists and cultural theorists have escaped the pitfalls others have faced. To begin with, music has generated more diverse and internally vexed responses from leftists than it has from other kinds of critics. The internal contradictions besetting the work of individuals or individual schools of thought (Bloch, Adorno, and other members of the Frankfurt school come immediately to mind) make difficult a tidy summary of a single Marxist position—if such a thing were possible in the first place. Another problem, and one to which I alluded earlier, has been the strong lingering influence of conventional musicology, which, interested as it is in great forms and great men, emphasizes history only insofar as it provides chronologies of particular composers or schools.

Another problem troubling music's position in Marxist criticism is its shifting place in the heated debates over mass culture, debates that are far from exhausted. Commodified forms like those of Tin Pan Alley, Broadway, rock and roll (and of course film music) have often given the impression of being inextricably yoked to the economic and cultural machinery that produces them. At the risk of stating the obvious, however, "higher" forms of art music are no more removed from the banal technologies of their culture industries than are these other, "lower" forms of music. And each is equally conventionalized. But I am speaking of impressions: the connection between mass-reproduced music and ideology *appears* to be more intense and immediate, a fact that helps explain its prominence as an object of study with cultural critics today. It should also be noted that the patterns of consumption and distribution that accompany forms like rock did not emerge *tout à coup* over the last several decades but were set into play more than a century ago when social relations were changing and the economic ideology of proprietorship, competition, and specialization was on the ascent.

What establishes the parameters of the current debate over mass culture are the *responses* to this milieu, in other words the claims critics have made about art's and music's function within this particular social and economic setting. The following questions have proven especially crucial (even if I pose them somewhat strategically here) and help separate the prevailing approaches to popular music: does popular music come "down from above," numbing and manipulating its consumers and co-opting their desires? To Marcuse, and even more so Horkheimer and Adorno, especially in their well-known critique of the culture industry, mass culture's involvement with capitalism makes it irredeemably complicit with capitalist ideology. How, then, to locate resistance? Adorno seeks momentary refuge in modernist practices, although even here the results are uneven, as his pointed preference of Schönberg over Stravinsky makes clear.

For others, "low" music forms are conceived of as a form of popular expression, a nonelitist articulation of mass desire, transgression, or even revolt. The argument is upheld with particular vigor by communication scholars like Larry Grossberg and John Fiske, who assert that rock music offers listeners strategies for resisting and for active participation in cultural production. Grossberg's explanation of how this is done is something less than convincing, however. "I know a woman," he writes, "who has simply erased (literally scratched beyond recognition) those songs which she finds objectionable on her records."[1] Fiske, in a move reminiscent of Barthes, argues, "MTV is orgasm—when signifiers explode in pleasure in the body in an excess of the physical."[2]

Clearly the opposing camps do not address all of the intricacies involved in the debates over how to read mass culture. Yet both have something to offer: on the one hand, as members of the Frankfurt School would tell us, mass-produced music does involve an amount of control and management since it, like all music, systematically controls and lends order to chaotic sound and "noise."[3] The organized sound that music gives us—like perception itself—needs to be considered as constructed, conventionalized, and therefore not natural (think of musical harmony). It follows that a degree of management and control of auditors is also involved: with tonality, for instance, listeners are afforded a pleasant, harmonic representation in which to psychically invest themselves, and this investment affirms larger patterns and relationships in which subjects continually find and re-find themselves.

Yet, as the second approach would tell us, mass culture offers resistance as well. This may not take the form of the radically decentered, free-floating "body without organs" envisioned by Deleuze and Guattari or the orgiastic bliss promoted by Fiske; it may, in fact, only exist as the *possibility* of resistance, but that is precisely the point. If something exists that is threatening enough—or rather, perceived as threatening enough—to have to be controlled (consider Hollywood's pressing desire to silence the film score), it would be difficult completely to contain or repress this object. As we have already seen, this renders music, whose abstract qualities preclude its being reduced to social and economic determinants, especially uncooperative. Unable to denote, reflect, or present a verisimilitudinous impression of social reality, it commonly gives an impression of exceeding or subverting its context, even in the most commodified of forms, such as the Hollywood film.

How then best to address the constantly shifting tension between the idea that film music replicates the ideological context in which it finds itself and that it offers a way to resist it? Adorno's work contains a number of interesting (and frustratingly contradictory) positions on this point, but before that a discussion of a few other lesser-known leftist scholars is in order. I turn now to the work of Antoine Hennion, János Maróthy, Christopher Ballantine, Donald Lowe, and John Shepherd.

Marxist Approaches to Music

For Antoine Hennion, the interests of capital largely shape and govern popular music. Yet because it lends expression to what he calls a "negative history of those who have a right to speak" and articulates the "minute desires" and "repressed passions" of people through its abstract, "unstable" codes, music is not entirely acquiescent or passive. But far from radicalizing this position or flatly assigning music a transgressive quality, Hennion is careful to note that its meanings speak from the margins of society and thus have limited, fleeting power; once mainstream industry commandeers it and makes it "official," in his words, its subversiveness is diminished. Punk music is a case in point: something of the edge of the movement was permanently lost once Lord and Taylor began selling torn T-shirts for sixty dollars.[4]

For Hungarian János Maróthy, popular and regional forms do not lose their subversive impact even when they are integrated into dominant culture. In fact, he maintains popular music is able to *contest* mainstream culture even as it is institutionalized. He cites jazz as a "process coming from below," one comprised of several "lesser" regional and marginal musics like traditional black music and workers' songs that collectively have changed the face of music culture.[5] Refusing to position folk and popular music as the perpetual adversaries of high art or of the economic superstructure more generally, Maróthy argues instead that they form a constituent part of it.[6] Maróthy's work, which is far from well known in the states, shows a theoretical sophistication that frequently eludes Western pop culture scholars, who often simplify the relationship of popular or indigenous music to dominant forms (with popular forms existing simply as a threat or repudiation of the mainstream or else as something completely absorbed by it). What is more, as Maróthy notes, just as the conventions of mainstream music can be changed through popular, low- or mass-reproduced forms, so can they be eroded by high art. He suggests a number of examples (e.g., disrupted major-minor relationships, untraditional rhythms, and the use of non-Western modes such as pentatonicism) which have upset the tradition of art music in the twentieth century. Maróthy's approach helps address the complex relationships among "massified" elements (such as the mass-produced cinema) and ostensibly elite discourses (such as "classical" music). Ironically, classical film music—like the classical art music against which it is frequently found deficient—is habitually constructed as a singular, unchanging constant (it *is* emotional, it *is* seductive, and so on). Until very recently, the classical mode of Hollywood film production was conceived of in much the same way, functioning, especially for leftist critics like Comolli and Narboni as a bastion of aesthetic and ideological conservatism, a monolith against which alternative practices like avant-garde, experimental, and documentary filmmaking were compared.[7]

In refusing to place popular or folk music into simple adversarial relations to mainstream music, Maróthy begins to break down the cruder binarisms that have characterized film music analysis. Adorno, for instance, dialectician though he may be, keeps many of these fundamental oppositions intact. For him, Western art music provides a stable and unshifting constant against which popular and marginal musical forms, along with the degrees of their subversiveness, are measured. In *Introduction to the Sociology of Music*, Adorno places a variety of nonclassical forms of music into a single, homogeneous category he calls "jazz" (Elvis Presley is here, for instance), without ever defining official, classical music to begin with. Given his bias against virtually all forms of popular music—a point to which I will be returning—this reductionism may not be surprising, but the move provides a striking contrast nonetheless to his simultaneous careful cataloguing of the various, different types of *listening* he believes contemporary music engenders: here his list ranges all the way from "expert" to "indifferent" listeners.[8]

Whereas Adorno stands somewhat alone in his pessimistic view of contemporary music as immune to differentiation, Maróthy and others comment on the radical changes *already* undergone by art music in the twentieth century. Christopher Ballantine has noted, for instance, that contemporary music's use of improvisation helps "overthrow [music's] pre-given fate" and that this kind of structural laxity "jolts signification."[9] But neither Maróthy nor Ballantine believe that popular, folk, or marginalized forms of music necessarily contain "subversive" effects or meanings, or that that is all they could mean anyway. For them, rather, these different types of music do not function as a system of cultural "others" binarily opposed to dominant musical traditions but as part of a complex network of mutually interactive forces. We have here the recognition of the differences that exist *within* musical forms. Yet for as much as this idea enables us to begin to challenge the uniformity of function and effect imposed on the classical Hollywood film scores, other ideas work to reinforce it.

Marxism's recent relationship to the ideas of totality and coherence has been, by all accounts, complex and uneven.[10] In aesthetics, for instance, many believe that a large part of music's subversive potential rests in its ability to *upset* the fragmenting and alienating effects of industrial capitalism; yet it is rare for leftist aestheticians, particularly in the West, to propose unity as any sort of goal. In fact, Western Marxists have largely abandoned Marxism's earlier advocacy of wholeness and totality at other levels, whether as an international communist movement, a projected historical finitude, the harmony of technology and nature, subject-object relations, and so on. The term *wholeness* itself has come be considered as tainted, an idealization, or as an element of false consciousness. When employed at all, it often tends to refer to a condition beyond the range of capitalist influence either as a harmonious, fully integrated social condition that supposedly preceded capitalism or one that will emerge with capitalism's withering away. Of the two, the former enjoys greater currency, and it is into this nostalgic setting that Marxist critics place much of their own work on music.

In this regard, as we shall see, Marxist commentators might not be terribly dissimilar to psychoanalytic-minded critics like Barthes and Kristeva—not to mention the classical proponents of film music. At the least, they encounter some of the same theoretical obstacles, obstacles produced largely by their efforts to nostalgize music as an object of study or have it stand in for an abandoned ideal. For Ballantine, Shepherd, and, especially, Adorno, this idealized moment is conceived of as an irrecoverable prior moment in history—just as psychoanalysts conceived of it as a lost period within the history of the subject. Moreover, both traditions associate the nostalgic condition with notions of lost wholeness, integrity, and cohesion, even when this wholeness is itself put into question.

An important issue cultural analysts have explored has been the relationship between perception and epistemology and how this relationship is conventionalized at any given time. The understanding here is that perception is discursively—and not naturally—shaped, in much the same way as our perceptions of perception are cued by the historically variable facts of society, economics, and technology. From this it follows that different senses and perceptions dominate certain periods in varying degrees, something Donald Lowe has argued in *History of Bourgeois Perception*.[11]

Drawing from categories devised by Walter Ong (to quite different ends, to be sure) in *The Presence of the Word*, Lowe delineates four phases in which knowledge and perception have been institutionalized, each marked by its own technological supports and assumptions about communication and the media. There is a discernible trend in each of these successive phases: Lowe associates hearing and sound with earlier cultures, and sight and the "ideology of the visible" with our own. In the first, an "oral culture," Lowe argues that information was verbally transmitted and preserved; in the second, chirographic culture, written language started to supplant this function, a move that was further consolidated in the next "typographic" phase when the printing press was developed. What is apparent is that with each passing phase, hearing plays a diminishing role whilst sight is increasingly associated with the intellect and its abilities to analyze, to judge, and to measure. In this way, as Lowe and others have argued, the eye appears more readily connected to the idea of objectivity than does the more "emotional," less discriminating ear. Reality becomes fabricated out of visual appearances, since "seeing is believing," after all.[12] Lowe's fourth and final phase, our own "electronic culture," tentatively begins to strip sight of some of this power: looking is now a detached "seeing out of context" thanks to the fragmenting effects of mass reproduction, even though it still retains its epistemological edge over hearing. Like the growing capitalist framework around it, perception is assessed in terms of a growing alienation and disunity. Subject-object relationships become increasingly separated and are no longer characterized in terms of immediacy or proximity—qualities that, along with experience itself, would seem to be affiliated with hearing or perhaps touching. (As Ong writes, "Sound is more real or existential than other sense objects, despite the fact that it is more evanescent.")[13]

For Hanns Eisler, the story is much the same. Although the social, economic, and technological supports of late industrial capitalism have encouraged the development and sophistication of human sight, he argues that this has been done at the expense of hearing, which has remained relatively undeveloped and oftentimes ignored.[14] He acknowledges, for instance, Western education's disregard for developing musical abilities and auditory skills in children, referring to the following passage in Goethe's *Dichtung und Wahrheit*: "According to my father, everyone should learn to draw. . . . [H]e also more seriously urged me to practice drawing than music, which, on the other hand, he recommended to my sister, even keeping her at the piano for a good part of the day . . ."[15] Although Eisler himself fails to explore the issue of gender, the passage clearly associates the male and his path of study with vision—and subsequently, with progress and enlightenment—whereas the female is identified with "historically outmoded domesticity" and is thus banned from the training that otherwise might serve her. Her father's orders bind her instead to music, an activity which, as Lowe's work has already shown, harkens backward.

Eisler, who is normally very aware of the ideological pressures impinging on music and listening, relies on an uncharacteristically essentialist understanding of sound to develop his line of argument. The failure of the ear to adapt to the rigors of bourgeois rationalism partly emerges, he argues, from the fact that it is less selective and "discerning" an instrument than the eye: hence hearing is deemed more passive and less critical than sight. Such assertions clearly take as their starting point the "givens" of biology and physiology, thereby diminishing the strength of Eisler's normally sharp cultural insights in the process. It almost seems as if sound were so natural a phenomenon that it precludes its own cultural inscription. (Even thinkers in precapitalist times associated listening with passivity and a receptive inwardness, something Kathryn Kalinak traces back to classical Greece when "Alcmaeon described the ear as an 'empty space' which resonates sounds of the soul[;] Democritus termed it 'a cavity'; Aristotle a 'void.' . . . In contrast, . . . the eye was absorptive and porous," and, of course, active.)[16]

Christopher Ballantine, for his part, considers the connection between music and the past in primarily social terms. In an argument reminiscent of Lévi-Strauss's belief (that music "rediscover[s] structures which already exist . . . on the mythical level"),[17] he maintains that societal and ideological ideas find expression in musical forms and structures. Of course this position runs the risk of lapsing into theoretical reflectionism, something which Ballantine is not always able to escape. In an analysis of the work of

J. S. Bach and other composers working just before the French Revolution, for instance, he finds only mechanical, predetermined musical forms and patterns of development. (He singles out the fugue as a particularly moribund form and ultimately condemns Bach for failing to escape the ideological rigors of the Enlightenment since, according to Ballantine, Bach's work adheres too closely to its rationalist ideology.)

Instead, Ballantine prefers music that he believes offers a respite or sanctuary from mainstream ideology and its aesthetic forms, and for him that refuge is supplied by music that appears to harken back to moments of prior unity. Ballantine highlights works that evoke "simpler periods" or that utilize allegedly more primitive social forms, referring approvingly, for instance, to the musical quotations in the work of Charles Ives, which he claims inject elements of popular, massified culture into now-canonized art forms. Yet Ballantine's own investment in unity becomes apparent here, for although the different kinds of music used in Ives do not interact with one another in harmonious, noncontradictory ways, they nonetheless construct a totalized representation of society—one that, in Ballantine's estimation, unmasks its "real foundations"[18]—an idea, of course, which assumes that a complete or "real" representation of culture is possible to begin with.

A methodological contradiction pervades Ballantine's argument. On the one hand, he lauds the music of Ives for its ability to reveal the relationships of its proper social and ideological context, yet his critique of Bach stems from the belief that his music fails to *transcend* its context or to offer the sense of a utopian refuge. One wonders if music is supposed to be excessive or not. Ballantine's assessment of Beethoven begins to clarify the problem.

For him, Beethoven's use of the sonata form musically exemplifies Hegelian dialectics: he believes that the sonata movements' differing themes and tonal activity dramatize the dialectical principles of conflict and tension. Just as Lévi-Strauss argued that the fugue reunites the kind of oppositional extremes found in myth, Ballantine maintains that through this musical tension a sense of unity and integration emerges. In fact, what ultimately attracts Ballantine to the sonata form is its alleged ability to synthesize materials (recapitulation, for example, does not repeat the earlier musical activity of the piece so much as modify it): "Sonata . . . like the unifying of opposites in Hegel, ends only when reason has organized the whole so that 'every part exists only in relation to the whole,' and 'every individual entity has meaning and significance only in relation to the totality.' "[19] So fully does Ballantine believe this to be illustrated in Beethoven's sonatas that, somewhat astonishingly, he stresses the coincidence of Beethoven's and Hegel's birth years.

But to Ballantine, Beethoven's work does more than parallel contemporary ideas and philosophical principles; it also transcends them. Somewhat romantically, he argues that in combining both "thought and affect," Beethoven exceeds the boundaries of standard sonata form. What this means for Ballantine in social and historical terms is that the composer first confronted important issues and then moved beyond them. Unlike Bach, for instance, who was unconcerned with social alienation in his counterpoint, "Beethoven *started* from alienation, then in musical terms transcended it."[20]

In spite of Ballantine's conflicting desires for music to "transcend" its social and aesthetic context and to reveal its "real foundations," he implicitly maintains that music's goal is not so much to reproduce contemporary social and intellectual concepts as it is to move beyond them and to represent more than what is immediately known about them. Perhaps then the ideas are not as contradictory as they first appear, since both assume that music responds, whether affirmatively or critically, to the society that gives rise to it. Yet even this modified position raises problems by implying that art and music are merely the effects of larger causes, the superstructural consequence of some loosely defined social base. Such a position dramatically limits music's semiotic possibilities and range: music is left either passively to reflect its base or to work in counterpoint to it—just as the classical conception of Hollywood film music argued that the score should respond to the "base" provided by the film image.

Ballantine pushes his concern for unity further, arguing that music and society are so closely tied as once to have been virtually linked in primordial unity. During medieval times, he argues, music was more closely connected to its society than it is today, since there was not the sharp separation of producers, consumers, and so forth. Nor does Ballantine find separation at other levels, like in the different *types* of music produced at the time (he perceives no radical distinctions among musical forms such as the plainsong, troubadour song, and folk song, for example).[21] In this way, the relations among different kinds of music as well as the relationship of music to society in general are both characterized by the notions of integration, cohesion, and homogeneousness.

Like other cultural historians, Ballantine argues that the advance of capital and the rise of the bourgeoisie put an end to this overall cohesion. But for him, as opposed to someone like Adorno, integrated relations are still possible in the fragmented world of contemporary capitalism, even if their existence is not immediately apparent.[22] As his analyses of Beethoven and Ives suggest, it is music that has the ability to make these relations known. And it is music that once again operates as the conduit through which the sense of wholeness and unity is allegedly apprehended. In fact, Ballantine explains that the problem facing music scholarship in general is to "recover the concept of the whole."[23]

Canadian musicologist John Shepherd casts the idea of wholeness onto what he calls "pre-literate" culture, a precapitalist, pretypographic feudal society.[24] According to his description, this culture is unified through a variety of mutually reinforcing systems—perceptual, economic, religious—and each makes its own particular appeals to homogeneity and unity. Shepherd argues, for example, that the physical and mental worlds of the time were relatively indistinct since advanced systems of measurement (such as measuring time) had not been developed; a spiritual unity also existed through the sense of a "oneness with God"; in the economic sphere, labor was relatively nonspecialized and undivided, and in government, according to Shepherd, the "political-economic power group was to a large extent, constituted by the entire society."[25] This last observation leads Shepherd to claim that generally a sense of consensus prevailed and that public opinion was largely undifferentiated, a point rather precariously made given that the culture he describes was based on the feudal system. Yet what is important here is that the unity Shepherd ascribes to pre-literate society is a discursive projection and not an historical actuality.

Like Lowe and Ong, Shepherd goes on to discuss the centrality of sound and hearing to the unity of this early period. In a comment reminiscent of Eisler, he remarks that while sight always focuses on a single source, hearing absorbs multiple stimuli at once, leading him to conceive of sound in general as all-encompassing, anarchic, and in flux. In the same vein, he insists that sound is immediately accessible to human perception and describes the relationship between human consciousness and sound as one of mutuality and fusion. Shepherd's account of pre-literate music comes within striking distance of Lacan's pre-linguistic imaginary, particularly in terms of the fusion and internal integrity crucial to his characterization. As Shepherd describes it, pre-literate music is structurally as unified as the culture which gave rise to it: "In pre-literate music any 'unifying factors' of form are 'intrinsic'. . . rather than extrinsic and externally imposed. Firstly, the most common melodic factor is that of the repetition and variation of short motifs. Secondly, we are told that 'most primitive polyphonic music employs identical or similar materials in each part.' "[26]

The kind of music Shepherd describes here contrasts dramatically with tonal music, which emphasizes movement and patterns of development, qualities which require a keen sense of memory and time—conceptual emphases, it must be added, that are unfathomable in an imaginary register. (As if to stress this difference, Shepherd writes that "pre-literate" music "depend[s] upon the immediately adjacent existence in the memory of the listener of material closely related to that which he is actually hearing.")[27] Tonality, unlike earlier forms of music such as pentatonicism, is rigidly and hierarchically structured: all of its fundamentals, for example, relate back to a single note. "In this fashion," Shepherd writes, "the architectonicism of the tonal structure articulates the world sense of industrial man, for it is a structure having one central viewpoint (that of the key-note) that is the focus of a single, unified sound-sense involving a high degree of distancing."[28] In this scheme, tonality is a music finally of cause and effect, of fragmentation and alienation, traits that sharply distinguish it from the more holistic music of the pre-literate era.

Yet, as Shepherd's earlier remarks reveal, pre-literate music suggests an idealized and relatively self-contained phenomenon. His comments about its "intrinsically" guaranteed unity indicate that, although this music may structurally duplicate the integrity of its society more generally, it does so in a noninteractive, autonomous fashion. In this light, it becomes difficult to see music as a truly social and historical phenomenon.

The problem is further compounded by an irony that emerges in Shepherd's otherwise excellent critique of Suzanne Langer. Langer, it should be recalled, argues that music externalizes—and in fact, structurally duplicates—inner human emotion, a position that clearly adheres to romantic and expressionist conceptions of music. But if music speaks an inner voice imbedded within subjectivity, as Langer contends (and as Silverman has shown in a different context regarding the female voice in cinema), then it cannot be logically connected to the external world of social relations. Shepherd shrewdly notes that what Langer initially posits as an interiority functions as an *externality* since her position removes music from the realm of a social, material world.[29] And yet, while Shepherd proposes to do away altogether with the "interior" and "exterior" opposition, his own conception of the integrated pre-literate works very much to preserve it by creating an external site of projected unity, an historically impossible "other."

Shepherd's argument echoes those of poststructuralists and psychoanalysts in its notion of subjectivity in pre-literate times. In the same way that he characterizes the society itself in terms of fullness and unity, so does he constitute its subject as integrated and fully cohesive, not unlike the centered subject studio composers found in romanticism. Apparently what enables the pre-literate subject to construct his own sense of wholeness (as well as the impression of a unified world around him) is the idea of sound and hearing. Shepherd states, "Pre-literate man . . . sees himself as being in the centre of a sound universe, which is dynamic and bounding with energy."[30] (The generic male term, I should add, is by no means insignificant here.)

Moving still closer to critics like Barthes and Kristeva, Shepherd goes on to argue that listening to pre-literate music offered a kind of liberation to its society since it had yet to undergo rationalization, temporalization, or abstraction. He describes listening as a fundamentally sensorial experience—a description not unlike Barthes's and Kristeva's conception of music as a somatic, erotic phenomenon.[31] And just as Kristeva associated music with a condition that precedes subject-object distinctions, Shepherd argues that in pre-literate culture it was difficult for listening subjects to distance or even distinguish themselves from the music they were hearing: "Since pre-literate man possesses neither the objectivity nor the high division of labour necessary to divorce music from the immediacy of its social context, it would seem highly unlikely that he would be able to distance himself to any appreciable extent from the musical experience." He then goes on to argue that this music was less "abstracted" and "manipulated" than it has become in industrial society, arguing once again for the immediacy music allegedly enjoys with human experience and consumption.[32] And while his reference to absorption anticipates Adorno's critique of the way popular music narcotizes and absorbs its auditors, Shepherd (distinctly *unlike* Adorno) appears to prefer this to the rationalized, distanced, and reified music and listening habits which emerged with later harmonic forms.[33]

Adorno, Popular Music, and an Ambivalent Nostalgia

It would be difficult to imagine the nostalgic impulse toward unity and totality in Shepherd, Ballantine, and Lowe playing much of a role in the work of Frankfurt School theorists, since theirs has been perhaps the deepest suspicion of the term. As I mention in chapter two, they no longer considered integration and unity possibilities in a culture that had allowed capitalism—not to mention fascism—to flourish and that had given rise to the Holocaust and to atomic warfare. To retain totality in this climate even as a theoretical possibility was not only intellectually disingenuous but politically naive. The extreme pessimism of Adorno and Horkheimer in particular has arguably transformed the concept of totality from a condition of utopian desirability—as it had once functioned in Marxism—into one that simply describes the pernicious ubiquity of the culture industry. Still, and in spite of his critique of the sense of forced integration and homogeneity it prompted, Adorno is surprisingly conflicted about the idea of unity in his own aesthetic theory, particularly where music is involved. Like Eisler, with whom he collaborated on *Composing for the Film*,[34] he advocated a critical, distanciated mode of listening and condemned the culture industry for making that impossible. He argued that romantic music had set the stage for that, and he chastised Wagner for weaving his own earlier spells of self-sufficiency and unity. Yet, curiously, he joins others, including Wagner, in situating music within lost periods of imagined wholeness and integrity.[35]

Initially Adorno maintains that art operates in a complex dialectic relationship with culture, on the one hand "commensurable, however indirectly, with the outside world of social reality," able to unveil its ideological machinations, and, on the other, refusing these things, "well-defined in itself" and "not unequivocally identifiable with any moments of the outside world."[36] Such a tension enables Adorno to argue for art's ability to perform "positive" (i.e., ideologically or culturally affirming) as well as critical, negative functions. Although this dialectic occasionally collapses into self-contradiction (what does one do, for instance, with the comment "There is nothing in art that is directly social"?),[37] it is important to remember that in the final analysis, Adorno strips popular music of any capacity for potential negative commentary, making out-and-out subversion of mainstream representational and social practices virtually impossible. For him, as well as for his collaborator Horkheimer, the culture industry of late industrial capitalism had fully recuperated music's oppositional edge. Moreover, if any work of art—musical or otherwise—were to be considered meaningful, its parts must integrally relate to the work as a whole. But for the Frankfurt School, it could no longer offer such a comforting promise, and any attempt to provide totality or unity was, in Adorno's and Horkheimer's estimation, bankrupt. (Jazz, the music that receives Adorno's greatest disapprobation, "never really disturb[s] the crude unity of the basic rhythm, the identically sustained metre, the quarter-note."[38]) If art is to produce knowledge at all, it must expose the conflicted facts of its own alienated state: "Art of the highest calibre pushes beyond totality towards a state of fragmentation,"[39] and Adorno's enthusiasm for Schönberg offers proof of this position.

Needless to say, the forms Adorno finds in greatest complicity with capitalism are the ones he considers to be the most dependent on its economic and technological supports, that is, items which are mass-produced and reproduced. Unlike Benjamin, who maintained that film, radio, and other mass-reproduced forms held the possibility of a negative critical function, Adorno argues that they reveal nothing more than the dismal fact of their own commodification. For him, the culture industry is the great homogenizer; the only difference between products has been manufactured solely for purposes of the marketplace. Even high, established art forms have fallen into the clutches of the culture industry, with Beethoven symphonies and other "great masterpieces" joining advertizing jingles and Muzak through their fragmented, fetishized, and trivialized circulation (Adorno cites the "Ode to Joy" movement of Beethoven's Ninth Symphony as an example of how high art music has been reduced to the status of an instantly recognizable popular theme—a comment made long before its release in the 1970s as "Song of Joy" on the pop music circuit). This meshing of high and low forms was perhaps the supreme expression of how the culture industry has standardized the entirety of its aesthetic and media output (although, it must be remembered, Adorno accomplishes much the same thing when he groups film music, jazz, rock, easy listening, swing, theater, and Muzak into a single, contemptible category). It is ironic that even forms of "autonomous" music, which Adorno defines as uninvolved in the tainted sphere of standardized production and reproduction, are, in the end, subsumed by the culture industry.[40]

In an article entitled "The Radio Symphony," Adorno argues that the blurring of "serious" and "trivial" musical forms begins with the technology that transmits them, recalling the technophobia of some classical film music commentators.[41] The "mechanical process" standardizes music; through it, "any symphony can be replaced by any other which has the same framework."[42] Beethoven's symphonies—Adorno suggests the Fifth or the Seventh, although he never really explains why—cannot withstand radio transmission; their broadcast, he argues, transforms them into something less than the original work. To be sure, the technology of early radio broadcasting (the article was written in 1941) did present less than ideal listening conditions since it restricted the dynamic range of the piece, its complexity of texture, and so on. Yet this is not what is at stake, for Adorno argues that the piece *itself* is altered and its actual existence changed by virtue of having been transmitted. In fact, he argues, "complex" works such as Beethoven's symphonies are not even suitable for radio broadcast in the first place (whereas Wagner's are, since Adorno argues that his work never attains the same level of seriousness as Beethoven's). Adorno's idea that "serious art" cannot be translated into, or transmitted by, mass-produced means shifts the terms of his argument considerably for, in fixing essential properties to different musical forms, his analysis abandons its ideological concerns in favor of less political, ontological ones.

What is more, his comments on the degradation of once-complex music invoke the same sense of phenomenal loss that characterizes classical discussions of film sound, especially those that argue that technology robs the cinema of its allegedly human dimension. Adorno extends this idea of loss into the listening situation itself, arguing that the broadcast changes the conditions of reception so dramatically that one cannot even hear the music in the same way as when it is performed live. In live situations, he maintains, listening is active and concentrated, with the performance "surrounding" its auditors, immersing and absorbing them in a sense of wholeness. Adorno characterizes broadcast music, on the other hand, in terms of fragmentation and dismemberment, features that for him engender passive, distracted modes of listening—much as London observed in regard to the audience's unconscious apprehension of film music. One notes here another similarity between Adorno's interest in live music as a means of humanizing the experience of music listening and Hollywood film critics who used sound and music as a means rhetorically to animate the cinema.

Adorno's assessment of live music also calls to mind Shepherd's description of pre-literate music listening. Like Shepherd's, his account signals a near-imaginary condition, something made apparent in the following passage on radio transmission: "[In radio, t]he sound is no longer 'larger' than the individual. In the private room, that magnitude of sound causes disproportions which the listener mutes down. The 'surrounding' function of music also disappears, partly because of the diminutions of absolute dimensions, partly because of the monaural conditions of radio broadcasting. What is left of the symphony even in the ideal case of an adequate reproduction of sound colors, is a mere Chamber symphony."[43]

Adorno goes on to argue that music has been reduced to a singular, commercial function in his well-known 1938 article, "On the Fetish-Character in Music and the Regression of Listening," where he writes that music signifies nothing but the pleasure it promises as a product. The consumer, in turn, comes to cherish the commodity value of the item, worshipping not the music but "the money that he himself has paid for the Toscanini concert."[44] Music's reification has reached such proportions that it is appraised for aesthetic qualities Adorno considers to be entirely bankrupt: lack of tension, simplicity, adherence to predetermined patterns of development, and flawless, standardized performances. The culture industry, in short, has assigned music a soothing, narcotizing function, appeasing instead of challenging its consumers (something he notes in reference to the aptly named "easy listening" music), equipping them with a self-deluded sense of aesthetic expertise and sophistication. The "regressive listening" Adorno ultimately affiliates with popular music arrests our abilities to listen at what he calls "infantile" and "retarded" levels; auditors, he argues, with no hope of resisting, cannot actively or critically engage themselves, nor consciously apprehend music.[45] It is as if the imaginary has very nearly taken over. Curiously, however, while Adorno clearly condemns the sense of immersion and passivity involved in the culture industry, he nonetheless restores an equally imaginary impression of plenitude insofar as it is offered by "complex," "serious" composers and live situations. In other words, he replaces what he considers to be a false, deceptive coherence with an allegedly genuine one. Yet it seems that both emerge from an equally imaginary impulse and are equally impossible, distinctly unreal phenomena.

Adorno's metaphor of immersion suggestively returns music to the idea of a lost moment and an idealized past, one that, as we have seen in chapter two, has been worked out as a reunion with the maternal body. Although Adorno does not follow through on the psychoanalytic dimensions of this idea, he nonetheless constructs a notion of original unity and plenitude that leans heavily on psychoanalysis's understanding of music. In the eventual disruption of this unity through radio transmission, it is as if Adorno fears being bodily severed from the site of musical origins (recall his remark that "the 'surrounding' function of music . . . disappears"), a fear that is at odds with his promotion of otherwise critically distanced modes of music listening. One cannot help but note the "regressive" and nostalgic strain of his own argument here. Indeed, his is a knotted lament for what he believes is a foreclosed unity—be it textual or otherwise.[46]

In order to critique the formulaic nature of contemporary music and the fetishism within music listening, Adorno posits different kinds of music which are defined in terms of wholeness and aesthetic integrity. By now it should come as no surprise that Adorno's conception of "serious" music very much establishes it as that earlier, correct, and, it must be added, livelier, less automated form: "In Beethoven and in good serious music in general . . . the detail virtually contains the whole and leads to the exposition of the whole, while, at the same time, it is produced out of the conception of the whole. . . . Nothing corresponding to this can happen in popular music. It would not affect the musical sense if any detail were taken out of the context; the listener can supply the 'framework' automatically, since it is a mere musical automatism itself. . . . Every detail is substitutable; it serves its function only as a cog in a machine."[47]

Significantly, the different music to which Adorno approvingly points emerges from earlier periods. Sometimes he goes as far back as ancient Greece—not unlike Wagner, whom he will be criticizing for this—at other times, he retreats only as far back as Beethoven or Mozart for examples of good, serious music. With these choices Adorno reconstructs the classic scenario in which artworks were supposed to have once enjoyed unified relations as texts (in terms of their formal construction) and as social products (through their distribution, consumption, and overall social position), using the past as a screen onto which present-day lacks are projected and made good.

If contemporary art can no longer achieve this synthesis, and if good art "pushes beyond totality towards . . . fragmentation,"[48] Adorno reserves a special harshness for the romantics (and for Wagner in particular) for their efforts to recapture unity within textuality, social relations, and subjectivity. His most extensive attack appears in his book-length essay *In Search of Wagner*, whose title alone hints at a certain nostalgic undertaking. In this archeology, which finds the origins of the culture industry in romanticism, Adorno argues that the movement is defined by the "notion that society would be able to regenerate itself if only it could find its way back to its unsullied origins."[49] He finds the culmination of this and other of romanticism's more deplorable tendencies in Wagner. Attacking Wagner's idealization of Hellenic times as a period in which the universal was united with the particular, Adorno argues that this is not only a regressive model, but one based upon a deeply fraudulent unity. As he writes in another context, "because [cultural criticism] fails to see through the apparatus [of material production], it turns towards the past, lured by the promise of immediacy."[50] Yet he himself commits a similar error in arguing that before romanticism—even as recently as Beethoven, if his examples are any indication—music might have been able to express a unified totality.[51] With the ascension of romantic ideology, music became increasingly involved in expressing the composer's subjectivity and so discouraged listeners from understanding the piece as a series of unified interrelationships.

The sentimentality of Wagner's music might deceive its listener into thinking it is conveying important social tensions of the composer's time, but for Adorno it did "nothing less than retract the historical tendency of language, which is based on signification, and to substitute expressiveness for it."[52] Adorno goes on to assault this expressivity by linking the word's etymology (the "pressing out" and externalization of an initial force) to the hard facts of capitalism: "The uncontrollably intensified expressive impulse can barely be contained within the interior, within historical consciousness, and finds release as external gesture. It is this that gives the listener the embarrassing feeling that someone is constantly tugging at his sleeve. The strength of the constructivist element is consumed by this exteriorized, quasi-physical intensity. This exteriorization then merges with the fact of reification, of commodification."[53]

It comes as something of a shock that in spite of Adorno's disdain for expressionist approaches to music, and in spite of his interest in the historical and economic pressures exerted on music, he suggests this same kind of immanent aesthetic purity, which is then subjected to and brutalized by the corrupting, external forces of capital. As we noted of Shepherd's analysis of Langer, the division between interiority and exteriority would also seem to suggest that aesthetic activity exists independently of culture and ideology. What is more, and not unlike the classical studio composer, Adorno indicates that externality threatens to invade the text, writing, ". . . a truly symphonic movement contains nothing fortuitous, every bit is ultimately traceable to very small basic elements, and is deduced from them and not introduced, as it were, from outside, as in romantic music."[54] Far more than his aesthetic dialectic initially suggests, Adorno adheres to the idea of self-contained, autonomous musical pieces.

Such a desire is revealed in his assault on Wagner's notion of the *Gesamtkunstwerk* for its promotion of a specious unity; this falseness in fact provides the linchpin of his critique. As Andreas Huyssen has observed in a different context, "The *Gesamtkunstwerk* is intended as powerful protest against the fragmentation and atomization of art and life in [early industrial] capitalist society. But since it chooses the wrong means it can only end in failure."[55] For Adorno, a genuinely synthesized artwork could simply never emerge; the notion of the *Gesamtkunstwerk* itself is self-contradictory, oscillating between the idea of collective unity and "the negation of everything with an individual stamp."[56] Adorno analyzes a few of the formal devices that he feels promote the particulars over the collective whole in Wagner's work (e.g., the leitmotiv), but he makes an interesting point at another level: Wagner could not have been really interested in a truly synthesized art form since the composer's musical dramas were never created by collective labor.[57] (At the same time, it should be recalled that most of the good, "serious" music Adorno upholds is also produced by individual artists like Beethoven and Schönberg.)

For Adorno, the elements of Wagner's music drama fail to interact with or mutually enhance one another: "In Wagner . . . the radical process of integration, which assiduously draws attention to itself, is already no more than a cover for the underlying fragmentation."[58] In this way too the *Gesamtkunstwerk* operates out of a fundamental homogeneity, not a real principle of synthesis, making it less akin to the Hellenic tragedy and its desirable aesthetic unity than to the present-day culture industry and its pejorative conformity.

Ultimately, Adorno considers the Wagnerian *Gesamtkunstwerk* as a promise that delivers false goods and he condemns Wagner for his inability to musically achieve these goals. To be sure, he does not entirely fault the composer since art under capitalism would, as he would argue, be hard pressed to achieve totality at all.[59] But his position remains vexed nonetheless. For although he clearly deplores romanticism's idealizing obsession with bygone epochs, openly ridiculing its metaphors of organic wholeness and unity, his condemnation of the movement—and its music—stems from its own failure to connect the part to the whole.

Idealism and the Past

It should be stressed that although Adorno and other leftist critics preserve the notion of unity, the radical edge of their observations is not necessarily diminished since the concern for synthesis and totality does not necessarily involve political or aesthetic conservatism, in spite of what film scholars in the 1970s asserted. E. P. Thompson makes this point clear in *The Making of the English Working Class*, where he argues that nostalgic appeals to the past can be progressive under certain circumstances (e.g., the building of a rebellious working-class consciousness toward the end of the late eighteenth and early nineteenth centuries).[60] The ways in which societies define—and project—unity can also help critics to target and challenge current problems and perceived lacks. Consider, for instance, Shepherd, Lowe, Eisler, and Ballantine, who collectively build a unified, highly aural past as a utopian alternative to the fragmented and visually oriented culture from which they write. In this regard it would be premature simply to jettison the utopian element of these kinds of theoretical observations and projections. Yet, before moving on to realign music with a different notion of utopia, it will help to review the main problems in the approaches to music covered so far: the classical approach to Hollywood film composing, poststructuralism, and psychoanalysis as well as Marxism. Three questions haunt these perspectives: the problem of reflectionism; music's so-called representational "difference," a difference usually tied to the idea of excess and femininity; and the pervasive association of music with a desirable lost past.

The first problem of reflectionism affects both the classical and Marxist schemes since they conceive of music as a primarily reactive phenomenon. In the classical approach, film music is believed to reinforce the visual material of the film; for Marxism, music—and its patterns of consumption—is often thought to reflect the social times of its production, an idea that constructs a certain structural parity between music and society (unified societies produce unified texts, alienated societies produce alienated ones, and so on). Or perhaps the relation of music to society responds to a simple cause-and-effect pattern between base and superstructure. Either way, by insisting on its basically illustrative function, assumptions like this make it impossible for music to be a socially active or productive discourse. Moreover, it maintains that music passively absorbs and mouths the dominant ideology of its time, enabling Adorno, for instance, to argue that popular forms like film music are fully assimilated into their industrial contexts and become subordinated to their ideological and representational endeavors.

By emphasizing music's untraditional ways of producing meanings to the extent that they have, psychoanalytic and poststructuralist approaches have constructed music as a simple representational other, the perpetual adversary of conventional symbolic operations. In this way music's utopian dimension has been made quite explicit. Champions of pop culture and high art elitists alike affiliate music with change or a critique of the status quo, the bourgeoisie, and so on. And although these utopian claims are far more apparent in critics like Grossberg who openly celebrate the seditious force of rock music, it is just as present in commentators like Adorno who cast aside pop culture in favor of other, more "serious" forms of music.

As I stated before, the utopianization of music forecloses its ability to interact within a larger social and discursive context and essentializes music for qualities it is believed to possess as standard representation's alleged other: it is seditious, sensual, pre-literate, pre-Oedipal, precultural—terms which all relegate music to something close to a Lacanian imaginary. (It is worth noting that music, rhythm, and other abstract sounds are placed within this irrecoverable sphere much more frequently than are other, more representational systems.) Not only does this assertion ontologize music by assigning it unchanging characteristics, traits, and functions, but it also makes impossible music's ability to operate within concrete representational forms like the cinema. What little effects music is permitted to have there are constructed as almost nonsensical in their "excess." Music, consequently, is barred from generating meaning and participating in discourse at all. What is more, and what raises the political stakes of the matter, is that femininity is often relegated to this "otherly" position.

The third theoretical obstacle is closely connected to the first two, posed as it is by the claim that music signals an idealized anterior moment and is able to conjure forth the lost qualities and goods associated with it. All of the approaches to film music we have covered so far participate in some form or another with this nostalgic conceit, associating music with one of any number of theoretically desirable souvenirs: a lost aesthetic wholeness, the early activity of subjectivity, pre-linguistic representation, precapitalist culture, and so on. This, like the problem of music's "difference," makes it impossible for music to participate in discourse.

But the association of listening and sound with earlier, precapitalist periods—ones characterized in terms of fulfillment, union, and immediacy—nonetheless makes some sense coming from a fragmented society in which proximity and cohesion are perceived as lacking. Moreover, and as postmodernists would remind us, because ours is a vision-dominated culture of flat surfaces and screens, hearing easily lends itself to this impression of fulfilled utopian restoration.[61] Unfortunately, critics do not often acknowledge these facts of their own context, leading critics like Lowe to extend observations on perception as if they were objective historical truths or facts.

Although John Shepherd leans in this direction, many of his more striking remarks about pre-literate culture and its music are made in order to distinguish it from the later, postindustrial era that he characterizes in terms of competing national interests and separate nationalisms, growing antagonism between classes, division of labor, hierarchized musical forms, and so on. Even its designated name makes clear that "pre-literate" culture offers a theoretical alternative whose utopian dimensions are specific to a rational, industrialized, and highly verbal culture whose own needs oblige us to produce utopia in the first place.[62] And although Shepherd makes the important point that the worldview of preliterate society *is* a discursive construct and should not be taken as objective reality, he fails to follow his own advice when he maintains that "unity" had its actual locus there and that it has subsequently been lost.

Shepherd's account makes clear the central problem for Marxist theorists: utopian projections need to be acknowledged as theoretical constructs; utopian fullness and integrity cannot be treated as if they had actually existed or could currently be actualized. The purported integrated subjects or harmonious cultures of utopia exist only as a result of critical interpretation; they are nothing more than discursive ideals and do not identify conditions that really existed. To maintain that they did is to court a theoretical naivete and, moreover, is to put at risk the political force that criticism of this kind offers in the first place.

And so, with exceptions, and with all their good intentions, a number of cultural critics and Marxists have idealized music to such an extent as to separate it from the material conditions of its production and consumption. And although we found this also to be at work among Hollywood classicists and poststructuralists, the irony here is noteworthy given Marxism's readiness to situate music within a social, historical, and ideological framework. Leftist critics have carefully—if unwittingly—preserved its status as a mythically removed, ungrounded "elsewhere."

In this regard, Adorno, for all of his conflicts with the concept of unity, offers a couple of instructive insights. Unlike Barthes and Kristeva, who argue that music's utopian dimension—its excess—can reveal itself through textual practice, Adorno maintains that although music might briefly activate our nostalgia for a lost totality, it can never fully restore it. For him, the possibility of utopia, be it within textuality or within historical and social practice, has passed.[63] And while this initially may appear to indicate little more than a deep political and theoretical pessimism, it yields a very productive observation as well, namely, that it is impossible to actualize a utopia so idealistically conceived. For Adorno, this is due to the ravages of late industrial capitalism and the culture industry. I would argue that it was never possible to begin with.

Toward the end of his life Adorno began to rework the concept of utopia. Its articulation, he conceded, might be possible in bits and pieces—that is, as negative critical moments or, in his phrase, "intermittent dialectics" in art or other cultural practices—but it could never be mounted as a fully elaborated, coherent system. "The utopian impulse in thinking," he wrote in 1969, "is all the stronger, the less it objectifies itself as utopia—a further form of regression—whereby it sabotages its own realization."[64] We will see how crucial these ideas will prove, even though they have met with their fair share of criticism, not the least of which from Siegfried Kracauer, Adorno's life-long colleague. Kracauer argues that Adorno shows "that the concept of Utopia is a *vanishing* concept when besieged; it vanishes if you want to spell it out."[65] When Adorno's conception of utopia is subjected to theoretical or philosophical logic in this way, Kracauer contends, it remains an "unstatable" (not to mention unstable) notion. Yet the "unstatability" of Adorno's utopia that Kracauer provocatively raises recalls the notion of ineffability that has proven so central to critical discussions of film music, and it will be a major concept in renegotiating the idea of musical utopias in the cinema. For, as we have already seen, it is with great difficulty that utopia is enunciated at all.

FOUR

OUT OF THE PAST

RECONTEXTUALIZING THE UTOPIAS

OF FILM MUSIC

ALTHOUGH THE CLASSICAL approach to film music dominated a specific historical and institutional setting, and although that setting, though fully situated in the twentieth century, adhered to the aesthetic ideology of late nineteenth-century romanticism, it is by now apparent that romanticism's influence extends well beyond the golden era of Hollywood film scoring. Virtually all of the approaches to film or popular music we have covered subscribe to at least one of its tenets: that music offers something more than conventional language; that it reveals glimpses of a better, more unified world (or a more profound experience of our own); that it unveils universal truths or essences and opens doors to exotic situations or lands; and lastly—and perhaps most importantly—that it can capture the sense of lost integrity and grandeur. Romantic ideology seems to have given critics the green light to remove cinema music from its discursive and institutional contexts and then to reassert its immunity from these same concerns.[1] In many ways, film music has been handed down to us as something ethereal, timeless, and deeply ahistorical. It is easy to see how a utopian understanding of it can emerge—and indeed has emerged—from this particular set of assumptions.

The ensuing conception of utopia, moreover, is utopian in the strictest sense of the word, a "no-place," an impossible, unrepresentable, and idealized condition with little in common with the facts of actual social and historical existence. Others before me, including (and especially) Marxists, have critiqued the concept of utopia for this reason. Orthodox Marxists have met the idea of utopian thought with special distaste; Friedrich Engels ties the concept itself to the ideology of the bourgeoisie. Yet there are sound reasons to retain and rework the idea. First, its very pervasiveness suggests that no matter how politically or theoretically problematic it might be, the concept cannot be wished away. Second, the idea is especially crucial for political critics to consider since it enables what is largely known as negative criticism to begin, as Fredric Jameson has influentially argued, a constructive, "positive" agenda. Even the pessimistic Frankfurt

School thinkers (especially later members such as Marcuse) preserved a philosophical sense of an eschatological goal that could be likened to the idea of utopia or utopian rebellion. Consider, for instance, the analysis of twentieth-century serial music by Ernst Bloch (whom I will be discussing in greater detail below): In contrast to Adorno and Attali, Bloch argues that serial music is not the structural expression of alienated relations under postindustrial capitalism but the fulfillment of this culture's desire for openness. Openness is created through the absence of set keys and prescribed paths of musical development. Thus, while it may be read as one of late capitalism's most fragmented, alienated aesthetic forms, serial music also constructs the hope for an alternative working against this same alienation.[2]

Of course the problem even with political criticism is its tendency to systemize the idea of utopia to such an extent that it becomes impossibly idealized, resting outside of history and culture as we know it. As we have seen, criticism often works to abolish difference, enclosing utopia within a sealed-off imaginary. It should be recalled here that even Thomas More located his utopia on a remote island. Indeed, utopias have consistently provided a womblike haven from the world, replete with their soothing waters—something as true today for feminists who glorify the maternal and its amniotic *chora* as it was in More's scenario. Femininized or not, however, the utopian condition is obsessively marked by escape, excess, and as something beyond discourse. The task of this chapter, as the title suggests, will be to rematerialize and reconsider the notion of utopia in regard to film music. For, as I have already begun to indicate, utopian thought serves an important critical function, one that provides commentary on the society it purportedly transcends.

It is difficult to recontextualize utopia without assigning it the same function it has always had simply in less troublesome terms. Indeed, the concept needs to be rethought in new ways altogether. Utopia does not always entail active resistance—to argue this implies a monolithic conception not only of dominant ideology but of the alternative or marginal practices that might oppose it. Instead, as I stress in the introduction to this study, utopia is fleeting and partial; its signs offer strategies and tactics, something akin to what Michel de Certeau has called "ways of making," ways of putting the practices of everyday life to different and unexpected ends.

De Certeau's discussion culls examples from the working class (for whom *la perruque*, "the wig," disguises workers' labor from their employers, e.g., writing notes on company time, using business equipment for personal projects, and so on) and from native Americans colonized by Spain (who, although subjected to a foreign culture brutally imposed upon them, "used the laws, practices and representations . . . to ends other than those of their conquerors").[3] De Certeau stresses the resistance expressed through the seemingly minor acts of everyday life, small rebellions against larger imposed dominants. Not surprisingly, he associates these activities with popular culture—certainly a significant gesture for any critic interested in the Hollywood cinema. Moreover, de Certeau's focus on the idea of the secondary production involved in using "already-produced" representations, images, and sounds firmly emphasizes the active role of interpretation, an emphasis we will want to preserve in our own study of film music.

Another way to begin to concretize film music and utopian thought is offered through Elizabeth Cowie's discussion of fantasy. Cowie argues that fantasy does not involve the objects of specific desires so much as the *process* by which desire is put into a scene, the staging "of what can never directly be seen."[4] Like de Certeau, Cowie emphasizes the actions and structures through which desires are set into play, bestowing importance upon the critical act of interpretation. Moreover, her remarks suggestively imply that sound and music might take up where vision, fundamentally impaired, leaves off, since, as she puts it, the things of fantasy "can never directly be seen."

Insofar as film music is concerned, it is important to recall that the untraditional traits associated with its utopian capabilities (its emotional pulls, abstractness, non-representationability and so on) *do* exist but that they remain, like the music itself, historically bound products of discourse that are not automatic or naturally guaranteed. The escapist, excessive, and utopian properties of film music must be considered in light of the cultural, institutional, and ideological functions it serves at a particular time.

Much of the utopian ideology of classical film music is founded on the idea of nostalgia, a word derived from the Greek *nostos*, to return home, and *algia*, a mournful or painful condition. Although the term was first coined by a Swiss doctor in the late seventeenth century, it did not come into prominence for a hundred years or so. Over time it has become more common, although its demedicalization even as a psychological disorder appears to have only been quite recent.[5] Significantly, the word's entry into our vocabulary corresponds to certain developments in the expansion of market and industrial capitalism, a system that, it should be stressed, also necessitates the idea of "homesickness" through its long history of colonization—the word *nostalgia* in fact was initially used to describe the melancholia of soldiers fighting on foreign soil—and through capitalism's slow but inexorable disengagement of private from public spheres. With the latter, as social historians are at pains to note, people began to lament a vanishing sense of mass community—a nostalgia, it should be recalled, that János Maróthy links to a bourgeois sensibility. Privatized notions of domestic life began to replace a more communal sense of home. During the era of the Enlightenment, domestic relations were considered primary, the family was idealized and individual needs were believed to supersede social ones. The public sphere grew to become an antagonistically defined other with supposedly less gratification to offer individuals and their families, and "home" functioned as an asylum, a cherished refuge from an allegedly hostile world. The trend, of course, continues, perhaps culminating with the self-contained nuclear family of the 1950s. (Interestingly, and as sociologist Fred Davis notes, it was soon after this that the word *nostalgia* came to be used as a matter of everyday speech.)[6]

Maróthy shows how this ideology of homesickness first began to take root in music. Tonality, for instance, always returns "home" to the tonal center of the piece. It also preserves the sanctity of this home by expelling "foreign" elements such as chromaticism or by domesticating those few that are allowed to remain. In an analysis of Bizet's *Carmen*, for example, Susan McClary has shown how the exotic, sexually "excessive" Carmen threatens the opera formally through the dissonant, chromatic elements associated with her, something which makes Carmen's final undoing as inevitable musically as it is does narratively and ideologically.[7]

The occasional inclusion of musically dissonant elements works to lend special force to the final tonal achievement of a piece. By retarding tonal resolution—and thus delaying the return "home"—Maróthy observes how Western music conveys the idea that this goal is truly difficult to attain, elevating what he rightly perceives as a banal conceit into a grand and noble conquest. This practice, as Maróthy and others have noted, historically helped lead to the gradual sentimentalization of Western music. Based on the idea of desire's impossibility, musical sentimentality relies on formal devices such as melismatics and rhythmic lengthening to stress the irretrievability of the object and to enhance its emotional weight. Lyrics also contribute to the sense of nostalgia and sentimentality, operating in forms as diverse as American folk tunes ("Red River Valley"), popular songs ("Those Were the Days" and "Yesterday" from the 1960s) and *lieder* (Mahler's "*Kindertotenlieder*," in addition to the Schubert mentioned by Barthes). Even the cynical Adorno was led to note that sentimental music caused people to weep over what he called their "missed fulfillment."[8]

And so film scores are not alone in generating the impression of sanctuary for their listeners or of extending a reprieve from currently perceived problems. It is also important to stress here how these problems and lacks enjoy concrete institutional support, as Marxists would remind us and, as psychoanalysts assert, involve some of the fundamental incoherences of human subjectivity. In these ways, utopian thought constantly involves a conceptual movement toward totality at the same time it moves away from a fragmented and lacking origin.

As far as popular film scores are concerned, according to certain Marxist perspectives, music functions not only as a "home" or sanctuary from capitalism (or Hollywood, or its films) but as a reprieve from its fragmenting and alienating effects (think of Lowe, Ballantine, Shepherd, and especially Adorno). The idea even enters into Maróthy's work, since he too refers to bygone communal epochs that preceded the entrenchment of bourgeois musical forms. But these past epochs function quite differently for him than they do for critics like Adorno, for unlike Adorno, Maróthy argues that this communality, this potential socialist utopia, can in fact be reactivated within existing social, historical, and representational orders. His position does not so much promote the actualization of an impossible otherworldly "no-place" as it uses portions of it as a model for future change. He associates the anticipatory condition that this involves with music: "The search for the lost mass experience turns the attention of the composers towards the ancient 'Dionysian intoxication' or the surviving collectivity of later periods, for instance Baroque polyphony (both are present in Beethoven). All this—the critical distortion of what exists or the search for the non-existent—is not only a crisis phenomenon, but a *tentative sensing of the future.* Of a future which is not behind the bourgeois world picture but *begins only beyond it.*"[9]

As this passage makes clear, Maróthy tries to move beyond connecting music to a regressive, backward-oriented condition, and, given the frequency with which music is linked to anteriority, this would appear to be an important first step. Yet, at the same time, Maróthy's enthusiasm for music's anticipatory abilities is somewhat difficult to share, for there is nothing automatically to link music's abstract nature—that which lends it what Ernst Bloch will label its *Ungleichzeitigkeit*—to the future any more than to the past.

Still, the idea has critical precedent, especially in the work of Bloch, for whom the arts—and music most particularly—could forecast the future and give anticipatory "traces" of it. Bloch, of course, is less widely known than Lukács, Adorno, and the other Marxists with whom he was loosely affiliated. This is partly explained by his longtime support of Soviet communism (even after Stalin), something that caused considerable tension between him and other leftists. Moreover, his interest in mysticism, aesthetics, and utopian thought (his magnum opus, *Geist der Utopie*, appeared in 1918) led to his further ostracization by more conventional Marxists. As Jack Zipes has recently pointed out in a volume of *New German Critique* devoted to Bloch, his largest audience in the United States has been among theologians.[10] Things, however, are beginning to change, most notably due to Jameson's work in the 1970s and 1980s (especially *Marxism and Form*) and special issues of journals like *New German Critique*.

Bloch's belief in music's anticipatory value stems from a dialectic aesthetics that, like Adorno's, holds that art is rooted in the age of its production at the same time it is estranged from it. (A good example of this would be Bloch's interpretation of serial music mentioned earlier. Music does, despite a potentially high degree of displacement, respond to the needs of its time. In regard to film music, one might consider how the score of *Gone with the Wind* discussed in chapter one plays out the threat of a nation divided at a time when global fascism was on the rise, when the Depression had scarcely retreated, and so forth.) For Bloch, the temporal and historical discontinuities involved in the process enables art to preserve the memory of what he considers earlier forms and "archetypes" while retaining sight of future ones.

To illustrate this point he borrows a passage from Nietzsche: "Music is of all plants the last to appear. Indeed, once in a while music peals forth into an amazed and modern world like the speech of a vanished epoch and comes too late. . . . Only with Mozart was the age of Louis XIV and the art of Racine and Claude Lorrain repaid in gold of the realm; not until Beethoven and Rossini was there a musical finale to the 18th century."[11] Initially, Bloch appears to endorse Nietzsche's remarks, particularly when he notes just how "shallow" matching Mozart with "Austrian Rococo" or Beethoven with the "Empire style" would be.[12] Yet he is critical of Nietzsche as well, protesting the suggestion that meaning in music is produced retrospectively (since for Nietzsche artists "sum up" earlier movements). For Bloch, this position not only relegates music to the past but requires it to reflect this anterior state, not actively building upon existing or future ones. In a gentle but significant revision, Bloch proposes instead that Wagner was the "fulfillment" of Mozart, suggesting less that Wagner's music summed up Mozart or Mozart's age than that it revealed traces (*Spuren*) of the future that had already been imbedded.[13]

The idea of future traces being latent within the social forms of the present has a crucial place in Bloch's theory of *Ungleichzeitigkeit*, or nonsynchronous or uneven development. The latter term is taken from *The Critique of Political Economy*,[14] in which Marx briefly alludes to the disparity between the activities of base and superstructure and between the development of economic and cultural phenomena (consider its usefulness in describing the uneven development in Third-World countries today). The idea, of course, challenges the notion that superstructural phenomena are determined solely by their economic base. For Bloch, *Ungleichzeitigkeit* offers a way to accentuate the temporal disphasure he deems so important to music, to stress the delays and deferrals he believes to be at work between music and its signifying potential.

Another component of Bloch's theory of nonsynchronous development involves what he calls "cultural surplus," a surfeit that enables music and other art forms to endure beyond their immediate socio-historical and aesthetic contexts. He argues, for instance, that art (along with nature and religion) will outlive capitalism and help articulate cultures that emerge in its stead. The notion of surplus suggestively calls to mind Barthes's and Kristeva's theories of poetic excess, since for them too poetic practices frustrate and surpass mainstream contemporary forms. Yet, whereas Kristeva and Barthes gauge excess chiefly in representational terms, Bloch casts it into a dialectic involving ideology and utopian thought: music then emerges from an historical and ideological base that, in exceeding that base, broaches the utopian.[15]

Art's negative relation to its own time causes Bloch to emphasize the idea of the future—the "not-yet-conscious"—in the artwork: "Every great work of art, above and beyond its manifest content, is carried out according to a *latency of the page to come*, or in other words, in the light of the content of a future which has not yet come into being, and indeed of some ultimate resolution as yet unknown."[16] Other critics have also argued for the anticipatory powers of music. Attali, for example, has somewhat extravagantly claimed that "every major social rupture has been preceded by an essential mutation in the codes of music, in its mode of audition and in its economy." (To him, 1950s rock and roll anticipates the social protests and upheaval that followed in the 1960s, for example.)[17] Attali argues that because musical codes are abstract, flexible, and change more easily than those of more concrete sign systems, the future is more readily inscribed in them than in other, more rigidly codified forms. His remarks that music is "ahead of the rest of society" and that "as a mode of immaterial production it relates to the structuring of theoretical paradigms, far ahead of concrete production" show the extent to which his ideas are indebted to Bloch's notion of *Ungleichzeitigkeit*.[18] One even finds the notion circulating in more popular arenas, as Timothy Leary proclaims, "Rock is the voice of the future. The old establishment will always hate it."[19]

There is, as I have already argued, a danger in arguing for music's prophetic abilities. Giving it an anticipatory function is, in a very real sense, much the same as assigning it a nostalgic one, albeit in reverse, with idealism being projected forward instead of backward. Yet the idea that music is "out of sync" with its immediate context is nonetheless quite important. To begin with, it frees music from the passive, illustrative function it so often has been assigned, especially in the classical film. And although music and other art forms are not obliged to reflect their time in this framework, they nonetheless remain connected to it. And giving the concept of utopia the sense of an historical ground relieves it of the abstraction it undergoes at the hands of Attali, Barthes, and other critics Bloch has influenced.

It is instructive to compare Bloch's discussion of music's physical properties with Barthes's, for, like the author of "The Grain of the Voice,"

Bloch stresses the material nature of music, maintaining—in a very Barthesian turn of phrase—that music "sings of itself." He also highlights music's actual source, be it somatic or instrumental, in considering the effects it produces. But Bloch draws quite different conclusions from these observations than Barthes. Barthes, it should be recalled, believes that the singing voice ultimately signifies a lost condition of subjectivity; for Bloch, it simply means different things within different historical moments. In the nineteenth century, for example, the tenor was equated with erotics, power, and youth, while in the eighteenth century, these qualities were associated with the tessitura and the body of the baritone (e.g., the figure of Don Giovanni).

Bloch upholds a notion of totality, but he refrains from naively endorsing it. For him, it is not something that is ever actual or complete, just as our present-day lacks cannot be projected onto a self-contained past. Instead he argues that traces of the future, traces connected to the utopian promise it holds, are latent within the *incompleteness* of the past and the social forms of the present. Maróthy's account of jazz illustrates precisely what Bloch means. Jazz, according to him, recalls and fulfills earlier, more "primitive" rhythmic forms, although it also surpasses them by creating new ones. And in spite of the adoption of jazz into the middle class, it still preserves its function as a "process from below" that Maróthy argues not only has changed the face of mass culture but extends a partial critique of bourgeois musical forms.

Art, and especially abstract art like music, is an especially appropriate medium through which the "not-yet-conscious" of Bloch's theoretical plan begins to take shape since its connotative activity is relatively unstable and unfixed. Because the aesthetic text houses elements of the non-representational it is able to suggest utopia, the dimension that knows no referent. But utopia's struggle to be put into discourse obliges it to rely heavily upon displacement and disguise in order to be conveyed, something described by Fredric Jameson: "The Utopian moment is indeed in one sense quite impossible for us to imagine, except as the unimaginable; thus a kind of allegorical structure is built into the very forward movement of the Utopian impulse itself, which always points to something other, which can never reveal itself directly but must always speak in figures, which always calls out structurally for completion and exegesis."[20] As Jameson makes clear, utopian thought requires critical analysis to uncover and activate it, much the same way that unconscious desires and meanings have to be decoded out of dreams. Curiously, Bloch does not address the role of interpretation, nor does he directly consider the role in this played by unconscious representational mechanisms such as condensation and displacement, in spite of their obvious applicability to the concept of *Spuren*.

Jameson, however, pursues it in *The Political Unconscious*, a work that repeatedly gestures toward Bloch, even though it never directly acknowledges him. Jameson advocates interpretation which makes use of what he calls a "reconversion process" that cuts through various displacements and disguises in order to locate the utopian energy and political direction of a given text. The choice of psychoanalytic terminology is, of course, deliberate on Jameson's part, but it should not be concluded that Bloch was completely unaware of its hermeneutic force. In Bloch's discussion of dreams, for example, concern is apparent. Bloch divides dreams into two groups, those analyzed by Freud, the "nightdreams" fueled by repression and memories of the "no-longer-conscious," and the "daydreams," or the dramatizations of wishes that are based on the "not-yet-conscious." For Bloch, Freud errs in associating the unconscious solely with the past, and he redirects Freud's emphasis on the unconscious onto the preconscious, which does not lose memories completely to repression but is able to bring them to light.

Since Bloch maintains that the arts, like dreams, do not directly represent their external reality, his special interest in music seems logical. Music plays an extremely prominent role in his conception of utopian thought, and its abstract quality is doubtless what leads him to make the claims he does about its prophetic capabilities. Comparing music's ability to project utopian thought to that of other arts, he writes: "Even as Gothic art, which crossed all boundaries, it contained something balanced, something homogenized. Only music, performed in open spaces, has an explosive effect, and that is why the art of music has always something eccentric in regard to the other arts, as if music were only transposed to the level of beauty and sublimity."[21] It is clear from this passage that Bloch intends to preserve music's distinctiveness as a sign system.

He clarifies the connection between the non-representational aspect of music and utopian thought in a piece on authorial expression. Bloch maintains here that the performance of a musical work yields more meanings than what the composer originally envisioned and, more pressingly, he implies that music's signification emerges most fully from its abstract, non-representational components ("the performer's inflexion, his manner of speech and musical gesture"). In contrast to this, the musical note, a more representational component, "is still empty and uncertain"; the score is merely a "rough indication" of meanings that might be actualized through performance.

"Let us assign to music the primacy of something otherwise ineffable," Bloch insists, "its enigmatic language does not want to hide from us what is already resolved supernaturally. On the contrary, the function of music is the most complete openness."[22] Here he once again anticipates Kristeva and Barthes by associating music with an alternative semiotic field. (No doubt Bloch would be pleased that his work had sufficient "cultural surplus" to reemerge later in poststructuralism!) The limits of conventional sight and vision encourage all of these writers to argue for music's special powers; Bloch casts the idea in especially mystical terms: "[M]usic's different magic resolves this loss of [conventional] sight in a favourable, personally intimate sense, in the more luminous sense of the concept of a spirit-realm."[23] Sight is no longer a reliable centering force and offers nothing in the way of utopian "vision." Years later Attali makes much the same point: "For twenty-five centuries," he writes, "Western knowledge has tried to look upon the world. It has failed to understand that the world is not for the beholding. It is for hearing. It is not legible, but audible. . . . Today, our sight has dimmed; it no longer sees our future, having constructed a present made of abstraction, nonsense and silence. Now we must learn to judge a society by its sounds."[24]

That earlier social and representational activity persists in contemporary forms as "traces" immediately brings to mind the work of Benjamin and Derrida. For Benjamin, however, as Jameson and others have observed, traces operate as signs of past disaster and barbarism, whereas for Bloch they are anticipatory, hopeful. Derrida concerns himself primarily with its signifactory aspects while Bloch places greater weight on their circulation within an historical sphere.[25] Indeed, Bloch's notion of the trace is important precisely because it equips the concept of utopia with this kind of context.

In a significant example, Bloch turns to dance and cinema to explore the non-representational component of movement in the utopian sign. He argues that movement produces an effect beyond conventional meanings; he speaks of its "unnatural eloquence:" "The cooking-pots swaying with the ship in Eisenstein's 'Potemkin' [1925] belong here, and precisely here the great rough stamping boots, shown in isolation, on the steps in Odessa."[26] This argument—even this choice of examples from Eisenstein—strikingly recalls Barthes's discussion of the third meaning. For both, the non-representational element of such signs exceeds standard signification, although Bloch makes this claim less explicitly than does his poststructuralist counterpart. Beyond this, however, the two diverge: Bloch maintains that the "cultural surplus" generated by these signs carries over to subsequent historical periods (and it should be added, interpretive contexts), an altogether different argument from Barthes, who claims that this excess evokes a lost, repressed moment.

For Bloch, a utopia based solely on the past is insufficient since it resurrects stagnant models and precludes future change. In fact, Bloch was as critical of the existing literature on utopia as more conventional Marxists were, and he noted the frequency with which the past had been yoked to what he called "false" or conservative utopias: consider the early Nazi movement, which fed off of a widely experienced nostalgia in Germany at the time—a nostalgia for preindustrial relations, a less urban culture, a more powerful sense of national unity and strength—to win grass roots appeal and promote its own agenda.

Film Music and Utopian Thought

Bloch's aesthetics enable us to sidestep three of the main obstacles that have plagued theories of Hollywood film music. First, he avoids the problem of reflectionism by insisting that music articulates more than its social, economic, or ideological underpinnings. By arguing that music points to cultural and historical frameworks beyond its own context, he implies, like Maróthy, that ideology works its way only obliquely into musical techniques and practices, *partially* uniting the musical works with the social realities of their time, but never fully integrating them into it. Also like Maróthy, Bloch's belief that utopia cannot be directly reflected or represented diminishes the problem of reflectionism.

Second, his notion that utopian thought reveals itself in partial, displaced forms preserves the important idea that music generates meaning, although in different ways from more conventional sign systems. A crucial component of this—and one which greatly influences the present study— is Richard Dyer's notion of the non-representational sign. Such a sign (involving, for example, rhythm, texture, color, or music) knows no real referent and therefore cannot convey the idea of utopia with any precision. Instead it gives the sense of, in Dyer's words, "what utopia would *feel* like, rather than how it would be organized."[27]

Like traditional notions of utopia, Dyer implicitly highlights its communal, social aspect, arguing that utopia is always generated out of the perceived lacks and deficiencies of any historical period (he offers an excellent example through his reading of "We're in the Money" from Depression-era *The Gold Diggers of 1933*, in which the glistening costumes of the dancers convey a sense of abundance and pleasure; in the same way, "Edelweiss" of *The Sound of Music* (1966) promotes the utopia of a rustic and natural landscape, its "noble white" untainted by Nazism, to members of an increasingly urban and high-tech culture). Although I will be taking issue with what is excluded by this, it remains an extremely important emphasis nevertheless. Moreover, although Dyer himself does not use the term, it seems appropriate to describe Hollywood utopias in terms of their being partial utopias, for these films do not promote a full escape so much as the promise or suggestion of one. In fact, Dyer seems to acknowledge this limitation when he emphasizes how the "entertainment industry" defines and hence constrains utopia for consumers. In other words, the sounds and images of "something better" do not necessarily pose a challenge to the status quo but often will reinforce its basic values. In this way, the Hollywood genre film cannot reasonably be expected to be entirely critical of the industrial and ideological machinery giving rise to it; its inscription of utopian resistance and alternatives must always be partial. So too the *alternative* component of Hollywood's utopian impulse must be apprehended in a tentative, limited fashion. To put this another way, music and other non-representational traces simply enable us to catch *glimpses and impressions of utopia*. This generates a promise or feel of utopia that will always be greater than the program it delivers, because utopia, in short, cannot be fully delivered at all.

The third contribution of Bloch's work is equally important. We have seen how theories of Hollywood film music have attempted to resolve at the level of discourse lacks or deficiencies of the present, be this at textual or social levels or within subjectivity, by projecting wholeness onto externalized, anteriorized sites and often "losing" the utopian element into an impossibly lost condition in the process. What distinguishes Bloch from other theorists in this regard is that for him the compensatory process is not fundamentally restorative, that is, it does not strive to regain the past, nor to maintain the present. Instead, it uses the "missing" elements—whether taken from the past or not—as active guidelines for change and social betterment.

The Subject of Utopian Thought

Dyer, who acknowledges Bloch's work, and Attali, who does not, inherit from their German precursor a strong concern for community and the belief that music is a key force in giving it shape and definition. As Attali writes, in a comment reminiscent of Eisler's remark on music's function as a "social cement," "All music, any organization of sounds is . . . a tool for the creation or consolidation of a community, of a totality."[28] Now given the Marxist convictions of these critics, the emphasis on community is hardly surprising. In fact, Bloch moves quite easily from the idea of community to that of communality and communism: "All Utopias, or nearly all," he writes, "despite their feudal or bourgeois commission, predict communal ownership, in brief, have socialism in mind."[29] Indeed, Bloch is at great pains to integrate Marxism's goals into his own recommendations for utopian change. Jameson, for his part, is convinced enough of this to use the words *utopia* and *classless* interchangeably in his work, and to argue that utopian thought is most solidly embodied—or perhaps one should say embedded—within working-class consciousness since the working class would be the first to perceive the need for social and economic transformation. (One is also reminded of de Certeau's examples of practices selected from the working class and other disempowered groups.)

Bloch's, Dyer's, and Jameson's emphasis on community and utopia's social dimension is in keeping with most utopian literature in that it designates utopia as a specific social program. Yet it fails to consider the role subjectivity and agency play in the formation of utopian thought. Their importance is twofold: first, the desires of a particular kind of subject—specifically, a gendered subject—help determine the content of any given utopian projection. In other words, an idea, a sign, or a piece of music is going to appear utopian only to certain listeners, much the same way that its overall significance will depend on its particular social, historical, and institutional context. (Recall here how Barthes's and Kristeva's notions of music and poetic language took as their organizational center the desires of a male subject.)

The subjective factor is equally important at the level of interpretation. Earlier I indicate how Bloch failed to address adequately the role played by the subject in deciphering utopian signs—or rather, in activating their meanings to begin with. Instead, he suggests that utopian meaning is fixed within the trace itself, that its significance is somehow immanent, already there in the text and not shaped by reading—think of his critique of Nietzsche's reading of Mozart, which argues that the sign is "in" the musical composition and realizes itself in later periods. Considered in this way, Bloch's trace is its own ruler, able to put itself into discourse, and shape its own interpretation: "the utopian function not only discovers the cultural surplus as something that belongs to it, but also fetches an element of itself from the ambiguous depth of the archetypes that is an archaically stored-up anticipation of something not-yet-conscious, of something not-yet-accomplished."[30] Although the phrase "utopian function" obscures the matter somewhat, it is clear that there is not much room here for subjectivity to intervene. (Elsewhere, Bloch focuses on the "subjective" dimension of utopian thought but uses the term only insofar as it opposes the allegedly "objective" facts of concrete social existence.)

Since interpretation involves a context, one with historical, discursive, and subjective dimensions, analyzing a text for utopian meanings is not a "subject-less" act any more than it can be neutral or self-effacing.[31] In this light, it is useful to approach the utopian traces of Hollywood film music as part of a utopian sensibility constructed *by* the analyses critics perform on them. For if utopia is, as Bloch avers, contingent upon its hermeneutic context, the subjects who shape and are shaped by this context have to be taken into consideration. Interpreting subjects and subject positions are never as absent as critics might have them be (as evidenced in the work of Barthes and Kristeva), nor are the utopian meanings of the trace fixed or immanent within the text (as Bloch's work suggests). Instead the trace produces meanings as a partial and tentative sign; it has no stable referent but nonetheless prompts certain readings by readers who project utopian functions onto it. It is, in other words, *given* utopian form. To turn Bloch's phrase a bit, it is the consumption of texts that is never complete. Mary Ann Doane, in a discussion of the woman's film, offers an astute quote from the managing director of the International Division of the Motion Picture Association in 1947: "The motion picture is one product which is never completely consumed for the very good reason that it is never entirely forgotten by those who see it. It leaves behind it a residue, or deposit, of imagery and association, and this fact makes it a product unique in our tremendous list of export items."[32] The emphasis of the cited speaker is on the successful commodification of such "residue," of course; Doane's focus falls on its subsequent defamiliarization; my own is on how we can appropriate and restrategize it as critics.

The question of subjectivity also raises the issues of gender and sexual difference, issues that have been conspicuously absent in most of the discussions so far. For Jameson, Attali, and Dyer, this is an especially noticeable omission since feminism has distinctly shaped the political and intellectual milieu out of which they write. Their failure to address these issues is all the more striking in light of their concern with other contextual factors—such as class and ethnicity—involved in the cultural production and reception of utopian discourse.

Writing from an earlier historical time, Bloch's scant references to gender are somewhat less surprising. Yet Maynard Solomon has recently broached the topic (if inadvertently) and suggests the stakes involved for contemporary feminists in Bloch's work. According to Bloch, he notes, archetypes function as expressions of utopian thought and possibility, and Medusa is cited as one of the few archetypes utterly "without hope."[33] Now given the frequency with which Medusa has been appropriated as a sign of feminine strength and resistance (Cixous's "The Laugh of the Medusa" comes quickly to mind here), and given the nature of the myth itself, it is obvious that any despair and "hopelessness" she suggests is going to involve a conventional masculine subject. We saw this "male" despair reach great proportions in Kristeva's work on music and the maternal body; we also saw it hinted at in Goethe when he consigned music to a feminized past. Since these—and other—accounts of music and its utopian pleasures are imbued with such a strong sense of nostalgia, the relationship of nostalgia to sexual difference and subjectivity needs to be raised and interrogated as well.

For a relationship *does* exist between the theories of musical utopias we have been covering and subjectivity, however implicitly they have appeared so far. In chapter two, the issue was inadvertently raised by John Fiske, for whom MTV was "orgasm . . . when signifiers explode in pleasure in the body in an excess of the physical." The question to pose at this point is, just *whose* pleasure was Fiske talking about? *Whose* body, *whose* orgasm? Since Fiske's claim is made in reference to a medium known for its heavy metal groups, rap, and "cock rock,"[34] the answers are not difficult to divine. A similar example can be found in an analysis of Warner Broth-

ers musicals from the 1930s written by Mark Roth.[35] Arguing that these
films are far from "escapist" (something earlier critics were prompted to
assert given the extravagant style of auteurs like Busby Berkeley, known
of course for his highly abstract, visually impossible geographies), Roth
ties them to the contemporary ideology of the New Deal. He goes somewhat too far in drawing exact analogies between characters of backstage
musicals (linking Jimmy Cagney, the director of the musical in *Footlight
Parade* [1933] or Warner Baxter, the director in *42nd Street* [1933]), with
the country's own political "director," FDR). More useful is Roth's emphasis on the collective nature of the films' utopian spirit, which suggests
that the show—and presumably, the United States at large—can be
pulled together only through group effort and cooperation. Yet, in spite of
this focus on united collaboration, the female form is depicted in curiously
fragmented forms, something Lucy Fischer has observed in her article on
Berkeley's *Dames* (1934). Severed from any notion of the whole, the
women appear, in the revealing words of the choreographer, "matched
like pearls" through the fetishistic repetition of isolated body parts.[36] Roth
tellingly remarks that these close ups "border on being foolish," presumably when compared to the coherent, unified efforts (and representations)
of the producers, directors, and backers featured in the film's story.[37] To
Roth, then, these films construct a utopian sensibility, a serious, "harmonious nation" that, as he notes, is definitively political (in replicating the
ideology of the New Deal) but, it should be added, is just as definitively
male.

The close analyses of the next chapter will insist on the involvement of
subjectivity and gender in the making and apprehension of film music's
utopias. Although this is not to diminish the significance of the factors
already taken into account by other critics, it is to redirect the path of the
investigation and ask how the sense of utopia comes to be "engendered" at
all. For it is apparent that women, to modify Jameson's comments on the
working class, have a tremendous amount at stake in creating utopias and
proposing social change. The theoretical issues involved are equally important since femininity is so frequently cast alongside music as a form of
representational excess or difference, and subsequently ostracized from
symbolic relations and social discourse.

With this in mind, it bears repeating that for as much as critics might
like them to, utopias do not always work toward politically progressive
ends or causes, just as I would argue that wholeness in and of itself is not
a reactionary concept. For instance, the communal and nostalgic dimension of utopia—so crucial to the Marxist theories we have been investigat-
ing—can be harnessed to reactionary political ends, as it was under German fascism. The non-representational utopian trace Bloch proposes offers no semantic or ideological assurances; its reliance on displacement

and disguise, in fact, would seem to insist upon the ease with which it can deceive. (Jameson has pointed out how fascist utopias masqueraded as a brand of socialism—literally, a "national socialism"—while courting a profoundly regressive, reactionary politics.) Thus utopian signs, like music, do not guarantee specific political readings or effects; they are not automatically subversive and may actually be bound to forces that seek to preserve and not better unjust social conditions.

Following this, Jameson, like Bloch before him, suggests that the utopia of fascism is a "false" one. Insofar as socialism was commandeered by Nazism as a disguise for its reactionary agenda, and to the extent that this agenda advocates restoration and return instead of actual change, this is true. But the problem here is that Jameson and Bloch assume that only utopias that promote change to the left are truly "authentic." To lay claim to discursive authenticity, however, is not necessarily to politicize one's argument. It seems far more useful to me to assess utopian thought in terms of its utopian and dystopian contours and to consider its abilities— as well as its inabilities—to conceive of change, rather than to categorize it as either true or false.

Although I am finally not interested in Bloch's questions of authenticity, two utopian impulses he associates with the true and false utopias may be usefully approached by comparing the emotional and psychological activity of each. This will prove important to our understanding of film noir and melodrama in the following chapter. What Bloch considers the *faux* utopia involves a restorative and idealized psychological model, something to which he aligns the idea of "filled affects or emotions," which in turn project an "inauthentic future," as he puts it (Jameson calls it an "unreal psychic space").[38] Here, future fulfillment involves simply the preservation of the present, changing it by redressing a few present-day lacks, adding objects as they are desired, and so forth. Jameson labels this approach "infantile" and "primitive," remarking on its inability to conceptualize substantial social change. It cannot, he argues, recognize the fact that change depends upon more than just remedying isolated problems; it needs to consider the interrelationship among worldly phenomena, something that the allegedly more "authentic," second utopian impulse is equipped to do.

The psychic activity associated with this second group is comprised of what Bloch calls "expectation affects," which can be, like those of the first group, either positive or negative, hopeful or fearful, utopian or dystopian. But, rather than promoting change at isolated or individual levels, they work toward organizing a new, different world. To be sure, one would be hard-pressed to find an example of this without recourse to a full-fledged blueprint of utopia, like those of More and other influential utopianists. But more to the point is the fact that this second approach does not have utopia replay the past but instead reworks it as a "way of making," an active *act de faire*.

Because utopian thought knows many forms, it must be stressed that film music, to which we now return, performs vastly different utopian functions in Hollywood genre pictures as well. These texts also engage competing forms of subjectivity. Moreover, although many are fueled by the notion of nostalgia, and although the films "themselves" take many of classicism's precepts as their starting base—especially insofar as they link music to an idealized past—the musical utopias that they construct are actually quite different. Much of that difference, as I hope now to show, depends on notions of sexual difference.

FIVE

MUSICAL UTOPIAS OF THE CLASSICAL FILM

Music is the voice of the past, of memory, of an idealized state,
of a lost moment frozen in time and left behind by its
inexorable advancement.
(Martin Rubin on Back Street *[1932])*

Music for me has always been a kind of refuge, a symbol of
hope. By not having it fit into the diegetic world, it gives
no hope or refuge for any of the characters.
(a student on Kiss Me Deadly *[1955])*

I**T IS EXTREMELY** difficult to find an anticipatory strain in Hollywood's classical film scores, since most lean heavily on the backward-looking model against which Bloch and others rallied so vigorously. Indeed the tendency cuts across a variety of films and genres. In Westerns like *Red River* (1948), for example, traditional folk songs recall America's "Old West"; the powerful main theme of *King's Row* evokes the pleasant childhood of its two male protagonists;[1] and "As Time Goes By" provides a musical souvenir of Ilsa and Rick's love affair in *Casablanca* (1942). The nostalgic utopia that influences so much of the theoretical discourse on film music has, in other words, enjoyed an equally strong hold within the films themselves.

It enjoys special force in some film genres in particular. For films with historical settings like *Gone with the Wind, The Sea Hawk,* and *The Adventures of Robin Hood,* the heavily orchestrated music helps evoke the grandeur of dramatically epic earlier times. To Western ears, scores like Korngold's and Steiner's offer an assuring regalness and stability. (Steiner's instrumentation relies heavily on the string section, Korngold's, the horns, and each of these pieces is composed in stable major keys.)

Steiner's score for *Gone with the Wind* typifies the classical style, consisting as it does of leitmotivs for Scarlett O'Hara, Rhett Butler, and the other characters within the film. ("Tara's Theme" works in much the same way, although it identifies a place and not a character.) But the score does much more than this. In the early prewar scenes, it establishes the grandeur of the antebellum South; later it provocatively recalls it, suggesting not only a homesickness for the period but a strength through the sense of identity the past seemed to offer. Just as the plantation home is used metonymically to convey this visually, "Tara's Theme" appears on the soundtrack when that home appears to be most deeply threatened.

In a similar vein, Korngold's award-winning scores for historical dramas *The Sea Hawk* and *The Adventures of Robin Hood* (as well for *Captain Blood* [1935] and *Juarez* [1939]) highlight the same sense of glorified pasts, although these films' constant warring and battling make it impossible for their scores to construct the same tranquil, peacetime utopia as does Steiner's. But even in these turbulent diegetic worlds the music assuages its listeners, offering a clarity otherwise unavailable to them through the sharply demarcated motifs for "good guys" and "bad guys." In the case of *The Sea Hawk*, even the titles of musical themes reveal a certain nostalgic telos, with the score moving from "Main Title" to "Finale" via the notion of a "Reunion."

Another connection between music and anteriority is often worked out at the level of narrative, where music is compulsively used to signal temporal disphasures, especially those associated with the flashback. Films whose flashbacks are inaugurated by musical performances such as the melodrama *The Enchanted Cottage* (1945) or the film noir *Detour* (1945) make explicit their function as gates of refuge from the diegetic present. More importantly, the music establishes the means through which that nostalgic desire is activated in the first place; it appears its very conduit. Music will also veil the jarring effects possible from such a break in chronological, linear narration, providing both text and spectator with a suturing illusion of fullness in the process.

Other connections between film scores and the past are made through the use of already existing compositions. *Red River* integrates variations of familiar old folk tunes like "Coming 'Round the Mountain" and "Red River Valley" into its score (their masculine orientation is suggested by the male chorus that occasionally accompanies them)[2]; *Gone with the Wind* features "Dixie" in a clear effort to authenticate the period as well as to confer upon its listeners, classically enough, the appropriate mood. "Dixie"'s upbeat tempo and melody make it readily enjoyed and easy for auditors to appreciate the initial carefree scenes of the film, and listeners familiar with its opening, wistful lyrics are even more predisposed to the song's nostalgic underpinnings. None of this is very subtle, of course. Nor is it very simple, for the antebellum utopia constructed is quickly deconstructed by the fact that the southern tunes are performed in minor keys. David O. Selznick reportedly required Steiner to do this, in fact, presumably to steer film auditors away from "improper" (i.e., southern) political allegiances, even in their listening habits. What this indicates is just how contrived musical utopias actually are—so much so that Hollywood producers like Selznick can consciously dictate them.

With this in mind, we can see how the nostalgic function of music was less *fixed* to films of the time than it was *affixed* to them. The formal styles of historical film scores, for instance, do not necessarily correspond to the time or setting of their diegetic worlds (Miklós Rózsa recounts how his score for *Ivanhoe* [1952] did not use music of Jacobean England, and he selected Elizabethan and not Roman music in his score for *Julius Caesar*).[3] Korngold's work for *The Sea Hawk*, a film that tells the story of the beginnings of the Royal Navy in Elizabethan England, intermittently makes efforts at period instrumentation, but beyond that is largely (if unsurprisingly) based on the romantic style. The same is true of countless other historical films of the time whose scores work do not try to send auditors back to the specific time of the film's setting, but get them to participate in a looser, more generalized sense of nostalgia.

Despite the fact that the connection between extra-diegetic music and historical verisimilitude is more apparent than real, so naturalized has music's ability to authenticate a period become that we assume an immediacy exists between them. In a bio-pic like *A Song to Remember* (1944), which uses the music of Chopin in a narrative about him, it is especially hard to distinguish between the two registers, even though the promotion campaign of the film arduously stressed the fact that well-known pianist José Iturbi was performing the Chopin.

Film genres like the musical exploit the discrepancy between scoring style and diegetic setting to an especially high degree. Given that the genre has always promoted music's utopian function, as Richard Dyer's work has shown, this should not prove surprising. Moreover, the musical provides a particularly interesting case study because its music (especially in diegetic numbers and performances) most often assumes contemporary, popular forms. Contemporary music is usually placed in competition with the "high" forms of art music in an apparent rejection of the class values and transcendence that art music signifies (e.g., *The Bandwagon*, which attempts at all costs to establish older, classical forms as moribund). Utopia, it would seem, is brought closer to home in the musical, made more down to earth, cast in the present tense. But, as we shall see, this is not really the case.

Vincente Minnelli's *Meet Me in St. Louis* (1944) offers an excellent case in point. Like the historical drama genre film, *Meet Me in St. Louis* tries to create the impression of an earlier time, specifically, the city of St. Louis at the turn of the century. Neatly opposing the then-small city and the family values it represents to New York, the land of bustling opportunity, Minnelli's film pays sentimental tribute to an allegedly simpler way of life. Only the father is associated with the city since he has a job offer there; St. Louis is governed by his discernibly matriarchal family, and dad is notably out of step with its rhythms, ways, and gossip.

True to Goethe's association of music to regression, *Meet Me in St. Louis* presents the eponymous town in a series of old tableaux, its story springing to life from a collection of still pictures, frozen as if from a storybook album. To press Goethe's observation further, the activity of the backward-looking town is, like the home itself, feminized, with singing, music, and performances and even the lyrics of the songs associated with women or a feminine perspective (consider "The Boy Next Door," whose melody appears more than any other as background music throughout the film; think also of the fact that many numbers are set in the home and performed by female characters).

The songs are accessible, popular tunes, and folksy to the hilt. Their structure is simple and in a basic ABA pattern, something especially discernible in the hymnlike "You and I" performed by Mr. and Mrs. Smith. Each song appears to promote the utopia of the small town in a clear, uncomplicated way (e.g., "Have Yourself a Merry Little Christmas," Tootie's cakewalk performance, as well as "The Boy Next Door"). Even their keys are strong, bright Major keys like F and F#, with the more disturbing minor keys occurring rarely, such as in the Halloween sequence (although even here, when Tootie is brought home with a supposed illness, the music is playful, suggesting things are not as serious as she pretends).

But the film offers a competing utopia as well, one associated with the world fair and the promise it holds of the newly arrived century. Signs of technological progress are strewn throughout the film and are emphasized in scenes like Rose's eagerly anticipated long-distance telephone call. In Esther's "Trolley Song" number, the assembled sounds of timpani, bells, the lyric's references to clanging and dinging, as well as the fast pace of Garland's singing create a vertiginous, mechanized energy that is very much at odds with the film's otherwise peaceful, nostalgic musical utopia. As Serafina Bathrick has noted (in one of the few applications of Bloch's ideas to the cinema other than Dyer's), it appears that the film's narrative is finally unwilling to keep these two irreconcilable utopias in competition: by the end of the film, the father decides to stay in St. Louis where he and his family will enjoy it all—a prosperous career, the world's fair, signs of the future, as well as the backward joys of small-town life.[4] (In the musical more generally, song will often reconnect men with their families; consider *Mary Poppins* [1964] and *The Sound of Music*, films whose fathers must learn to benefit from the joy and playfulness music supposedly represents.)

Meet Me in St. Louis shows the extent to which Hollywood genre films cannot be entirely critical of the industrial and ideological machinery that gives rise to them. Utopia, in other words, may be put into play in ways that *conform* to the precepts of the classical model as much as *challenge* them. Utopian resistance, in other words, as a true alternative, can never be more than partial in the classical cinema. In *Meet Me in St. Louis*, this is made doubly clear, not only by naturalizing the relationship of people to technology, but by preserving the traditional, middle-class family as well. Even the "Trolley Song," where non-representational signs work so strenuously to convey an advanced technological utopia, the representational component of the lyrics reassures listeners of a very simple, down-home quality since they convey, after all, the simple pangs of young love.[5]

As Jane Feuer has argued, it is the reflexive aspect of the musical that enables it to treat music with such lavish sentimentality.[6] Musicals, after all, are frequently *about* entertainment and the idea of putting on a show, and they routinely quote from earlier entertainment forms, tunes, stars, and shows (e.g., *Singin' in the Rain* [1952]). And while the music certainly does not generate this nostalgia single-handedly, it plays a key role in the genre's staging of lost and longed-for desire. The longings will often take the form of a nostalgia for a rural American folkland, as in Minnelli's 1943 *Cabin in the Sky*, where songs like "Life's Full of Consequences" and "In My Old Virginia Home" function as anthems for the film's black diegetic community, a folk group constructed as especially rural and "earthy." (At the same time, the music in this film effectively *dematerializes* the community by connecting it to a second, spiritual utopia, which is embodied in the film's sundry angels, devils, and assistants.) Another Minnelli musical, *Brigadoon* (1954), though relatively late in the classical cycle, imbues its music with equally religious, otherworldly qualities. The exotic status of the music is made apparent through the occasional use of Scottish folk rhythms and bagpipes; its nostalgic dimension is secured through the film's eighteenth-century setting (although here too the style of the music itself is largely twentieth-century). The utopia engendered in this way is made all the more precious by virtue of the fact that the town appears only once every hundred years.

The town of Brigadoon, we are told, exists by the grace of miracles, most notably the miracle of Gene Kelly's seemingly omniscient love for Cyd Charisse since his love enables the town to materialize again even though the usual century has not passed. The ideology of this utopia is illuminated through the film's absented church fathers (who made Brigadoon's temporal miracle possible in the first place), its constant references to Christian faith, and the sound of "angelic" choirs—all male, curiously enough, until once the town is first sighted. Unlike *Meet Me in St. Louis*, where music emerges from a feminine source, the songs here are masculinized, with most written for male voices or with lyrics like "I'll go home, go home, go home with Bonnie Jean."[7] Curiously, though not surprisingly, the female voice is primarily reserved for calling forth Brigadoon once Kelly has left for New York, a city depicted primarily from within nightclubs, its background music a mere abrasive clamor of conversations. A return to Brigadoon, for Kelly at least, would effect a return to the woman, a return to the past and the promise of never having to cope with the future. Although writing in reference to *Singin' in the Rain*, Clive Hirschhorn could well be describing *Brigadoon* when he says "even to those not seduced by nostalgia, it remains an invigorating musical, perfect in its reconstruction of a world gone forever."[8]

Music is put to equally nostalgic ends in George Seton's *The Country Girl* (1954), a film Rick Altman appropriately calls an "anti-musical."[9] A touching popular song by Gershwin and Arlan, "The Search is Through," isolates an idealized moment in the past of now alcoholic singer Frank Elgin (Bing Crosby). The moment is marked both by professional achievement (the song, a huge hit of Frank's, is depicted in flashback in a recording studio where he is accompanied by a full studio orchestra) and by personal happiness (he sings there to his wife, Georgie [Grace Kelly], and their young son). When the song is later played on the radio, it reminds Frank of all that had once been his. At the same time, however, it recalls his distance from that ideal state and its ultimate remoteness to him. As in psychoanalysis, musical sounds here remind the subject of his present losses as much as of his former glories: immediately following the old recording session, Frank's son is killed by a car when Frank momentarily releases the boy's hand during a photo session. Not coincidentally, this loss is absented from the image track and is depicted solely through sound effects. What is more, the radio transmission of "The Search is Through" distorts its original sound quality, chipping away even more at its utopian dimensions. Adding to this is the disc jockey, who introduces it as the original version of "another oldie" currently climbing the charts.

But musical utopias—and dystopias—do not confine themselves to musicals. In some of Hitchcock's films, music is used thematically to highlight a sense of danger, otherness, or suspense. In *The Lady Vanishes*, as I have already mentioned, a melody is briefly hummed by the matronly woman who "disappears" from the train. Not only does the tune offer her young neighbor an important key to the woman's espionage activities but it also provocatively suggests a maternal figure that has been absented (this idea, so pronounced in psychoanalytic theory, is taken up in other genres, as we shall see momentarily).[10] Similarly, when the protagonist of *The 39 Steps* (1935) hears a tune whistled at the outset of the film, only later when he hears it again does he recognize its full significance (just as Wagner maintained in reference to the leitmotiv). In *Strangers on a Train* (1951), diegetic music cloaks the murder that occurs on the carnival grounds, even though this is only depicted through the murderer's subjective, acoustic "flashback."

Music's connection to the idea of utopian excess is worked out in other ways as well. Music becomes literally foregrounded in terms of spectacle and excess (think again of *The 39 Steps*, which opens and closes in a music hall). As we shall see, even film noir uses music for its spectacular value, although its presence usually introjects an odd, unsettling quality into the film. Consider the extravagantly stylized jazz combo number in *Phantom Lady* (1944) in which the Elisha Cook, Jr., character very nearly orgasms as he plays the drums, or the production number of the government agent/nightclub performer (Veronica Lake) in *This Gun for Hire* (1942) in which she "casts" for a man in what can only be described as S & M fishing apparel. There is Gilda's famous "Put the Blame on Mame" (non)striptease in the film of the same name (1946) and Vivian Rutledge's singing of "Sad Sister" in *The Big Sleep*, a low-key, relatively styleless performance that always prompts the question "what is it *doing* there?" Certainly spectacle—or at least the sense of exuberant display associated with it—does not automatically point toward the utopian, a point Dana Polan has made:

> Spectacle works not by the delivery of that which it promises, but by the endless making of promises that are not always kept. In the musical, for example, the endless parading on- and offscreen of spectacular sights can encourage a certain sense of loss, the notion that no image can stay eternally in place. There is a tragedy in musicals: the tragedy of an art whose most spectacular moments are always moving into the past. . . . [I]n the melodrama or in *film noir*, the full spectacular moment is held up as incomplete, transitory, even impossible.[11]

Music and hearing are often tied to the notion of a "special sight" that accompanies, even in postclassical films, blind characters (*Don't Look Now* [1975] and *Peeping Tom* [1960]). And although its special vision may be associated with a form of epistemological insight, it is more likely to be aligned with unusual creative abilities of an individual (*The Enchanted Cottage* and *Night Song* [1947]). It often, in other words, appears as something no less than magic. There is *Brigadoon*, of course, but even as cynical a film as *Rear Window* (1954) briefly links music to the miraculous salvation of a character when the piano playing of Miss Lonelyheart's neighbor (who bears an uncanny resemblance to Oscar Levant) saves her from suicide. At the end of the film, she tells the composer, her new beau, "I can't tell you what this music has meant to me." Such sweetness makes a striking contrast to the overall score, which is an uncharacteristically discordant, jazz-influenced work of Franz Waxman.

At the same time Hollywood music provides refuge and salvation, it also pushes these utopias to their logical conclusion, to an escape marked by withdrawal and death. This is forcefully exemplified in *Christmas Holiday* (1944), a little-known film noir that features Gene Kelly in a non-dancing, sinister role of bad guy Robert. The bizarre casting decision immediately suggests that the film is trying to divest itself of the utopian sensibility its title might initially suggest. Robert's girlfriend, Jackie

Lamont (Deanna Durbin), a nightclub performer, sings a highly synco-
pated version of Irving Berlin's "Always" with virtually no affect or accompaniment. (Immediately afterward, Robert nearly kills her.) Earlier, the
two fare better by music and in fact are first brought together because of
it. As they leave a concert—a performance of Wagner's "*Liebestod*," of
course—they share their different impressions of the music:

> ROBERT: Sometimes when a concert's over I get a feeling I've left myself for
> a long time. Of course you wouldn't know it, but that's the greatest thing
> that could happen to me—I'm the most wonderful person in the world to
> leave. Unfortunately you can't make a living out of being absorbed in
> music. Y'know, sometimes when I listen to it I feel that there's nothing
> man is capable of that I can't do. Then it stops, and then it's over.
>
> JACKIE: Well, not for me. When I hear good music I feel, well I feel as if
> something had been added to my life that wasn't there before.
>
> ROBERT: I'd like that. Think you could teach me?

Robert's and Jackie's divergent responses oblige us to consider the
influence gender has in shaping the utopian conception of music in Hollywood film. In so doing, we return to the question of subjectivity. We also
return to the notion that as readers, we lend shape to these anterior utopias as much as our subjectivity is shaped by them.

Film Noir and the Maternal Melodrama

Film noir and the melodrama offer especially illuminating ideas about the
connection between utopia, music, and gendered agency, and I will be
examining these film groups in some detail.[12] There are several reasons
that prompt my selection: first, and most generally, as genre productions
they provide the very backbone of the classical cinema's output. Unex-
traordinary in aesthetic ambition, formulaic in nature, and easily mass
produced, genre films are mainstream texts in every sense of the word,
with virtually nothing in common with the modernist works to which
Barthes, Kristeva, and Adorno turn for examples of musical innovation or
radical semiotic activity. It is partly because of these critics' refusal to
consider such texts seriously, however, that prompts me to use them to
explore how tension can exist within conventional narrative forms. What
is more, musical utopias, although rarely straying far from the classical
model, contain significant variations across films and genres, suggesting
that the classical mode of Hollywood film production and scoring is not
nearly as monolithic as it has been conceived.

The second feature drawing me to film noir and the maternal melodrama is their relative historical coincidence. Both of these film genres
were initially popular at about the same time, with the maternal melo-

drama emerging slightly before World War II and film noir during and just after it. Cinema scholars since the late 1970s have argued that because these films initially gained momentum during a time of widespread social, political, and ideological upheaval, they were able to convey the crisis and emerging unrest of this period. For Michael Renov, for example, these film genres show how the dominant ideology of wartime America was in fact not so dominant, but could be easily unraveled, contested, and exposed as incomplete.[13] Dana Polan argues that "the period figures a certain breakdown of narrative" which may be profitably aligned with the "breakdown of the studio's ability to confidently tell its stories,"[14] and Maureen Turim observes the increasing unreliability of narrators of the time (e.g., *Laura, Mildred Pierce, Sunset Boulevard* [1950]).[15] What this recent scholarship does is equip film noir and melodrama with a second historical context, since the films have been literally re-written through these kinds of new readings, meanings, and other forms of critical intervention. Their prominence in this latter critical context draws me to them even more.

One of the key interpretive strategies used in regard to these films has been the "reading against the grain," the goal of which has been to locate potentially progressive or "subversive" elements in texts that first appear to be situated within the confines of mainstream ideology. Like the work of Barthes and Kristeva (but distinctly *unlike* them in their choice of examples), most of these analyses proceed by isolating moments of representational excess, in this case, stylistic patterns that deviate from the Hollywood norm of seamless invisibility. Such occurrences of representational excess are believed to yield a more fundamental, ideological excess. In this fashion, critics have come to affix the label of "subversive" to film noir, melodrama, and other film genres (e.g., science fiction, horror, and the musical) that rely on greater stylization than do most of their classical counterparts. Scholars argue that the increased sense of artifice in these films undermines classic cinema's project of life-likeness, and hence frustrates dominant ideology's interest in passing itself off as transparent, natural, or real. Stylistic excesses and unconventional formal practices have often been identified as the purported means by which cinematic content (e.g., story lines) can be politicized and rendered subversive, as Comolli and Narboni have so influentially suggested.[16]

Methodological similarities, most of them psychoanalytic in conceit, exist between the idea of readings against the grain and Bloch's interest in unearthing utopian traces from the text. Like them, Bloch ties his concept of the trace to the idea of ideological surfeit and excess; yet, unlike them, and as we have already observed, Bloch does not maintain that the utopian trace is necessarily progressive. Representational "excess" does not ensure certain effects or readings—something not always remembered in recent readings against the grain, which tend somewhat perfunctorily to equate stylistic or formal extravagance with a radical political agenda. Music's representational and semiotic differences do not, in other words, have an automatic bearing on the politics of a text.

Curiously, if not too surprisingly, few readings against the grain of film noir, melodrama and other genres have been concerned with their sound-tracks.[17] Mise-en-scène criticism, which by definition excludes issues related to sound, has dominated the scholarship of both film noir and melodrama. Film noir criticism reveals this bias in article titles such as "The Primacy of the Visual" and "Some Visual Motifs of Film Noir"; indeed, the genre's very name stresses its visuals, with *noir* obviously referring to a scarceness of light. Certainly the "ideology of the visible" Comolli observed operates here. But at the same time, it is puzzling that the search for excess in 1970s and 1980s film criticism exhibits this bias since Kristeva's and Barthes's work, so influential at the time, insisted that the auditory component of excess was one of its most compelling features.

My final reason for concentrating on film noir and melodrama has to do with their obsessive investment in anterior moments and lost objects. Film noir reveals this in titles such as *Out of the Past* (1947) and *The Postman Always Rings Twice* (1946), melodrama offers us *Since You Went Away* (1944). Both genres make use of the flashback plot structure (*Sunset Boulevard, Double Indemnity* [1944], *Rebecca* (1940), and *The Enchanted Cottage*); and preexisting past events are used to explain or lend meaning to the diegetic present and to our comprehension of the film at large (*Gun Crazy* [1949], *White Heat* [1949], *Back Street, The Locket* [1946]). True to the classical style, music is tied to the anterior moments in both of these genres. Previously known characters, places, and relationships have their individual leitmotivs; flashbacks (as we will observe in *Detour* and *Penny Serenade* [1941]) are often initiated when the protagonists hear songs that send them back to what presumably were better days. In the film noir and melodrama, music signals this sense of lost pleasure and stability, echoing the function it serves in so many theoretical accounts.

Furthering their connection to theory—and to psychoanalysis in particular—melodrama and film noir tend to associate femininity with lost, musical moments. In films noir, this usually spells trouble in the form of a "duplicitous dame" who has betrayed or otherwise undone the hero, a woman who has left him with psychological scars or with marks of actual physical disablement—consider Phyllis Dietrichson (*Double Indemnity*), Elsa Bannister (*The Lady from Shanghai* [1948]) and Kathy Moffet (*Out of the Past*). Each of these women emerges from "out of the past" of her partner to destroy him, effecting a return of the repressed that both terrifies and attracts her male partner. The female protagonists of the maternal melodrama (consider *Stella Dallas* [1937] and *Now Voyager*'s Charlotte Vale [1942]) are likewise bent on resecuring relationships with women, although these relationships are usually defined more in terms of maternal comforts than by threats. Because of their relationship to music, femininity and memory provide the key in determining the subjectivity behind the nostalgia and utopian sensibilities of these films. We turn first to *Detour* and to the case of film noir.

Film Noir: Grade B but with "Vision"

Critics interested in subversive readings have paid special attention to films produced by B studios like Monogram, Republic, and Grand National since their output tends to be more pared down and formulaic than standard genre pictures. Because of this, these films were believed to expose the ideological foundations and contradictions that other, more expensive productions veiled over and neutralized. Critics argued that the literal lack of investment on the part of producers allowed these films to deviate from the constraints normally imposed upon Hollywood films, constraints involving both style and ideology.[18]

The B picture most routinely enlisted for these kinds of readings has been film noir. Paul Kerr, in an insightful and influential article, demonstrates how the technological demands of the genre (its spare use of lighting, for example) readily lent themselves to low-budget productions—and consequently, to these kinds of analyses. Although any number of B films noirs could be used for these readings, it is Edgar Ulmer's *Detour* that critics herald as "King of the B's."

Produced by Producers Releasing Corporation, a "beehive" studio formed in March 1940 and dissolved in 1946, the film cost less than $20,000 to make. *Detour* was shot in six days and released five months later, at a final running time of sixty-nine minutes. No retakes were done, and, according to Ulmer, slates were not used to identify takes (they took up too much footage of the fifteen thousand feet allotted; reportedly, Ulmer differentiated shots by putting his hand in front of the camera at the start of every take). The costliest and most sophisticated special effect appears to consist of several optically printed wipes. *Detour's* low budget reveals itself in a number of ways: it has few backgrounds and scene changes, scenes are rear-projected, it uses borrowed footage, and it has a very small cast. There are but two main actors, Tom Neal and Ann Savage (the latter a star of B extravaganzas such as *Two Señoritas from Chicago* [1943] and *Midnight Manhunt* [1945]), two secondary actors, and brief appearances by only a handful of others.

Like the cast, *Detour's* plot is skeletal at best. Al Roberts (Neal) narrates in flashback from a roadside diner in Nevada. His narration begins when "I Can't Believe That You're in Love with Me" is played on the diner jukebox. The song had been a popular favorite at the low-grade Break o' Dawn club where Al had worked as a pianist. In his words, it was like "heaven" to work there because of his romance with one of the club singers, Sue Harvey (Claudia Drake). When Sue suddenly announces her plans to move to Hollywood to advance her career, however, Al's spirits are dashed. Miserable on his own, he hitchhikes to Los Angeles to join her.

The first significant character to pick him up is Charles Haskell, Jr. (Edmund MacDonald), a puzzling man who tells Al about a female hitchhiker he had picked up earlier. In fighting off Haskell's sexual advances, this women had left scars now visible on his hand. (He calls her "the most dangerous animal in the world"; Al has no trouble agreeing.) Later, Al drives as Haskell naps, but is unable to awaken him when the weather grows threatening. He stops to open the passenger door and Haskell falls out, hitting his head on a rock. Panicked, Al tells us that the police would never believe his story. He hides the body and drives on, assuming Haskell's identity. Later when Al has a nightmare about the death, he tries to calm himself with the realization he had come to after going through Haskell's things: Haskell was a crook and a gambler.

On the road again, Al picks up a female hitchhiker, Vera, who turns out to be the same woman with whom Haskell had ridden. She scoffs at Al's implausible story and threatens to turn him into the police. He is forced to stay with her, and they rent a room in Los Angeles. Vera devises several schemes for increasing their wealth (one of them involves Al masquerading as Haskell in order to get money from the dying Charles, Sr.). Al is morose and passive, and the two bicker constantly. After one row in which Vera locks herself in the bedroom, threatening to call the police, Al inadvertently strangles her by pulling the telephone cord from the other room. With two freakish deaths now on his hands, Al (who never contacts Sue), quits Los Angeles, and his flashback ends back in the Nevada diner. When he walks outside he is apprehended by the police.

Detour has become a bit of a darling among popular critics and cultists, in many respects because they believe it exploited or transcended its severe budgetary limitations. The editors of *Kings of the Bs* refer to it as "probably the greatest B ever made"[19]; Andrew Sarris writes that it "is not so much an example of a B that rises unexpectedly in class . . . as a poetic conceit from Poverty Row."[20] Curiously, however, few scholars have performed readings against the grain on *Detour*, even though its rock-bottom budget and threadbare narrative might lend themselves easily to this type of analysis.[21] It is almost as if it were too obvious an object of study— something which propels my own interest in it. But, and as the quotations above indicate, the film's formal "excesses" have by no means gone unaddressed. Instead, they have been considered a testimony to Ulmer's creative genius. Sarris, for instance, refers to the director as "one of the minor glories of the cinema . . . a genuine artist"[22]; Peter Bogdanovich's interview reveals an admiration of a quasi-religious nature (Ulmer was a "legendary figure," "miraculous")[23]; Myron Meisel adds to the encomia: "Ulmer transformed his camera into a precise instrument of feeling, and his convulsive abstractions of screen space intensify that feeling by investing it with particular gestures of light, form, and motion that define his own director's soul, and none other."[24] In this way, Detour has been appreciated mainly as an expression of its auteur's renegade vision. And we might wonder at this point what there is about this "vision" that recent commentators find so appealing.

Following the tradition of most criticism of the genre, the bulk of Detour's commentators praise the film noir for its visuals. Meisel's comment about the camerawork certainly demonstrates this (as does the title of the piece from which it is taken: "The Primacy of the Visual"). Variety similarly applauds the "outstanding camerawork that helps the flashback routine come off well."[25] The book Cult Movies refers to Ulmer's overall work as "beautifully filmed and ornately designed"[26]; Sarris writes that "Ulmer's camera never falters even when his characters disintegrate."[27]

I am not interested in challenging the visual achievements of Detour. But I find it nonetheless curious that the praise which has been lavished upon its visual style has been made at the expense of quite a number of other elements—virtually nothing has been written on the film's soundtrack, for instance, or on its composer, Erdody. For Andrew Sarris, the object of opprobrium is the film's characterizations; for others, the plot. As Meisel writes with revealing simplicity, "The story is beneath trash."[28]

The widespread investment in denigrating the "trashiness" of Detour's plot is not insignificant, and scholars seem to take great pains to distance themselves from it. Blake Lucas, a film noir critic, writes: "The story of Detour, fraught with outrageous coincidence, would be ridiculous in most hands," and then goes on to compliment Ulmer for rescuing it.[29] To an extent, Lucas's observation is correct, for there are indeed many coincidences in Detour's strange tale: Al just happens to pick up the handscarring hitchhiker whom Haskell had previously encountered, Haskell and Vera just happen to be the only people whom he befriends, both happen to die in bizarre accidents that appear to be Al's fault, and both even suffer from mysterious fatal ailments.

Al is keenly aware of the unlikelihood of these events and repeatedly stresses the intervening role of fate: "something else stepped in and shunted me off in a different destination than the one I had picked for myself" and "just when you think you're on your way fate sticks out its foot and trips you." He is convinced no one will believe his story. When Haskell is killed, Al considers what to do and sighs, "The cops would laugh at the truth; they would say I did it anyway." He directly projects this response onto the film spectator, remarking in voice-over: "But I know what you're going to hand me even before you open your mouths. You're gonna tell me you don't believe my story about how Haskell died. You'll give that 'don't make me laugh' expression on your smug faces." The character of Vera makes good his predictions. After Al tells her his story, she pauses (as if sympathetically) and then blurts, "That's the greatest cock and bull I ever heard." To be sure, the story's incredibility helps firmly establish Al's passivity (he blames fate for his misfortune), but at the same time it also conveys his strong paranoia and sense of persecution (he thinks no one will believe him). But it discloses even more than this: by acknowledging its improbability, the story codifies itself as a fantasy.

But it is a fantasy over which Al has no control. Indeed, it seems to control *him*. One is reminded of the oneiric quality of other films noir, like *Out of the Past*, in which Jeff's (Robert Mitchum's) sleepy, cynical voice-over wonders, "Maybe we thought we were in a dream and would wake up in Niagara falls." In *Detour*, spatial features establish Al's story as highly dreamlike: He is portrayed against a number of undefined, dark backgrounds as he hitchhikes across the country; the camera, which tracks across a United States map to indicate his progress, stops at Oklahoma, at which point we see Al in a decidedly non-Oklahoman setting of cacti and palm trees. The few specific locations that *are* given, thus, are mendacious, unreliable. It would appear that spatial verisimilitude does not matter at all. As John Belton has observed: *"Detour*'s travel montage denies specificity and purpose. The camera pans westward over a succession of maps superimposed with shots of Al's feet walking; there are no arrows or lines to indicate where Al is. Somewhere past Chicago [actually, Oklahoma], the maps cease to appear, eliminating even this abstract index of the hero's spatial progression. The journey has taken Al into an uncharted no-man's land."[30] If Al is thus "lost" to a geographical vagueness, it is a vagueness then that signals not mobility and free play but confinement. Moreover, Belton's reference to it as a "no-man's land" anticipates the ways in which this hostile space ultimately serves a feminine function.

Al's predicament is also confined by its strong Oedipal dimensions. Bloch, in an essay on the detective narrative in general, notes the genre's preoccupation with origins and its obsession with the past. He writes: "What is true about all these various versions of the Oedipal metaphysic, above and beyond their mythological content, is that they reflect, if not, certainly, any initial dreamed-up *crime*, then at least the very *darkness* or *incognito* of origins themselves. Every fundamental type of research is related to the Oedipus form in the way in which its incognito is treated not so much as an unknown of a logical type but rather as something monstrous, something unclear even to the bearer himself."[31] What this passage fails to acknowledge is that the maternal plays a pivotal role in constructing these generic, "monstrous" searches. To be sure—and decidedly unlike the maternal melodrama—few films noir actually literalize their interest in the mother (noteworthy exceptions include the protagonists of *White Heat* and *This Gun for Hire*, whose criminality is supposedly explained through their relationships with castrating maternal figures). Film noir displaces this desire for the maternal onto younger women whose romantic affections, if once available, have since—like the mother's—proven impossible to retrieve (e.g., *Laura*, *The Killers* [1946]).

Tania Modleski's psychoanalytic reading of *Detour* is one of the few that addresses the film's much maligned story and considers the Oedipal basis of Al's woes. *Detour*, she writes, "derives its emotional force not . . . from the hero's failure to accede to the symbolic, but from his failure to remain at the pre-Oedipal stage of development."[32] In other words, the source of Al's trauma lies, according to Modleski, in his overinvestment in the maternal, pre-Oedipal element. Unwilling to leave it in order to follow the routine path of Oedipalization, Al remains confined within and ultimately destroyed by it. His repeated misfortunes and final capture by the law demonstrate the extent to which this resistance is not without repercussion, although Modleski argues otherwise on this point.

Despite this, Modleski's reading remains extremely compelling. The utter passivity of Al and his constant "bellyaching" (as Vera puts it) certainly weaken his claims to traditional masculinity. Moreover, he refuses to identify fully with the father figure symbolically represented in Charles Haskell. When given the chance literally to assume Haskell's identity, he does so only with the greatest reluctance and discomfort. His guilt over Haskell's accidental death (which, like the killing of Laius in the Oedipus myth, occurs on the road) resurfaces in his nightmare that replays the traumatic event.

In fact, father-son relationships do not fare well in *Detour* at all. We learn that Charles Haskell, Jr., left home for good after an incident involving his father's sabers, one in which Charles, Jr., had plucked out the eye of a young dueling partner. Scarred from the accident and afraid of further symbolic castrations, he leaves. Years later, as an adult, Charles takes his revenge on his now invalid father by conning him in a scheme involving bogus church hymnals. Music—here, in the form of the hymns—is beginning to point to a sense of deceit and fraud.

The film makes elaborate connections between femininity and music. As Al's initial voice-over begins, we see an odd, extreme close-up of his coffee cup. Because of its exaggerated size and illumination, the cup's roundness is highlighted over any of its other features or functions. After this, the camera moves to the spinning record playing in the jukebox, emphasizing once again its roundness. The shot then dissolves to another brightly lit circular object, one that is first so abstract as to be virtually unidentifiable (when the camera pulls back we realize it is the front of the bass drum of the Break o' Dawn combo). Although these shapes playfully reinforce the circularity of *Detour*'s plot, they also suggest the presence of a non-representational trace, a displaced sign that signals for Robert both memory and anticipation. More specifically, it is the circular trace of an yonic presence, a feminine force which first sets Al's reminiscences into play.

Although Al never refers to his relationship with his biological father (a fact which sets the stage for its symbolic reenactment in his exchange with Haskell), he *does* mention his mother. He speaks of her but once, and in an off-the-cuff manner, but the reference is charged nonetheless. Dodging the conversation of a garrulous fellow diner at the beginning of the film, he mumbles, "My mother taught me never to speak to strangers." Neal's flat delivery of the clichéd line conforms to film noir's familiar use of ironic, deadpan speech—a device that "speaks" to the fatalism of its protagonists (recall the male voice-overs of *Out of the Past* and *Sunset Boulevard*). But here the content of the lines reveals even more: it tells us that Al follows the rules, advice, and proscriptions of the mother rather than those of the father ("my mother taught me . . ."). Even more telling is her order "not to speak to strangers," which demands that speech, sounds, and the voice stay within her jurisdiction. If Al is to remain there and enjoy its benefits, he must respect this command, a move which clearly enforces psychoanalysis's connection of music to the maternal. Another detail develops this line of thought: when Al calls Sue just before deciding to join her in Los Angeles, we hear a brief portion of Brahms's lullaby playing non-diegetically (it subsequently dissolves into motives from "I Can't Believe That You're in Love with Me"). Music appears to cradle and soothe the beleaguered protagonist. And it seems to me no accident that Sue—a vocalist, after all—serves the maternal role.

Modleski comments on the mother-son quality of the relationship between Al and Sue: "The sullen way in which he accepts Sue's announcement, his forlorn bearing as he walks slowly away after reluctantly kissing her goodnight, suggest a child being abandoned by its mother. . . . Al goes from would-be husband and future father to lawless and faithless adventurer, as he takes his fatal cross-country journey to be reunited with the 'mother.' "[33] Modleski goes on to note how Al bifurcates the maternal element, setting up Kleinian objects that function as "good" and "bad" objects in Sue and Vera. Sue is the idealized mother who is a source of goods, Vera the "bad" one who denies him those goods.[34]

The musical idealization of Sue (the "good" object) begins as soon as the flashback starts. From the beginning, music is a sign of their past, since "I

Can't Believe That You're in Love with Me" launches Al into sentimental reverie when it is first played on the jukebox. Their very identities in fact are tied to the idea of music: Sue is a singer (defined, like the mother in psychoanalysis, by her soothing, melodic voice); Al is a pianist. "I Can't Believe That You're in Love with Me" is "their" song ("she loved it too," the voice-over informs us) and metonymically stands in for the union they once had. Motives from the song appear in variation throughout the film, most commonly when Al fantasizes about Sue or prepares to call her. It would seem that it signifies a lost utopia for him, one whose reminder appears at his every turn.

Significantly, while performing "I Can't Believe . . ." in the flashback, Al is seated and gazes adoringly up at Sue, whose upright figure suggests her near phallic control over him. Literally looked up to in this scene (Al's perspective is emphasized by a slightly low camera angle), Sue is also idealized on the level of mise-en-scène: glamorously dressed, she is well-lit and given all the representational cues that Hollywood procedurally bestows on its stars. Her dominance over Al is further revealed by the fact that she sings while he only plays the song—a division that associates woman with language and man with the supposedly more "meaningless" sounds and rhythms, reversing Hollywood's standard paradigm.

Although the weight of its significance will be developed later, we need to comment briefly on the regressive character of Al's musical utopia. The title "I Can't Believe That You're in Love with Me" itself is charged with the idea of improbability much the same way that the incredibility of Al's story is established. What is more, the song is performed at a club called the "Break o' Dawn," a name which, as Modleski has noted, suggests more than a little concern with origins. (One also notes that the circular o' suggests another feminine presence and that its conspicuously missing letter also indicates that the utopia the club might represent is broken or otherwise incomplete.) Such details flagrantly contradict Al's insistence on the utter desirability of this moment ("like working in heaven"). For him, as for so many of the film music theorists we have examined, the musical delights of the Break o' Dawn Club are falsely believed to offer a self-contained, complete plenitude.

Before Sue's departure, Al performs Chopin's well-known Waltz in c# minor at the club piano. Sue joins him and the two fantasize about his becoming a concert pianist. (Again, Sue is positioned standing over him, with Al once again looking upward at her.) The scene appears stiff, as if it were frozen in time, musically inscribed upon Al's memory as a special moment of intimacy and union with the now-lost woman. The selection of music is especially noteworthy since beyond the Chopin, identifiable classical music is seldom used in the film. Its presence here is explained by the fact that Al and Sue are contemplating the likelihood of his going to

Carnegie Hall as a concert pianist. Al, in other words, once nurtured ambitions of entering the world of high art and classical music. Yet, although the bastion of high culture appears to offer a utopian hope for him, it simultaneously reminds him that this hope has already been foreclosed. "Contained" within the film's flashback as it is, the hope is lost to memory and provides a dramatic contrast to Al's current situation.

The use of the Chopin also enforces the idea of looking backward, of raiding history for utopian models of the future (much as Wagner turned to ancient Greece for the "artwork of the future" and Adorno to Beethoven and other "pre-culture industry" artists for examples of aesthetic integrity and wholeness). Chopin functions for Al in precisely this way, as an emblem of better times. (In a detail that strikingly recalls Adorno's work, he finds contemporary music annoying: a barely audible saxophone player playing jazz outside the hotel room "gets on [his] nerves." To both Al and Adorno, jazz functions as the art of a decaying culture, a music that fails to deliver the unifying comforts of classical works.)[35]

Chopin's Fantasie Impromptu in c# minor is played non-diegetically at the end of the club scene. Although at one level it appears to further close off and frame Al's own "fantasie," its effects are more open-ended than that. "I'm Always Chasing Rainbows," a song written in 1918 and widely popular when revived in the mid-1940s, is based on Chopin's Fantasie and would probably have been recognized by *Detour*'s original audience. The theme, in fact, recurs throughout the soundtrack (most notably, when Al is on the road) and suggests not only the conflict between the realms of high and popular cultures but, I would argue, the irreconcilability of Al to his own utopian fantasies.

When Sue leaves, Al masochistically abandons himself to the so-called decadent forms of contemporary music in an astounding scene. He performs Brahms's Waltz in A Major at the Break o' Dawn, looking terribly forlorn. It is immediately apparent that the refuge classical music may have once offered him has, like his girlfriend, left him. At this point, things go from bad to worse. Initially Al follows the melody of the waltz but then relinquishes himself to a maniacal bass-line improvisation that literally takes over the melody. Replacing the "harmonic" pleasures of the earlier classical period of music are the far less stable rhythms of boogie-woogie. Al revels as he plays a repeated chord sequence that literally goes nowhere. One critic makes clear the connection between this musical performance and femininity, writing: "Bitter at his fiancée, Al would certainly like to punish her for abandoning him, as demonstrated in his punishment of the piano during his crazed interpretation of a Brahms waltz."[36]

One would suspect that if Chopin and Brahms—masters of high art—finally represent displeasure to Al, a popular tune like "I Can't Believe That You're in Love with Me" would offer its pleasurable opposite. But as the example of "I'm Always Chasing Rainbows / Chopin's Impromptu" reveals, this is not the case. Here too the history of the song is significant. Penned in 1927, "I Can't Believe . . ." was a Tin Pan Alley song that was very popular during the 1930s when it was performed by people like Count Basie, Earl Hines, Ella Fitzgerald, and Bing Crosby. By the time of *Detour*'s production in the mid-1940s, however, its popularity seems to have been played out. In other words, to 1945 audiences, "I Can't Believe . . ." was not a current hit, but one of the past. Its position in the film thus works along with the Chopin piece to point out the regressiveness of Al's utopia.

There is one moment in which music suggests a future-directed utopia. Al remarks as he drives Haskell's car down the road "I began to think of the future . . . with Sue." He "sees" Sue reflected in his rear-view mirror. He imagines her in Hollywood, performing "I Can't Believe That You're in Love with Me" with accompaniment. Here Sue's idealization is even more pronounced than in his earlier flashback: her costume is more lavish and glamorous, the lighting produces especially dramatic, high-contrast shadows and the camera is more attentive to *her*, revealing fewer backup musicians. Yet the progressive elements of Al's anticipatory vision remain meager at best, for not only is the song tied to the past, but his entire anticipated utopia is framed in a rear-view mirror. His idealized scenario is shown to be inaccessible. The fantasy is likewise framed acoustically. As Al begins to "think of the future," the motive associated with Haskell (and with Al's road troubles more generally) is played non-diegetically, imbuing Al's projection with an element of doom and even fatalism. In all, the scene dramatizes the idea that Al's utopia is one of "filled affects": his one anticipatory fantasy shows that he is not interested in the future so much as in the retrieval of an element from an idealized past.

But the music soon starts to turn on him. The strains of "Home Sweet Home"—a tune directly pitched to Al's nostalgic sensibility—are played non-diegetically as he enters the Los Angeles hotel room—what he calls his "prison"—with Vera. Music mockingly reminds him of his distance from Sue—his real "home" and mother—and becomes increasingly charged with a sense of loss. His responses to the loss are deeply embittered, as is dramatically illustrated at the opening of the flashback when "I Can't Believe . . ." is first put on the jukebox. Al becomes nothing short of hysterical. Telling the other patron that the song "stinks," he comments passionately in voice-over:

> That tune—that tune! Why was there always that rotten tune? Following me around, beating in my head, never letting up. Did ya ever want to forget anything? Did ya ever want to cut away a piece of your memory and blot it out? You can't, ya know. No matter how hard you try. . . . You can change

the scenery, but sooner or later you'll get a whiff of perfume or someone'll say a certain phrase or maybe hum something, then you're licked again. "I Can't Believe That You're in Love with Me." I used to love that song once.

A number of non-representational elements here—smells as well as sounds—work to torment Al with the memories they carry; still it is clear that music bears the brunt of most of his disappointment and hostility.

As Michael Renov has observed, Al's recollections are initially catalyzed by pain. Moreover, he does not enter into them voluntarily:

This song . . . triggers the flashback through painful and unwanted reminiscence ("Did you ever want to cut away a piece of your mind?"). . . . This process of mind, the uncontrollable recollection, offers illustration of the Nietzschean formulation, the eternal return of the same, forerunner to Freud's return of the repressed. Nietzsche theorizes memory as lack, an unwished for inability to forget: " . . . only that which never stops hurting remains in (the) memory." And Al cannot forget his and Sue's "special song" which is simultaneously the self-taunt of the paranoid: "I Can't Believe That You're in Love With Me."[37]

Renov's observations are well taken. In many ways "I Can't Believe . . ." functions as an instrument doggedly set on Al's torture, virtually overwhelming the text, appearing whenever he thinks of Sue and often when he does not. It is inescapable, immuring Al in much the same way that the film's claustral visual style and narrative structure confine him. The song's ubiquity divests it of its initial utopian function; it appears with such frequency that it can no longer simply signify Sue and Al's love. It does not, in other words, unequivocally conjure forth the halcyon days when Sue and Al were united. Once it even appears mixed in with Vera's motive.

True to the claims of psychoanalysis, *Detour's* music plays out some of the fundamental ambivalence of the male subject. In Al's case this is revealed by the good and bad functions assigned to Sue and Vera. Initially, Vera appears to be defined as Sue's simple binary opposite: Sue is a chanteuse, defined by a pleasantness of sound; Vera does not sing and speaks harshly (says Al: "Each word coming from her lips cracked like a whip"). Significantly, however, once Al's musical utopia begins to fade, the distinctions between these "good" and "bad" women become increasingly less clear.

Moreover, the score firmly establishes that Vera is not the simple, nonmusical opposite of Sue. First, she has her own leitmotiv—a sort of non-lyrical equivalent to the song which is linked to Sue. What is more, this leitmotiv is in fact quite pleasant, a short, romantic melody that harmonically interacts with other musical activity (in some ways it is the most attractive motive of the film). It is evoked at times when she is both out of sight and out of mind—suggesting a flexibility of meaning and function. And Vera's voice—though harsh in its delivery—is not of itself unpleasant. Non-representationally, it is, in sum, difficult to consider Vera as purely "evil."

But the film's representational signs do everything they can to construct her as the singly bad, punishing mother who in turn must be punished. After all, she is "a dangerous animal" who inflicts wounds on Haskell's hand as severe as those made by his father's saber.[38] The castration anxiety engaged here has special resonance for Al since, as a pianist (and as a hitchhiker), his hand—his "member"—is essential to his livelihood. But as we shall see, Al is not the only subject terrified by Vera.

The Subject of *Detour*'s Dystopia

At this point, it is worth returning to the "vision" that critics have championed in reference to the film. It was noted earlier that the idea testifies to the visual orientation of most film noir criticism. Given this bias, the interweaving motives of Vera and Sue or music's combined utopian and dystopian functions might seem to mean little. But we have also noted how most of *Detour*'s commentators associate the idea of the film's vision with its director. Yet it seems to me that this "vision" entails a far wider way of seeing, one with specific notions of utopian and dystopian thought. For a great number of *Detour*'s enthusiasts share Al's sense of utopia-gone-wrong, and most of their negative projections inevitably fall upon Vera. The following discussion by Danny Peary is worth quoting at length:

> Ann Savage had a lackluster Hollywood career, appearing in such marvelously titled non-classics as *Two Señoritas From Chicago* (1943) and *Pygmy Island* (1950). But as Vera she was able to play the character who is quite possibly the most despicable female in movie history—even she admits she was born in a gutter [this line is delivered with great irony in the film]. *A truly memorable character.* The nicest compliment he [Al] can give her is "She had a homely beauty." The truest thing he can say is "Vera was just as rotten in the morning." . . . Her looks remind me of a vulture—not because she's ugly but because she appears to be thinking she'd like to rip you apart with her teeth and devour you piece by piece. Ian and Elisabeth Cameron correctly describe her: ". . . when she turns and looks at the camera, she has eyes so terrifying that one wonders how those who beheld her in the flesh managed to avoid getting turned to stone."[39]

Obviously Peary is conflating Vera the character with the actress who portrays her, Ann Savage. First he transforms Vera/Savage into a predatory vulture (but this comparison, he insists, is not based on her appearance), and then goes on to detail extravagantly the bird's abilities to disfigure ("she'd like to rip you apart with her teeth and devour you piece by piece"). Needless to say, a certain anxiety weighs heavily upon this passage. Peary even evokes Medusa (the only archetype, remember, "without hope"), whose castrating "looks" turn male subjects to stone.

More remarkable still is the manner in which Peary continues:

> Even more terrifying than her face, in my opinion, is her voice. Rarely does she simply deliver a line; instead, she screams. She is loud, scratchy, intolerable. All the time. And worse when drunk. The only screen characters whose voices are similar are the insane wife in John Waters's *Desperate Living* (1977) [another cult classic] and Susan (Dorothy Comingore) in *Citizen Kane* (1941) when she gets bad notices for her opera debut and screams at Kane until you want to put your fingers in your ears. It is fitting that Vera dies with a telephone wire around her neck, unable to finish her final sentence. The scene in which Vera is killed is doubtlessly the highlight of the film. Not only because it shuts Vera up once and for all, but because it exhibits Ulmer's most audacious use of the camera in the entire film.[40]

Peary makes it altogether clear that Vera's greatest threat is her ability to produce sounds, to "make noise."

It is striking how eagerly *Detour*'s characters and critics cut off woman's speech, strangling her sounds and her music. (One also recalls the conclusions drawn by Kristeva and Barthes about the maternal, musical realm of signification that they argue is ultimately articulated by the male artist.) Even Sue's "good" voice is subjected to this censorship. When Al phones her long distance, she is pictured wordlessly holding the receiver, as if she were being silenced for having earlier "spoken up" to him. Now Al repeats all of her presumed lines ("What? You're working as a hash slinger?"), a detail which is a consequence of *Detour*'s shoestring budget, to be sure, but one which also demonstrates the extent to which the film recuperates the ability of women to speak. The strangling of Vera, as Peary observes, achieves this with even greater determination.

Peary's contention that Vera's death is the film's best scene is of course more than a little disturbing. But it is also revealing. For it makes clear how real-life commentators have adopted the same fantasies—the same dystopic "vision"—as *Detour*'s wretched protagonist, and the extent to which this occurs is nothing short of remarkable. Al is not the only one who romanticizes the hard facts of his incredible story: One writer erroneously refers to Vera as Haskell's "ex-mistress" and then spares Al of a murder charge by arguing that Haskell "dies of a heart attack")[41]; *Variety* reveals similar compassion: "Director Edgar G. Ulmer achieves some steadily-mounting suspense as the pianist becomes implicated in two murders, neither of which he's committed."[42] By exonerating Al of Vera's and Haskell's murders, these critics exhibit an identification with him. In the case of Vera, this identification is engaged, quite literally, at the expense of femininity.

Moreover, what little power Al exerts over women does not go unnoticed. In contrast to my own analysis of the scene in which Al "attacks" the Brahms waltz which stresses Al's masochism, another critic writes: " . . . the closest thing to a moment of freedom in the movie (though the character doesn't perceive it as such) comes in the extraordinary sequence in which, working in a nightclub he professes to despise, he plays a brilliant, disjointed piano improvisation."[43] What I have argued as a display of sheer masochism is for these other commentators either a show of deserved revenge on woman, as in the case of the writer who spoke of Al's "punishing" the piano for Sue's departure, or, with the critic above, a moment of utter spontaneity and freedom.

It should now be apparent that *Detour*'s resentful nostalgia far exceeds the boundaries of the film. Moreover, the organizing force behind this fantasy is not so much the sense of community that Jameson, Bloch, and others claim unifies utopian thought, but the male subject who first would esteem woman and then debase her for the control she is believed to wield over his happiness. Characters and critics alike converge on the ultimate undesirability of Vera. Even within the film, a consensus is quickly reached by Haskell and Al who, just after they meet, agree that "there oughtta be a law against dames with claws," referring to her as a "little witch," a loose "tomato" who had been asking for more than a ride—after all, "what kind of a woman hitches? Not a Sunday school teacher."

An interview Ulmer granted late in his life discloses his own sympathy for Al Roberts. In fact, Ulmer's comments suggest that Al's tale fulfills a personal utopia of his own: "I was always in love with the idea and with the main character, a boy who plays piano in Greenwich Village and really wants to be a decent pianist. He's so down on his luck that the girl who goes to the Coast is the only person he can exist with sex-wise—the *Blue Angel* thing."[44] Ulmer goes on to state his preference for films told from a single point of view: "I'm trying very hard not to achieve something specific but to give it a viewpoint. Tell it from somebody I can feel for: don't do it from five viewpoints . . . *never switch from the boy to the girl*, because the screen cannot tell two stories at the same time" (my emphasis). Clearly the preferred viewpoint here is that of the masculine subject, one whose experience is then extended to members of the audience. In the same interview, Ulmer asserts that directors should also try to "identify ourselves with our audiences."[45] The collapse between filmic and extrafilmic subjectivities is revealed even further in a strange anecdote about Ulmer's pre-*Detour* studio days: "Apparently Ulmer was the victim of a [*sic*] elaborate on-set prank: An argument was staged, the lights went out, a gun was fired. 'When the lights came on again,' [Director William] Wyler recalled, 'one of the fellows was lying in his blood and Edgar stood over him, dumfounded, with a gun in his hand. As he stood there watching his "victim" in horror, a studio sheriff, who was in on it, put a hand on his shoulder, telling him he was under arrest for murder.' "[46]

In what ways does *Detour* restage Ulmer's own experiences? Where does his story end and Al's begin? These biographical coincidences are even more sharply—and grotesquely—played out in the personal drama of Tom Neal, the actor who portrayed Al Roberts. With him, much more than a studio vagary was involved: some time after the release of *Detour*, Tom Neal was imprisoned for killing his own wife.

The Dystopic Past

It is extremely curious that Al Roberts believes in the past's ability to save him as much as he does, given the frequency with which he expresses his incredulity over other aspects of the story. His romanticization of its earlier moments has the effect of confining his utopia to an isolated, irretrievable sphere—much as music has been situated in so many theoretical accounts. Like these theorists, Al fails to recognize that the moment of musical utopia exists as a projection, one that cannot be concretized since it is not derived from the realities of social and subjective existence. Because Al's fantasy is as idealized as it is (consider his comment about "heaven"), its dystopic unraveling seems its only logical outcome.

Yet this failed musical utopia gives way to some interesting observations. First, it shows the extent to which Hollywood's nostalgic conception of film music is preoccupied with the losses of subjectivity—in *Detour*'s case, the losses of male subjectivity. To be sure, film scholars before me have read *Detour*—and film noir more generally—as an exposé of the limits of patriarchy, and *Detour* certainly relies on the generic tradition of physically or psychologically disabled male heroes, of subjects eventually killed by their own obsessions (*Kiss Me Deadly*, *Touch of Evil* [1958]). Indeed, and as Modleski and Renov demonstrate, *Detour* may be said to expose the limitations of male subjectivity under patriarchy in other ways as well—one need only remember the difficulty with which Al attempts to undergo his own Oedipalization.[47]

But for however much film noir's male subject struggles, and for however lacking his discursive control seems to be, he is, in the end, the one who provides film auditors with their primary source of identification. It is his subjectivity that orchestrates the utopian enterprise of the genre, and music and femininity are linked and only made to perform for this male desire. In this way, the discursive and symbolic impotence of film noir's protagonist is not nearly as extensive nor as subversive as commentators before me have indicated.

As film noir's subject learns that the past and its feminine, musical charms can never be attained, he projects its now dystopic sensibility onto the feminine and musical figures that initially offered him the promise of utopian fulfillment. Doing this obliges him to condemn the very objects on which utopia relied to represent itself, a fact which reveals the fundamentally unstable, fragile nature of this particular kind of utopian thought. Even so, this does not seem to have diminished the widespread appeal of the fantasy: one need only recall the initial bond drawn between Haskell and Al (who agree that women are "dangerous animals"), or the relief of the one critic when Vera is strangled, or Ulmer's compassion for Al, or the reviewers' adoration of Ulmer. Given the range of responses it would indeed be difficult to argue that *Detour* has generated (either historically or discursively) truly subversive effects, for its utopia appeals to very traditional masculine social and theoretical constituencies.

Importantly, however, although *Detour*'s characters and critics project their failed utopias onto Vera, the soundtrack makes clear that she is only superficially the "bad" opposite of Sue. (That critics have overlooked this enables them to preserve the basic "goodness" of the maternal fantasy and the desirability of Sue.) In this way, the film's music works within binary oppositions, that is, those of "good" and "bad" women, utopia, and dystopia, at the same time it undermines them.

Thus, for as overdetermined as *Detour*'s misogynist utopia may appear, its non-representational acoustic signs also acknowledge its limitations: they demonstrate the impossibility of satisfying a utopia constructed from "out of the past." Not only is the musical activity surrounding Vera and Sue confused, but one notes that once Al's hopes are represented, music starts to question—and even withhold—the utopia he desires: "I Can't Believe That You're in Love with Me" tortures him as soon as he hears it on the jukebox. Even after provoking his nostalgic reverie, its pleasures last but a short while, and every time the song is performed it reveals more and more the repetition compulsion governing Al's fantasy. One is reminded of Adorno's culture industry as it is indiscriminantly paired with other music: character leitmotivs become intertwined, their functions fused and confused, and classical, jazz, and popular music all work to convey the unobtainability of the past they allegedly conjure forth to the listening subject.

Excess and the Melodramatic Tradition

Melodrama, like film noir, has come to be associated with an excessive quality that is usually perceived as an effect of style or mise-en-scène, and that, according to recent critics, indicates a deeper ideological surfeit which questions the assumptions of the classical narrative text. Excessive though the style of both film noir and melodrama may be, however, there are important differences in how cinema critics have come to terms with that excess. For film noir's non-representational components have largely been understood as phenomena that replicate the fundamental instability of the genre's narrative and diegetic world, while melodrama, on the other hand, has usually been characterized by the relative *distinctiveness* of its style from narrative themes and diegetic situations. Even the genre's etymology keeps this distinction intact with *melos* (its non-representational, musical element) functioning as the counterpart to the narrative and representational *drama*. Melodrama critics assert that the non-representational register reveals elements which cannot be conveyed through representational means alone, a fundamental split that seems to guarantee the genre's potentially "subversive" effects. Robert Lang places music firmly within this realm, for example, writing "In [melodrama]'s use of music, especially, we identify an impulse to fly free of the codifications of the symbolic"[48]; and Thomas Elsaesser, in his now classic essay, "Tales of Sound and Fury," argues even more forcefully that melodrama's music and other non-representational elements "punctuate" its narrative activity and work in "counterpoint" to it.[49] In an equally influential work, Geoffrey Nowell-Smith contends that melodrama's exaggerated style imposes an excess on the text that cannot be contained, accounted for, or resolved at the level of narrative. To him, these stylistic markings, which violate the norm of a natural, verisimilitudinous style, appear on the body of the film text in much the same way that somatic symptoms present themselves on the body of the hysteric patient: both "bodies" lend themselves up as texts that must be explained, interpreted, understood, and read.[50] Peter Brooks builds on this reference to psychoanalysis even more, calling the melodramatic text a "drama of pure psychic signs"[51] that strives to break through repression and to say the unsayable. He argues that melodrama is generically opposed to traditional modes of expression and to language as we know it. Like dreamwork, it disguises its articulation, condensing and displacing its affect; it engages its concerns symbolically and without referentiality or logic in mind. Melodrama's non-representational component, in short, has proved crucial to theorists and scholars of the genre.

As feminist critics before me have amply demonstrated, the woman's film and the maternal melodrama present special problems to wider generic studies of melodrama, especially insofar as its non-representational component is concerned. Stylistically, they are very much at odds with more mainstream melodrama. They are far less striking than their flamboyant 1950s counterparts, for example (compare Douglas Sirk's works to what Doane calls the "zero degree" or "non-style" of the woman's film).[52] Indeed, their emphasis on claustration and the domestic sphere makes extravagant sets and large casts unnecessary (Back Street; Gaslight [1944]); most of the woman's films were shot in black and white and with rather unremarkable lighting techniques. These subgenres make it necessary to reexamine the claims made for melodrama's extravagent representational excesses.

Scholars pin most of the excess and surfeit of the woman's film on its narrative and narration. It is, after all, not uncommon to hear these stories labeled excessive, hysterical, or (in what is only superficially a contradiction) banal. The New York Times, for example, reproached Penny Serenade's plot on two separate occasions: one article refers to director George "Stevens' victory over the material" (which it calls "high-grade soap opera")[53]; Bosley Crowther's review maintains that "you can't help but feel that somebody has slipped a fast one over on you. . . . Stevens . . . has put together a film which employs not one but six or seven of the recognized sob-story tricks." Regarding the music, Crowther is but brief: "Noel Coward once drily observed how extraordinarily potent cheap music is. That is certainly true of Penny Serenade."[54]

At an historical level, the woman's film and maternal melodrama flourished in the 1930s and 1940s, well before the period to which prominent melodrama scholars like Elsaesser and Nowell-Smith turn for most of their examples. Any contemporary conflicts their 1950s examples might be said to expose would have to be recontextualized in terms of an earlier—and predominantly female—audience. What is more, and as I have already stated, the heyday of the woman's film preceded that of film noir by just a few years—although the former, as Modleski has noted, has only recently attracted critical attention and acclaim. Film noir, on the other hand, has been receiving the lion's share of critics' attention and praise for some time. As Modleski argues, this is because these films trace masculine anxieties, anxieties derived partially from problems men experienced in readjusting to civilian life, and from finding their prewar jobs now held by women. She maintains that the woman's film lends expression to the fears women may have experienced during this period—fears involving, for instance, their position within the family, their desire for careers, or their reentry into the homes after having gained some economic and vocational independence.[55] Molly Haskell, for her part, stresses the utopian element these films tentatively suggest, writing: "[T]he woman's film, like other art forms, pays tribute . . . to the power of the imagination, to the mind's ability to picture a perfect love triumphing over the mortal and conditional. . . . [Its characters] are transfixed at the sublime moment of their love (denying yet improving on reality) by the power of the imagination, by the screen, and by their permanence in our memories."[56] As Haskell's remarks intimate, these films also tell us something about our contemporary fantasies and fears as well. Doane goes so far as to suggest that part of the contemporary feminist interest in the woman's film is because "for many of us, these are the films of our mothers' time."[57]

Another distinguishing factor between the women's melodramas of the 1930s and 1940s and the so-called family melodramas of the 1950s is the former's insistence on a female subject (something that separates it from its film noir contemporary as well). In her essay on the two competing forms of melodrama, Laura Mulvey writes: "One is coloured by a female protagonist's dominating point of view which acts as a source of identification. The other examines tensions in the family, and between sex and generations; here, although women play a central part, their point of view is not analysed and does not initiate the drama."[58]

Pam Cook differentiates male ("tragic") melodrama from women's melodrama in much the same way: the more "properly" Oedipal male story features the desire to take the place of the father (*Written on the Wind*), a battle in which tremendous suffering is usually involved, whereas the female version engages a search for knowledge and understanding (*Suspicion* [1941]).[59] Thus the family melodramas are male coming-of-age stories that fit easily into the masculine Oedipal narrative prototype that critics from Bloch to Barthes to Bellour have observed (consider *Bigger than Life* [1956] and *Home from the Hill* [1960]). Robert Lang has noted in particular how melodrama tends to restage and repeat original family relations.[60]

Women's films like *Stella Dallas, The Old Maid* (1939), *Dark Victory* (1939), *Gaslight*, and *Now Voyager*, on the other hand, feature female characters in search of their social and familial identities and concentrate on allegedly feminine themes such as romance, suffering, and mother-daughter relationships, even if the last of these is something less than ideal (e.g., *Rebecca*) or involves horror and death (e.g., *Dragonwyck* [1946], *Gaslight, The Strange Love of Martha Ivers* [1946]). Feminine desires and actions propel these narratives—something which, as Mulvey demonstrates in her now classic "Visual Pleasure and Narrative Cinema" essay—proves to be the exception rather than the rule in Hollywood's classic output. In other words, the excess associated with the women's films emerges as a perceived violation of a masculine, narrative norm. Not only are the stories themselves considered indulgent but so are the female desires and subjectivity which lend shape to them.

A central theoretical issue regarding this last point has centered around the way these films dramatize women's "vision," either as narrating subjects or as producers of discourse under patriarchy. The issue is thematically engaged by films like *Dark Victory* and *The Enchanted Cottage*. *Dark Victory* features Judith Trahern (Bette Davis), a wealthy, high-spirited woman prone to comments like, "I generally keep my eyes open" and "I am used to looking after myself." Ailed by blurring vision, she is shortly diagnosed as having a brain tumor that will eventually kill her. In contrast to Judith's ocular problems, her male physician, Dr. Steele (George Brent), "sees" clearly enough to forecast her blindness and to perform brain surgery on her (correcting her mind as well as her sight), falling in love with her in the process. Although the film has prompted feminist critics like Doane to insist upon the violence with which patriarchy obliterates or otherwise disempowers the female gaze, there are other ways in which it may be read. One could argue, for instance, that the medical gaze of Dr. Steele is not nearly as omnipotent or as all-seeing as it initially appears since, in the end, he is finally unable to help or cure Trahern. In fact, he does not even realize she is dying as he takes off for an important medical conference. Moreover, Trahern's best friend, Ann King (Geraldine Fitzgerald), displays an alternative gaze in the film that arguably encompasses a far wider epistemological and visual field than Steele's—or any other characters'. She is perfectly attuned to Judith (she recognizes when her death is near, for example), and extends a tremendous amount of empathy to both Judith and Dr. Steele. Perhaps this way of seeing—which relies less on voyeuristic distance than on emotional proximity and identification—suggests an altogether different mode of knowledge and vision at work in the film. Ann even describes this kind of "insight," if you will, remarking once that "I'm psychic, I'm Irish, I'm funny."

Feminists like Tania Modleski and Linda Williams have also argued that the woman's film opens up ways for female spectatorship to be theorized. In Williams's already influential recent essay on *Stella Dallas*, she shows how the woman's melodrama enlists a specifically feminine mode of reading or reading "competence" which she defines in terms of recognition, familiarity, and proximity—unlike the male spectatorship theorized by Mulvey, which presumes an antagonistic distance between viewing subject/voyeur and perceived object.[61] Yet, in spite of the diversity of feminist positions on the woman's film—or perhaps because of it—one thing emerges clearly: the genre's explicit focus on a female subject. And interestingly, this focus works in neat inverse to film noir, which strains so hard to construct a male one. Commenting on this relationship, Maureen Turim maintains that "noir and the woman's film are two sides of the same coin in Hollywood's forties symbolic circulation."[62]

Indeed there are some striking correspondences. Criticism pertaining to both genres has conceived of their excess—be it discursive, stylistic, narrative, ideological—as a predominantly visual phenomenon. Although this tendency could be partially accounted for in film noir studies (given its definitional reliance on vision, for example), its presence in melodrama criticism is less easily explained. Indeed, it is extremely odd that criticism has shown so little concern for what Claudia Gorbman has aptly called the "drama's melos" since melodrama generically requires the presence of music in order to exist at all. My selection of *Penny Serenade* for close analysis is partly a response to this "oversight"—the film's title alone suggests that music will play a significant role. *Penny Serenade* also demonstrates how the non-representational, auditory signs of a melodramatic text may work alongside—and not opposed to—visual and narrational ones. It shows that the workings of music, as well as those of other non-representational signs that convey utopia, need not be radically opposed—made ironic or counterpuntal—to the narrational or representational activity of the film. In fact, the interaction of the two shapes not only a film's ideological operations but the utopian sensibility that can be derived from it.

Penny Serenade and "The Story of a Happy Marriage"

Penny Serenade opens with "Apple Jack" (Edgar Buchanan), an avuncular friend of Roger and Julie Adams (Cary Grant and Irene Dunne), pulling a volume of record albums called "The Story of a Happy Marriage" from a shelf. When he places "You Were Meant for Me" on the phonograph, Julie enters the room and demands he remove it, since its memories upset her. She is preparing to move out. After Apple Jack leaves, however, Julie puts the record back on. The camera focuses on the spinning disc and with a circular wipe flashes back to a record store where she used to work. The song catches the ear of Roger, a journalist, who enters the shop to meet Julie, and what follows might be called "love at first sound." The smitten Roger purchases a boxful of 78 r.p.m. records even though he has no record player, as he tells Julie while walking her home. The flashback closes as the two enter her apartment to listen to them. Julie plays a number of other records throughout the film (popular tunes, waltzes, and birthday songs). Each prompts a separate flashback of her life with Roger, a story that is relayed elliptically, though in loose chronological sequence.

Their courtship reveals Julie's desire for children and Roger's initial lack of interest in same. Soon after they marry, when Julie becomes pregnant and joins him in Japan where he has been transferred, she is disturbed by his lavish lifestyle and chides him for "acting like a child" and for not "thinking about the future." The two quarrel and an earthquake—accompanied by very loud sounds and music—strikes, terminating Julie's pregnancy and making future ones impossible. Apparently sobered by the incident, Roger vows to become a more responsible provider and purchases a small-town newspaper back in the States, where Apple Jack joins them.

With Apple Jack's encouragement, Julie suggests to Roger that they adopt a child. Initially hesitant, Roger then decides that a two-year-old boy would be alright. Instead the adoption agent, Miss Oliver (Beulah Bondi), presents them with a newborn girl. Christina quickly "walk[s] into [their] hearts," as Roger will later claim when he has to fight a judge to keep her after his business has soured.

In another flashback we see Christina, now about five, perform the role of an angel in a Christmas pageant. She sings as "an echo" to the chorus and is obscured behind a makeshift cloud. The subsequent flashback shows Miss Oliver reading a letter from Julie: Christina has died—nearly a year later—of a brief and "hopeless" illness. The couple, particularly Roger, is devastated; we see them in silent, motionless poses in their living room. A woman and her son, stranded on their way to the annual Christmas pageant, happen to come to their door for help. As Julie and Roger give them a ride to the performance, the boy's sneakers indicate that he will be performing as this year's echo. A child's voice is heard singing the same phrase from "Silent Night"; Roger leaves the car, saying he does not "want to see anyone or anything" that reminds him of his daughter. This final flashback ends with "You Were Meant for Me" playing. Julie is making her last preparations to leave when Roger returns and for the first time acknowledges his feelings of defeat, blaming himself for their marital problems. Julie says that their tragedy simply overwhelmed them; she is resigned to their basic incompatibility. All of a sudden, Miss Oliver calls with news of a two-year-old boy whom she thinks they might want to adopt. Mesmerized by the idea, Roger and Julie lock arms and walk into the darkened room that had once been Christina's.

Unlike *Detour*, *Penny Serenade* is not a B film, but a feature production from Columbia Studios by well-known director George Stevens, with name stars like Grant, Dunne, Edgar Buchanan, and Beulah Bondi. Four years earlier, Grant and Dunne had appeared together in the successful *The Awful Truth* (1937), and Grant's performance in *Penny Serenade* was nominated for an Academy Award. The credited composer of the film is W. Franke Harling; the musical director is Morris Stoloff, and the orchestration of the Edward MacDowell music (see below) is Thomas Frost's. Beyond its initial reviews, however, *Penny Serenade* has prompted surprisingly little commentary. It has nothing like the cult status *Detour* enjoys, a rather surprising fact given the prominence of melodrama in recent readings against the grain. Perhaps traditional critics have cast the film aside for its pessimistic outlook on marriage and family life; feminist critics may be disinterested in its apparent use *of* the family and marriage as a means of resolving the problems it raises.

Music, Narrative, and Non-representational Signs

Penny Serenade immediately impresses upon its viewer / listener that music will perform a significant function in the film. The 78 r.p.m. records Julie plays divide her story into a set of discrete flashbacks, much like book chapters, an analogy suggested when Apple Jack first takes "The Story of a Happy Marriage" volume from the shelves. Through song, we learn of Julie's courtship with Roger, the accident in Japan, Trina's adoption, and so on. Music actively prompts the narrative, giving it its basic form and structure; it does not impede or oppose it in the way that most of the scholarship on film music or melodrama has claimed.

At the same time the records govern the movement of Julie's tale, they bathe their auditor in its affect. The songs—not all of which are recognizable or familiar—vaguely suggest an emotional state: instrumental music accompanies Miss Oliver as she reads the news of Trina's sudden death; "My Blue Heaven" initiates the sense of Julie and Roger's early happiness with the child; even "Happy Birthday," a tune with some connotative reference, works more to suggest a feeling of festivity and family togetherness than it does to mark the passing of a given year. Although these examples appear to perform film music's classic function of emotional embellishment, they also foreground this affective function, making it noticeable and not "invisible," silent, or unconscious as classicists would have it. We see close ups of spinning records and dramatic wipes opening each of the flashbacks. Small trinkets (cards, booties, etc.) are attached to the pages of the record album, emotional souvenirs that, like Lacanian *objets petits a*, function as partial signs, reminders of earlier fulfillment.

Music's non-representational qualities also bond Julie with the other characters in the film, unlike *Detour*, in which music severs Al Roberts from others. Special links are made between the films' three family members: the leitmotiv associated with Julie is often played when Julie longs for Christina (the piece is "To a Wild Rose" from Edward MacDowell's *Woodland Sketches*), and is usually performed through Julie's auditory point of view; the girl's performance as the echo in the school play draws Roger and Julie closer together; she is the "baby" that "makes three," according to the lyrics of "My Blue Heaven." At her mother's birthday,

Christina presents her with a record "because you love records and because you and daddy love each other so much."

Indeed, music initially brings and helps keep Julie and Roger together.
In Julie's second flashback, which begins as she puts a waltz on the phonograph, we see her and Roger dancing as the waltz continues in the past. So
pleasurable is this moment that words, in a very real sense, escape them.
Their happiness is conveyed solely through nonlinguistic sounds and gestures: the two dance wordlessly to the music, whistling, humming, and
grinning. The unidentified waltz not only recalls Julie's lost romance with
Roger, but it also non-representationally signals an earlier historic moment in a more general way. Its structure evokes turn-of-the-century
Americana, a supposedly simpler period unthreatened by war and economic hardship (one is reminded of *Meet Me in St. Louis*). The music is
assuring and comforting, its carefully measured form and rhythms creating a sense of order and stability. From this a utopian desire emerges for
a homespun stability, one which will become increasingly elusive to the
young couple. In this way, the nostalgic waltz, like the Chopin in *Detour*,
creates the impression of lost, better days. What distinguishes the two is
that in *Penny Serenade*, the waltz reminds its listening subject of a once-
held stability—Julie's actual relationship with Roger—whereas in *Detour*,
the Chopin points Al to the inability of high art ever to accommodate him.

The utopia that *Penny Serenade* musically constructs is specifically
based on the stability of conventional marriage and family life, more specifically, on the institution of motherhood. While these ideas—marriage,
the family, motherhood—hardly present subversive alternatives, *Penny
Serenade* does acknowledge how the traditional conceptions of motherhood and marriage are just that, concepts, constructions, and that once
recognized as such, they can be provisionally reshaped and reorganized.
This, I would argue, provides the base of the film's forward-oriented utopia.

Yet the film qualifies the comforts of this domestic setting through a
number of dystopian acoustic signs that help to keep Julie's utopia
grounded in the "real" facts of her personal history. Critics have long
noted melodrama's debt to its social underpinnings, and have relied heavily on the fact that the genre emerged in the eighteenth century as the
power of the middle class was firmly consolidated.[63] These social roots, as
Martha Vicinus has argued, have had considerable bearing on the reception of these texts. In her essay on nineteenth-century melodrama,
Vicinus has noted that part of its popularity with women and the working
class was because the genre provided "temporary" resolutions to conflicts
experienced in their daily lives. By stressing the growing rift between
domestic, private life and the public arena of this period, melodrama
"seemed to demonstrate how different circumstances could be endured
and even turned to victory."[64]

Since it launches a utopian sensibility from an historical base, melo-drama seems a likely site for the expression of utopian thought. But at the same time, and because the genre is so conspicuously engaged in a strug-gle with realist aesthetics, an internal dialectic is put into place. Melo-drama situates contemporary social problems into recognizable, "realis-tic," familiar settings (the difficulty of being a "kept" woman in *Back Street*; *Possessed* [1931]; the problem of cortisone addiction in the 1950s in *Bigger than Life*) at the same time it representationally strains in the direction of fantasy (consider the missed rendezvous in the park that Ray imagines at the end of *Back Street* or the nightmarish red used as James Mason is about to make a sacrifice of his son in *Bigger than Life*). As melo-drama scholars are at pains to note, this latter activity suggests that some-thing more is work than the mere staging of contemporary problems of social life, something that can be provisionally tied to some form of alter-natives based on hope and desire. In melodrama—as in the musical to which it is frequently compared—the utopian element in many ways over-rides its "realistic" one, although melodrama tends to defer or purloin its moment of utopia, while musicals preserve it (compare the conclusions of *Back Street* and *Meet Me in St. Louis*). Vicinus puts the matter quite nicely: "Melodrama is concerned not with what is possible or actual, but with what is desirable."[65] Nostalgia, unsurprisingly, plays a big role in this, and even though *Penny Serenade* aligns anteriority with music in a highly classical fashion (as Apple Jack says at one point, "Those songs sure can take you back, can't they?"), it also exposes the extent to which the relationship is mediated and made difficult.

Penny Serenade uses sounds to generate warning signals, anticipatory signs that point not to utopia but to how that notion of utopia may be troubled. For example, when Julie and Roger vow to remain together "till death do us part" on New Year's Eve, the scene erupts in an unpleasant outburst of non-representational signs. Confetti is strewn wildly through the air; party guests descend on the couple on the fire escapes outside; the scene is claustral and visually grim. Cacophonous non-diegetic music is heard; diegetically, noisemakers, horns, and whistles clutter the sound-track.

Although music comes to stand for the child Julie wants, sound disrupts this fantasy as well. When the earthquake strikes after Julie and Roger's argument, for example, their love theme is drowned out by the score's extremely loud noises. Later, when Miss Oliver makes an unannounced home inspection, Julie is "caught" dancing to a Charleston record she has put on the phonograph while cleaning house—a non-representational decadence that presumably displeases the staid agency worker (who, sig-nificantly, does not have her own leitmotiv). When the couple first brings the sleeping Trina home, the film comically exaggerates their noisy shoes, the squeaky stairs, and the alarm clock that threaten to wake her. Later, as she tries to bathe the child, Julie is noticeably unsettled by the noise of men cracking walnuts in the next room.

Most of the signs of this dysfunctioning utopia rally around the figure of Roger, immediately putting into question the kind of fatherhood and marriage he represents. Indeed, he is treated harshly by patriarchy ("you've had the regular opportunity to prove your fitness to provide," the judge tells the unemployed man); questions are raised about his virility (he is not, after all, the natural father of Christina); and his ability to generate discourse is similarly thrown into question (after buying a stack of records from Julie's store, he impotently tells her that he has no instrument, "no machine at home" on which to play them; Julie, by way of contrast, is always playing them).

Roger's most telling inadequacies, however, are finally not evaluated by patriarchal standards but by Julie's. The terms of their relationship, for example, are far from ideal. Apple Jack initially warns her "not to get involved with a newspaper man." Roger often is extremely petulant, behaving like a spoiled child with confusing mood swings and contradictory actions. First he states that he will not work for others, later he tells the judge he will take a job from anyone in order to keep his daughter (significantly, this is never depicted). He is a happy-go-lucky spendthrift at the same time he is a responsible family man; he dislikes children but is altogether crushed by Trina's death. He proposes to Julie only when he learns his business trip to Japan may result in losing her ("Julie, I've got to have you") and treats his newspaper as if it too were a possession—or a child-commodity—calling it "the fastest growing little newspaper." Curiously, the film barely tries to explain or diminish these contradictions. One senses that Roger's newfound sense of responsibility after Trina's arrival is never really convincing or complete since so many vestiges of his earlier, prefamilial personality remain. When Trina dies, this becomes especially clear as he is overtaken by a hostile sullenness and refuses to speak to Julie.

The figure of Roger elaborates both the utopian and dystopian sides of Julie's fantasy. That he is willing to change, and that he soon thrives in the family and occupies an active parental role within it establishes him as the utopian "sensitive male" that feminist critics from Molly Haskell on have observed in woman's melodrama (consider the Paul Henreid character in *Now Voyager*, George Brent in *Dark Victory*, et al.) Yet, because Roger never relinquishes all of his ties to conventional masculinity he also functions like the threatening, enigmatic male characters of traditional gothic narrative (Grant again in *Suspicion* and Laurence Olivier in *Rebecca* and *Wuthering Heights* [1939]). He is strange, ominous.

During their wedding, for instance, he has an inexplicable glassy stare on his face. When he begins his trip to Japan and Julie boards the train to bid him good-bye, the camera stays in the corridor as she enters his compartment. What occurs non-representationally is nothing short of haunting. The cabin door is left ajar, splitting the screen and separating the characters on its either side (we see only the character who appears to the right of it). At first Julie is revealed but, as Roger moves to the right to embrace her, his large body literally obliterates hers in a remarkably stylized, disturbing moment.

But *Penny Serenade*'s dystopian activity never entirely overtakes the utopian. In other words, it qualifies the film's utopia, but does not destroy it. Roger's shifting characteristics suggest in this regard not just an unsettled character but, more importantly, that the terms of his fatherhood are themselves being loosened. At times he is nothing short of feminine, rocking Christina to sleep (after Julie is unable to do so), choking on tears as he pleads with the judge, and so on. Apple Jack shares some of these maternal characteristics (he gives the infant her first bath, appears in aprons and so on), moving with self-effacing gestures and appearing confident only when with the child. It is Apple Jack in fact who first proposes that the couple adopt the girl and, later, who tries to keep the two together. In some ways, he is the most conventionally maternal character of the film.

It must be noted that the maternalization of the film's male characters arguably deprives the woman of one of the few roles admissible to her. But at the same time, that Apple Jack and Roger share in this maternal function demonstrates how arbitrary and social a phenomenon mothering actually is. From the start, *Penny Serenade* refuses to define motherhood as mere biological fact, since Christina is adopted, but as something regulated through a variety of discursive and social institutions. Here Julie's motherhood is not only mediated by Apple Jack and Roger, but by the adoption agency which makes her parenting possible in the first place. The most influential character here is the masculinized Miss Oliver, who functions much like a patriarchal God, giving the young couple two children (who appear miraculously as if from nowhere) and establishing the rules of parenting for them (it is she who first chastises Roger for his inability to make a living). Her stern, rigid appearance recalls that of Mrs. Danvers in *Rebecca*, another mouthpiece of domestic tradition that dictates the way households and families ought to be run. Unlike Danvers, however, the law that Miss Oliver ultimately represents is benign and poses no real threat to Julie's maternal fantasy. Even the unsympathetic male judge who threatens to take Trina from the couple eventually sides with them.

Penny Serenade's traditional family—and the refuge it purportedly offers—are not naturalized or idealized; they provide only limited refuge for

Julie. In this way, the film's maternal utopia extends only a partial alternative, one that does not escape or exceed its ideological perimeters so
much as rely on them for definition. To put this another way, the maternal
fantasy of *Penny Serenade*'s female subject does not subvert the ideology
that gives rise to it but arises out of it, rearranging and unwrapping it for
inspection.

Signs of Mediation: Narration and Time

The mediation of utopia also occurs at the enunciative level of the film.
Julie's "telling" of her tale is quite unlike Al Roberts's in this regard since
Penny Serenade acknowledges how her recall is just that—a re-calling or
re-presentation of past events. Hers is a subjective fiction, merely the
"story of a happy marriage." An unbridgeable gap separates Julie from her
past, her present situation from reverie, a distinction that of course eludes
Al Roberts. Moreover, Julie's flashback in *Penny Serenade* is continually
filled with breaks as her story struggles for articulation. In this way, there
is a continual oscillation between present and flashback scenes: the past
never overtakes the diegetic present. (Because *Detour*'s protagonist
rarely allows the present to interrupt his flashback, he is, in a very real
sense, unable to escape the past.) *Penny Serenade* does not extend its
memories as verisimilitudinous or regainable; they are cast simply as nostalgic reverie (Julie's first flashback closes on lyrics which stress that the
lover is now but a memory). Many of Julie's flashbacks end with songs
different from those that had initiated them, conveying not only the sense
of discontinuous time but also acknowledging that the past and present are
woven out of different temporal modalities.

One non-representational device in particular draws attention to the
fact that the story Julie is about to relay is merely representation. The first
flashback closes on the notes of a different popular song ("Just a Memory")
to the one she first puts on.[66] In fact, when Julie initially plays "You Were
Meant for Me," the record begins to skip, reminding her of how the song
skipped when Roger first came into her music store. But it more importantly reminds us that music will not be re-presenting the past smoothly
or without interference. In other words, the skip non-representationally
articulates the difference between what used to be and what is no longer
possible, and stresses the difficulty with which utopian thought is put into
representation at all.[67]

As I have already indicated, Julie's debt to the nostalgic scenario of
classical film music is great, as great as Al Roberts's. But unlike Al's, her
memories are voluntarily and actively set into play: she chooses to put the

records on the phonograph; her flashbacks are not the result of painful, involuntary recall.[68] As a narrating agent, she is somewhat active (a control that is qualified, to be sure, by the observation that the records have others speaking—or "singing"—for her, a point even more dramatically addressed in the 1982 film *Pennies from Heaven*). The popular songs that prompt her memories remind us that utopias are not entirely our own but are culturally produced as well. As Adorno would no doubt observe, these disks show that Julie's desire for a happy family life is mass-produced and ideologically sanctioned for her, highlighting nothing short of the typicality of Julie's experience, of her "desire to desire."[69]

Like *Detour*, *Penny Serenade* is fraught with odd coincidences and in ways is a tale of repetition compulsion: Miss Oliver repeats dialogue (both of the two infants up for adoption are "like no other child") and at the end of the film she just happens to have a young boy who fits the description of the one Roger initially craved; there are the mother and son stranded at Roger and Julie's on the way to the same Christmas pageant where Christina had performed the year before, and the boy walks on tiptoe the way Christina had. *Penny Serenade* boasts a number of other significant acts of fate: the earthquake that renders Julie barren; the babies that are immediately available for the couple at the adoption agency, the "hopeless illness" that kills young Christina; Miss Oliver's timely phone call about the new child that arrives just as Roger and Julie are about to separate for good. Fate seems to intervene either in the form of an act of God or as an act of Miss Oliver. Now, Brooks and others have stressed the important role fate plays in the melodramatic genre—and to this we should add film noir, since the characters of both genres do not act so much as they are acted upon. But unlike the example of *Detour*, where fate is cruel (it "sticks out its foot to trip you"), *Penny Serenade*'s fate is usually benevolent, in spite of its occasional tragedies. Compare, for example, the main songs of the two films: while "You Were Meant for Me" has fate playing a friendly hand, "I Can't Believe That You're in Love with Me" reveals only insecurity and doubt.

Just as the two films differ in the way they handle fate—the fixing of the future before it happens—so too do they differ in creating the sense of temporal progression. Dana Polan, along with a number of feminist critics, observes this in a number of films of the 1940s and connects it to the different forms of subjectivity they engage. He writes: "Men's time, women's time, enter into a nonsynchrony in so many films of the forties. There seems to be no single space in which all desires can come together in permanent and euphoric triumph."[70] For her part, Doane observes that in the woman's film, time is often marked by a sense of waiting and a lack of progression, a stagnancy she maintains emerges from a fundamental disphasure between women and discourse.[71] Regarding the maternal melodrama, she writes:

> The films obsessively structure themselves around just-missed moments, recognitions which occur "too late," and blockages of communication which might have been avoided. . . . The woman . . . will always wait for that moment (scenarios in which the woman *waits* abound in the woman's film) [this waiting, Doane notes, ultimately pertains to woman's exclusion from full subjectivity whose privileges, she accurately observes, are awarded only to adult males]. . . . What the narratives demonstrate above all is the irreversibility of time . . . [their ability to move us] is tied to a form of mistiming, a bad timing, or a disphasure.[72]

For Doane, the female subject is always out of sync with full subjectivity, a condition which certainly knows no respite in the woman's film—in fact, Doane argues, the genre exploits this condition. But, given that the past only partially governs the generation of discourse in *Penny Serenade*, one wonders if woman's disphasure might be read differently—less as a theoretical problem than as a preliminary articulation of utopia, an exploration of Bloch's idea of nonsynchronous development. For it seems to me that the female subject of *Penny Serenade* is far less bound to the past than is *Detour*'s male subject. And while the latter's condition is marked by dramatic stagnancy and lack of progress, the former moves forward through time.

Modleski has made a similar point in her illuminating analysis of *Letter from an Unknown Woman* (1948).[73] She argues that the protagonists, Stefan (a mildly amnesiac pianist and womanizer) and Lisa (one of his forgotten paramours who remembers their affair all too well since she bears a son as a result of it), operate on dramatically different temporal modalities. The memory of their romance commandeers Lisa's life. The perfect Victorian, she suffers a lifetime for one night's abandon. Before Modleski, critics largely considered Lisa as an hysteric since, true to Freud and Breuer's definition of the term, she appears to "suffer mainly from reminiscences."[74] The movement of Lisa's life could certainly be placed within Doane's mode of constant, obsessive, and cyclical return, a point well dramatized in the famous scene in which Lisa and Stefan take a train ride in an amusement park that "revisits the scenes of our youth" while actually going nowhere.

Arguing against these readings, Modleski maintains that Stefan is the film's true hysteric because of his inability to lay claim to the past. Incapable of grieving, unable even to remember (he fails to recognize Lisa when she returns to him), he is the one who truly suffers from reminiscences. He asks the same questions, repeats the same lines, courts women he cannot remember, and botches his career as a pianist. According to

Modleski, Lisa, on the other hand, "takes up the challenge of loss" and accepts her past without obliterating it.[75] There are several suggestive correspondences we can make between *Letter* and the present comparison of male and female subjectivities in *Detour* and *Penny Serenade*. Like Stefan, Al Roberts is a slave to his memories and thus cannot generate the kind of utopian thought that would enable him to move forward and ameliorate his situation. Similarly, Roger Adams is stifled, incapacitated by Christina's death: he will not talk about it and cannot bear to "see anyone or anything that reminds [him] of her." Because he is unable to move beyond the event, he is sullen and incommunicative (and silence, we are told, is the mark of hysteria). When Roger says "if there was some way you'd know a day or two before things happened," his desire to master time becomes clear. The fear of being controlled by time appears in other contemporary films, most strikingly in films noir like *D.O.A.*, *The Big Clock* (1947), and *Phantom Lady*; in *Out of the Past* the protagonist is out to assail his own history.[76] Critic Michael O'Pray extends this observation into the realm of the visual, arguing that the mise-en-scène of classical films (again he uses film noir as an example) is a fantasy of control over objects in a diegetic universe.[77]

Moreover, while protagonists like Al Roberts and Roger Adams both view their pasts with a degree of regret, Julie treats hers with gentle respect. Her sense of temporal progression and memory are tenderly revealed through flashbacks that do not organize themselves according to goal-oriented, linear time. Important is not only the fragmented nature of their successive unfolding but the way in which each one proceeds. Consider the non-representational signs in the waltz scene already mentioned, where the absence of dialogue, the languorous movement of Roger's and Julie's bodies, and the rhythms of the music itself convey a sense of profound slowness. A similar thing occurs when the couple first brings Christina home, when the unusually bare soundtrack is punctuated by the sporadic noise of the squeaky steps, dropped packages, and alarm clocks. Although this opposition between silence and sound strives mainly for comic effect here, it also works to suspend time, as if it were holding onto the affect of these emotionally laden moments and preserving its utopian traces for Julie.[78]

Such an interruption of linear time is accompanied by a temporal pattern that Doane, Modleski, Cixous, and Kristeva would doubtlessly associate with "woman's time" and female subjectivity. Yet, as I mention above, the cyclical time that Doane discusses need not be cast in terms of stasis or regression. True, Julie's past "returns" to her, but it comes back in fragmented forms and signs—in musical bits and pieces—and she never relinquishes herself to them as Al does in *Detour*. *Penny Serenade*'s score does not extend the fantasy of plenitudinous unity or utopian regression but offers the past as a series of partial signs to be reactivated. Consider how the lack of coherence of Julie's nostalgic utopia is even relayed by the diverse forms of music that prompt her story (popular songs, waltzes, instrumental neo-romantic works, and so on). Moreover, her willing return to the records indicates her readiness to embrace memory, to "take up the challenge of loss" with an eye toward future change (i.e., the dissolution of her marriage). The loose chronological order of her reminiscences further highlights a disinterest in logical causality, deceptive order, and linear progression. The nonsynchronous time and the disphasure associated with the female subject provide her with a nascent form of utopian alternatives, the beginnings of a rewrite of the "story of [her] happy marriage."

Detour, like film noir more generally, offers a strong degree of resolution. Melodrama is hardly less ambiguous, since it is known for its "extremes" (being, as Brooks dubs it, the text of the excluded middle), and its clarity of moral and ethical imperatives (embodied in the archetypal evil landlord or the chaste young heroine). But the woman's film offers no such easy oppositions or black-and-white solutions (consider the open-ended and ambiguous endings of *Now Voyager* or *Stella Dallas*). *Penny Serenade*'s denouement is similarly built around a set of competing, contradictory utopias that together work to defer any sense of final resolution (similar narrative strategies operate within contemporary soap operas as well). Of course, Julie's story ends with her returning to Roger and their adopting another child, something that diminishes the film's previous claims to alternatives and change. (This is powerfully dramatized in the closing shot, which shows the couple entering Christina's dark, gloomy room.) Yet, in many ways, *Penny Serenade* suggests that things will *not* be exactly the same for Julie, and that what she and Roger are about to embark upon is yet another "story," another version of "a happy marriage." It may not be clearly demarcated—it may not even be happy—but it will, hopefully, be different.

The Road to Utopia

Certainly the soundtracks of *Detour* and *Penny Serenade* participate in the larger classical tradition of Hollywood film scoring, especially in using music to link their subjects to the past and the subsequent feminization of this anteriority. But *Detour* is concerned with change only insofar as something lost to the subject is then restored to him. It is, in Bloch's terms, a regressive utopia of "filled affects" that craves the restoration of missing objects (in this case, Sue), and in this way Al's vision is doomed from the start. Even before his flashback begins, Al tells us that his is a subjectivity tortured by reminiscences. In fact, his past not only fails to comfort him, but actively betrays him, and in the end proves far more terrorizing than welcoming. Perhaps he knows that in turning backward for salvation, he forecloses his chances of moving ahead. At any rate, it could be said that the lack of change involved in Al's utopian impulse reveals his inability to fathom it in the first place. *Penny Serenade*, though not entirely innocent of that restorative vision (again one recalls the closing scene), generally uses its past to move beyond it and offer its subject the hope of change. Its highly mediated "story of a happy marriage" makes it impossible for Julie's nostalgic reverie to be construed as a real or utterly reclaimable "truth." At the same time, since the film's female subject finds within this past ways in which her role as a mother is also mediated and constructed—and thus reconstructible—the film acknowledges motherhood as a site for potential utopian alternatives. This is how *Penny Serenade* begins to articulate its partial utopian hope for a different future and give a glimpse of a utopia that offers new ways for aspects of family life—namely, mothering—to be redefined and reworked. What *Detour* does, on the other hand, is raise the partial trace of utopia only to shatter it. In fact it is questionable whether any straightforward utopian signs exist at all since everything in this film becomes entrenched within an overall sense of gloom and pessimism. It offers a dystopic, negative utopia in the fullest sense of the word.

Because the musical signs of *Penny Serenade* qualify Julie's domestic utopia throughout the film (just as they construct it in the first place), it is important to stress that these reworkings remain only at the level of suggestion. Serious questions are raised about whether they in fact will ever materialize or not, if Julie and Roger's new life together will be any different than before. It is within these qualifying signs that *Penny Serenade* exposes the limits of what marriage and traditional masculinity can offer. Julie's domestic utopia extends an offer of hope at the same time it acknowledges the difficult conditions that make necessary the existence of such fantasies to begin with.

In other words, Julie's utopian projections of new forms of mothering do not exceed their place within the family, but emerge as a consequence of it, much like the strategies de Certeau described in *acts de faire*. Although this necessarily restricts their subversive potential, the partial and negotiated nature of these projections also keeps them from positing falsely idealized, "otherly" conditions. The film's non-representational, acoustic signs of utopia do not urge its subject to lose herself to romantic memory. By not romanticizing Julie's lost ability to bear children, the film challenges theoretical traditions like psychoanalysis that insist on lost feminized, musical pasts as sources of boundless pleasures and escape. Instead, the score non-representationally points to a relaxation of conventional family roles (e.g., Roger's maternal streak), at the same time it reveals the difficulty of their actual realization or representation (e.g., his morose response to the couple's sudden childlessness). Moreover, like the utopia it cautiously establishes, the acoustic activity of the score does not work in opposition to the film's narrative or image track but articulates its utopian impressions alongside these other elements. Utopia is not externalized, nor rendered magical.

In this way, the woman's film works within and beyond the structures of the classical Hollywood film text to articulate its partial utopias. Though not subversive in any full-blown sense of the word, it does propose the beginnings of a difference from the status quo. But it is important to stress once again that this proposal or articulation is necessarily incomplete and tentative. And whereas the subject of *Detour* is unable to develop it (he seems only to respond to it), the subject of *Penny Serenade* is actively called upon to open up its partial utopia for completion. Julie takes up this challenge from within the diegesis, and, as critics "outside" of the film listening in, so do we.

In this spirit, the responses and readings I have offered here are not so much contained within the filmscores "themselves" as they are produced by the audition and analysis of a specific critic. Certainly my own position as a female subject, writing as a feminist in the early 1990s, brings with it its own utopian drive and agency to these readings. True, the soundtracks of the two films may seem to generate some sense of resistance on their own. And although this resistance might expose the misogyny of Al Roberts's maternal fantasy, or the nonbiologized version of Julie's maternal fantasy, the "traces" of utopian energy it leaves exist only insofar as they are activated through a particular vantage point of reading and listening. In fact, this is the only way that utopia is broached at all—as a strategy, a way of reading and of negotiating the texts around us.

SIX

MUSIC AND INTERPRETATION

As long as we choose to consider sounds only through the
commotion they stir in our nerves, we shall never have
the true principles of music and of its power over our
hearts. Sounds in the melody do not act solely as
sounds, but as signs of our affections.
(Rousseau)

IN 1977, SIMONE SIGNORET released her autobiography entitled
Nostalgia Isn't What It Used to Be.[1] Perhaps it isn't, although more
likely, it never was. The point is, it is still going strong today. Contemporary art music audiences get more opportunities to hear Beethoven
performed than they do Steve Reich; commercials promote everything
from regional health centers to champagne using the tried-and-true war-
horses of Western art music. Pop culture in the United States takes us
back through retro dressing, contemporary television shows like *China
Beach* and *The Wonder Years* (not to mention reruns), and the golden
oldie programs that saturate radio airwaves on weekends.

The current American cinema is also a gracious host to this idea, and its
sense of nostalgia is at least as pervasive as it was during the classical era.
Over the last fifteen or twenty years the United States has been virtually
inundated by films that reconstructed first the 1950s (*Grease* [1978] and
American Graffiti [1973] and then the 1960s (*The Big Chill* [1983]). More
recently, we have seen remakes of earlier classical films: *Xanadu* (1980),
a remake of 1944's *Cover Girl*, *Stella* (1989) [*Stella Dallas*], and *Always*
(1989) [*A Guy Named Joe* (1944)]. Although the focus on the 1940s as an
era is strong—and we will be returning to this point in a moment—there
are plenty of other nostalgic scenarios available. In the late 1980s, the
American market was given to a number of films in which men were allowed, to quote from *Letter from an Unknown Woman*, to "revisit the
scenes of their youth." In *Big* (1988), the adult male's body houses an
impish, younger boy; in *Back to the Future* (1985), the young male protagonist goes back through his family's history in order to preserve it in all of
its nuclear glory (replete with Oedipal anxieties and a father whose masculinity is in jeopardy).[2] Curiously, the next year, in *Peggy Sue Got Married*
(1986), Kathleen Turner returns to *her* familial past in order to rewrite it
and to avoid mistakes like her failed marriage. With these last two films

(competing versions of the same story, really), questions of subjectivity, gender, and nostaglia reemerge. Dramatically different circumstances send each of their protagonists back: in *Back to the Future*, it is a scientific experiment gone awry; in *Peggy Sue Got Married*, it is the emotional overload experienced at a high school reunion. The protagonists also have radically different relationships to the family, the past, and their reasons for returning to both. In many ways, the characters seem reworked, updated versions of the protagonists of *Detour* and *Penny Serenade*, with the men wanting to fix and preserve their pasts and the women expecting to change and to learn from theirs.

Regardless of the fantasy at hand—or *whose* fantasy is at hand—nostalgic utopias will always send their subjects back to supposedly better times, with romantic twists and turns. But these derailments are important, for they foreground the difference between the past and the present. Moreover, this difference, as I have stressed, has all too often been feminized for the hopes and/or threats it signifies. Classical and contemporary accounts alike riddle their conceptions of the present with lacks and deficiencies, obliging the past to function as a site of comparative cohesion, authority, and the hope, in Dyer's words, of "something better." Sometimes the pasts are punished for their failure to do so, other times, they are cherished.

Music continues to play a key role in triggering this widescale yearning for yesterday. Each week, for example, *The Wonder Years* starts with Joe Cocker singing "I Get By with a Little Help from My Friends" and concludes with a different song from the same era, for example, "Circle Game," by Joni Mitchell or "Bookends," by Simon and Garfunkel. *The Big Chill*'s soundtrack well outperformed the film and secured the latter's material success with the thirtysomething crowd, and Hollywood since then has increasingly and aggressively promoted its films through their scores. In this light, it would be foolish to argue that the classic score's "background" function still prevails (consider how the booming pop recording industry has enabled rock and roll to supplant classicism's romantic-influenced music). Yet, even so, contemporary film music still bows to a great many dictates of the classical approach. The score will still provide a conduit to idealized states and pasts, be this through the rock music of *American Graffiti* or in John Williams's neo-classical theme for *Star Wars* (1977). In fact, the *Star Wars* score offers a special case in point, since it non-representationally constructs the impression of nobility in a film that at more general levels restages old-fashioned heroism through state of the art pyrotechnics.

Part of *Star Wars*'s lost grandeur involves the appeal of the Hollywood cinema itself. The film, as Fredric Jameson has argued, takes up many of the elements of earlier, classical Hollywood genre features; indeed, as he claims, it is a virtual pastiche of stylistic and generic references.[3] Although Jameson believes this borrowing and raiding of the past exemplifies a general postmodern condition, the film's nostalgia for a lost golden era is revealed with special particularity by the score. Its principle theme bears an uncanny resemblance to Korngold's title theme of *King's Row*, following the same basic melodic movement (such as the opening, heavily stressed fifth interval) and instrumentation (a prominent brass section). And even though one might well question whether John Williams is quoting Korngold or stealing from him, the point to be made here is how contemporary cultural production actively banks on the utopian value that earlier, "classical" American culture—especially cinema of the 1940s—holds for us.

The films of the 1940s, and of the classical era more generally, serve an extremely important contemporary function. There are a few contemporary examples of remade women's films (*Romancing the Stone* [1984], *Stella*), but there has been a virtual onslaught of noir releases over the last twenty years, many of which are remakes of earlier films: *Cat People* (1982), *The Big Sleep* (1978), *The Long Goodbye* (1973), *Chinatown* (1974), *The Two Jakes* (1990), *Against All Odds* (1984), *The Grifters* (1990), *Body Heat* (1981), *The Postman Always Rings Twice* (1981), and even the "pastiche noir" of *Blade Runner* (1982), *Brazil* (1985), and *Dead Men Don't Wear Plaid* (1982). The attention paid to this era by film scholars is equally staggering. But why? (Or, as a student once asked me, "Why do all film teachers just show old movies?") In one way, because film studies as a discipline did not emerge in the United States until after the demise of the studio system, its obsession with Hollywood's classical era seems understandable, if not fully logical.

One connection that is immediate apparent, though, is that both contemporary film scholars and the classicists before them use the past in order to retrieve something found presently lacking. The desire is no less forceful in the 1990s than it was in the 1940s, especially insofar as film music is concerned.

For the studio composer in the 1930s and 1940s, the reversion to a nineteenth-century romantic model offered the promise of plenitude and unity on aesthetic levels because music supposedly rounded out the mass-produced film text through an ability to engender emotional, verisimilitudinous, and humanizing effects. It also prompted the same illusion on subjective levels, supplying the composer with a more individuated and potent notion of his own discursive production. For contemporary critics today, like the composers and lawyers of the classical period that preceded them, utopian hopes and dystopian fears are pinned onto earlier, idealized moments. Certainly our own "return" as critics to the film noir and the maternal melodrama of the 1940s reveals as much about our contemporary situation as it does about the times of the films' production.

Unlike the classicists, however, contemporary critics are more heavily influenced by poststructuralism and postmodernism than they are by nineteenth-century romanticism, and so the utopian projections gridded onto the past operate in conspicuously different ways. For most theorists, the 1940s is valued less as a site of prior unity and plenitude than as one marked by the appearance of rupture and disturbance. The notion of representational and subjective disturbances provides a utopian refuge to those who perceive a homogeneity—an "abundance" of unity, to defer to Adorno's critique of the culture industry—within their own discursive milieu. Because unity has come to be associated with the ideas of illusionism and false security, contemporary utopian thought activates signs that appear to dissolve it in order to promote the sense of an improved alternative condition.[4]

In this light, popular genres like film noir and the maternal melodrama have suggested to critics not only a diminished coherence within classical representation but a splintering of subjectivity as well—consider the ways in which both genres have been said to upset traditional notions of masculinity and the consequent loosening of gender identification. I think it is this sense of fragmentation that explains much of these films' utopian pull for contemporary critics and leads commentators to assign a politically progressive agenda to the genres. Such strains of utopia, coming as they do from the pens of cultural and political critics, produce in turn a nostalgia for a radicalized past, a privileged lost moment that gives the impression of acknowledging, for instance, the disenfranchisement of male subjectivity (consider film noir and *Detour*), or the limitations of traditional marriages and child-rearing situations for women (in *Penny Serenade* and the maternal melodrama).

It is important to recall, however, that these projections are produced solely through reading and that the radical sites they construct never actually existed. Still, as projections, they are crucial. Contemporary critics have been writing in extremely conservative times (Bush and Reagan's United States; Thatcher's Britain), and their readings of films from the 1930s and 1940s constitute a strategy, an act that does not radicalize earlier films or national history so much as it tries to reroute and resist the contemporary status quo. Such resistance does less than escape from ideology than point out, in however displaced a fashion, its perceived injustices and shortcomings. The partial and preservable traces of these utopias are more humble that conventionally conceived utopian thought. They are simply fragmented moments of hope, of desire. But they also raise the possibility of change, returning to representation, discourse, and perhaps even social action the fantasies and hopes that were prompted by these circumstances in the first place.

The Subject of Interpretation

It still remains for theorists to account for what Bloch and others have observed to be the disphasure between utopian thought and its actual historical context. Bloch, of course, tries to disengage utopia from its restorative function to involve it actively with present and even future contexts by claiming that the utopian sign contains within it traces of unrealized meaning, of the "not-yet-conscious." But it seems to me that the mechanisms of utopia are not contained or activated within any particular set of textual signs (no matter how abstract or "excessive" they may be), so much as they are set into play by the interpretive situation. They are, in other words, effects of discourse and, as such, the consequences of critical interpretation. Moreover, the tension created between the act of its production and any sort of point of original reference enables utopian thought to shift with time. Richard Dyer, it should be recalled, argues that utopian sensibilities arise from lacks perceived during the time of a film's production; by contrast, I am arguing that the utopias mounted to redress these apperceived lacks are created at the moment of reading, even if those utopias are then simply thrown backward. Only the interpreting agents performing that reading can render what Bloch calls the "not-yet-conscious" conscious. In my analyses of *Penny Serenade* and *Detour*, for instance, I have shown that the preoccupation with the lacks of the present day is in large order a preoccupation with the lacks of contemporary subjectivity. In this way, the utopian plenitude, the "excesses," and the subversion associated with melodrama or film noir are utopian, excessive, or subversive for *some one*, and the "something better" offered by their music is not something of another world, as some utopianists have implied, but that which we bring to it as actual listeners.[5]

My argument sharply curtails the extent to which film music—as well as Hollywood's other representational and non-representational elements—may be considered uniformly subversive, although in a very real sense it asks us to reconsider the term and its strategies altogether. Throughout this book I have tried to sustain the idea that representational excess and utopian thought are not necessarily progressive, but merely offer (and even then, only impressionistically so) alternative agenda through a series of non-representational signs. The case of *Detour* amply demonstrates this. For some, *Detour*'s score dramatizes utopian moments of unbridled freedom for its male protagonist (consider the comments provoked by Al's boogie-woogie improvisation), and in this way avails a glimpse of a liberating utopia for a certain kind of masculine subject. My own reading, on the other hand, stresses how the score has been indentured to a misogynist project that brusquely severs the female subject from the production of discourse, even if it does offer some initial resistance to Al's regressive fantasy.

Penny Serenade's utopian signs, on the other hand, lend partial expression to the desire for shared maternity, changed structures of the family, and the redefinition of fatherhood. Its understanding of these issues emerges from a specific historical and intellectual context, namely, one which has been shaped since the 1970s by feminism. To be sure, feminist criticism has deeply influenced recent film scholarship, but the point here is that it—along with other forms of political criticism, like Marxism—does not simply expose and *deconstruct* the machinations of ideology but actively *constructs* a sense of utopia through the analyses it offers.

The scores of films like *Penny Serenade* and *Detour* then offer very different strains of utopia for their interpreting subjects, even though both are entrenched within the wider, overarching nostalgia of the classical approach. *Penny Serenade*, through its elliptically rendered narrative and dystopian sounds that qualify Julie's auditory reverie, acknowledges that music cannot retrieve unity and points out that that idealized fulfillment never existed in the first place. And in the same way that *Penny Serenade* constructs its utopia on the basis of a female subject, *Detour*'s dystopia is based on her destruction. In fact, the contemporary critical response to *Detour*'s unsuccessful utopia can be interpreted as a dystopian response to the "progressive" representations and readings that film critics sympathetic to feminism were advocating in the 1970s. True, it would be difficult to pinpoint this position as a specific reaction against feminism of the 1970s, 1980s, and 1990s, for misogyny knows a far wider history than this, but the correspondences are there nonetheless.

I stress the notion of partial utopias to emphasize the negotiation involved between traditional representational systems—such as the classical Hollywood film—and utopian thought. I also use it to cast the irrational, poetic, excessive, and "utopian" elements alongside and within these classical texts—and not render them foreign or "otherly." At the same time, utopia's "partial" nature insists that utopia can never be directly represented, only alluded to and gestured toward. It is my hope that the notion will generate some flexibility in the way we understand what film scores can do and will give cause to rethink the different ways in which the apparently monolithic "classical" Hollywood score really functions. Moreover, it will require that some sort of historical ground be considered alongside any notion of the utopian.

Although I have been concentrating on the problems involved in associating music with utopia throughout this book, I am not, finally, suggesting that the connection is impossible. Rather, I want to stress the *difficulty* of this relationship as it has been posed within contemporary theory and within the classical studio system and film scoring practices. For film music scholarship, as I argued at the beginning of this work, has conspicuously ignored the historical and cultural parameters of its object of study, and even the most sophisticated cultural approaches have underplayed the important roles of gender and subjectivity in their accounts. By bringing these issues into sharper relief in the study of film music, it is my hope that we can more productively engage the strains of utopia in other artifacts around us. And since utopia stems from our own subjective hopes and fantasies, we have more than mere signs to work with, but the actual desire to materialize them.

NOTES

INTRODUCTION

1. Dmitri Tiomkin and Prosper Buranelli, *Please Don't Hate Me* (Garden City, NY: Doubleday and Co., 1959), pp. 253–54. My thanks to Barb Hall and Val Amenderez for making this source available to me.

2. Ibid.

3. The reference is to Claudia Gorbman's *Unheard Melodies: Narrative Film Music* (Bloomington: Indiana University Press, 1987).

4. Roy M. Prendergast, *Film Music: A Neglected Art* (New York: Norton, 1977).

5. This kind of inconsistency, as I will argue in the following chapter, suggests that the influence of romanticism on Hollywood scoring of this period was taken somewhat for granted.

6. Maurice Jaubert, "Music on the Sceen," in Charles Davy, ed. *Footnotes to the Film* (New York: Oxford University Press, 1937), p. 111.

7. Mary Ann Doane, "Ideology and the Practice of Sound Editing and Mixing," in *Film Sound: Theory and Practice*, ed. Elisabeth Weis and John Belton (New York: Columbia University Press, 1986), p. 55.

8. Several essays in the recent collection *Music and Society: The Politics of Composition, Performance, and Reception*, ed. Richard Leppert and Susan McClary (Cambridge: Cambridge University Press, 1987), develop this idea. See especially Janet Wolff's "The Ideology of Autonomous Art" and McClary's "The Blasphemy of Talking Politics During Bach Year."

9. "The School of Giorgione," in *The Renaissance: Studies in Art and Poetry* (London: Macmillan, 1919), p. 135.

10. "[L]a musique a bon dos." Vladimir Jankélévitch, *La musique et l'ineffable* (1961; reprint, Paris: Editions du seuil, 1983), p. 19.

11. For a discussion of this problem in light of current developments in critical studies, see Janet Wolff's "Foreword: The ideology of autonomous art" in Leppert and McClary, *Music and Society*, pp. 1–12. Although mainstream musicology is still under the sway of this tradition, scholars like McClary, Simon Frith, Angela McRobbie, and John Shepherd are beginning to raise the long overdue questions of music's relationship to its social, cultural, and ideological contexts. But even as early as the 1930s, critics were noting music's slow break from noncultural approaches. Historian Barbara A. Zuck quotes from one: "In this country music has been perhaps the last of the arts to break away from the 100 per cent reactionary art for art ideology. Only since the Depression . . . has the great rank and file of musicians and music lovers begun to feel that something is wrong somewhere." Quoted in *A History of Musical Americanism* (Ann Arbor: University of Michigan Research Press, 1980), p. 113.

12. Suzanne K. Langer, *Feeling and Form* (New York: Scribner's, 1953), p. 27.

13. See Book Six of *St. Augustine's De Musica*, ed. W. F. Jackson Knight (London: The Orthological Institute, n.d.). My thanks to Dudley Andrew for referring me to this source.

ONE

1. See, for example, the discussions of film music by Mark Evans, *Soundtrack: The Music of the Movies* (New York: Da Capo, 1979), Prendergast, *Film Music*, and Roger Manvell and John Huntley, *The Technique of Film Music*, 2d ed., revised by Richard Arnell and Peter Day (New York: Focal Press, 1975). David Bordwell, Janet Staiger, and Kristin Thompson's discussion of the classical Hollywood style situates its beginnings earlier, in the 1910s. Yet, although many conventions and techniques used in relation to film music were set in place by then, their extensive support and elaboration could not have been fully consolidated until after the advent of sound. See their excellent *The Classical Hollywood Cinema: Film Style and Mode of Production to 1960* (New York: Columbia University Press, 1985).

2. As this definition suggests, it is not altogether clear when classicism is prescribing a function of film music or when it simply describes a role music is believed to perform automatically.

3. Gerald Cockshott, *Incidental Music in the Sound Film* (London: British Film Institute, 1946), p. 1.

4. W. Stephen Bush, "Giving Musical Expression to the Drama," *The Moving Picture World* (12 August 1911): 354.

5. W. Stephen Bush, "The Music and the Picture," *The Moving Picture World*, 16 April 1910, p. 59.

6. Sigmund Spaeth, quoted in Charles Merrell Berg, *An Investigation of the Motives for and Realization of Music to Accompany the American Silent Film, 1896–1927* (New York: Arno Press, 1976), p. 62. The obviousness between music and image will, in the classical era, be reidentified as "mickey mousing." In mickey mousing, music assumes its most extreme and hyperbolized shadowing of the image. The consummate example is offered by Dumas's "The Sorcerer's Apprentice" in *Fantasia* (1940), where Mickey Mouse's movement down the stairs is accompanied by a descending scale on the sound track. See my discussion on page 34.

7. See Kurt London, *Film Music*, trans. Eric S. Bensinger (London: Faber and Faber, 1936).

8. Quoted in Berg, *An Investigation*, p. 18.

9. The work of early film scholars like Thomas Gunning is interesting in this regard. See, for instance, his "The Cinema of Attraction: Early Film, Its Spectator, and the Avant-Garde," *Wide Angle* 8, nos. 3–4 (1986): 63–70.

10. Berg, *An Investigation*, p. 52.

11. Quoted in Berg, *An Investigation*, p. 149.

12. See George Antheil, "Hollywood Composer," *Atlantic Monthly*, no. 165 (February 1940): 165.

13. From an interview with Johnny Green, head of the music department at MGM. See C. Sharpless Hickman, "Movies and Music," *Music Journal* 12, no. 1 (January 1954): 31.

14. *Who's Who in Music*, 5th ed. (New York: Hafner Publishing, 1969), p. 122 and *The New Grove Dictionary of American Music*, vol. 2, ed. H. Wiley Hitchcock and Stanley Sadie (New York: Macmillan, 1986), p. 283.

15. For a fuller discussion of Herrmann's work with Welles, see Kathryn Kalinak, "The Text of Music: A Study of *The Magnificent Ambersons*," *Cinema Journal* 27, no. 4 (Summer 1988): 45–63.

16. Quoted in Robert Faulkner, "Dilemmas in Commercial Work: Hollywood Film Composers and Their Clients," *Urban Life* 5, no. 1 (April 1976): 12.

17. Quoted in Prendergast, *Film Music*, pp. 67–68.

18. This was normally done through the "click-track," a technique developed by Steiner which used a metronome device that sounded at regular intervals as the film was passed through a projector so that the composer would be able to break down and analyze scenes for his music to appear exactly at the appropriate moment in any given scene.

19. Nick Roddick, *A New Deal in Entertainment: Warner Brothers in the 1930s* (London: British Film Institute, 1983), p. 59.

20. This is poignantly and humorously suggested in Visconti's adaptation of Thomas Mann's *Death in Venice* (1971), where the hapless Gustav von Ashenbach is musically linked to Gustav Mahler.

21. Newman first articulated this in "The War and the Future of Music," *The Musical Times* 55, no. 859 (1 September 1914): 571–72. This same perspective informs the music history of, among others, Richard Shead in *Music in the 1920s* (New York: St. Martin's Press, 1976), especially chapter one, "Precursors."

22. One of the early advocates of this romantic understanding of music was Jean-Jacques Rousseau, whose debates with classicist composer Jean-Philippe Rameau gave him ample opportunity to put forth this early romantic position. See his *Ecrits sur la musique* (Paris: Editions Pourrat, 1838; reprint Paris: Stock, 1979).

23. Curiously, however, this musical Americanism emerged at a time when the United States played home to many modernist composers who had emigrated from fascist Europe: Schönberg, Milhaud, and Eisler were said to have had little influence on *America's* musical development of this time, even though the presence of more traditional composers like Korngold, Steiner, and Rózsa in Hollywood has frequently been used as a means of explaining *Hollywood's* musical style.

24. For an extended discussion of the activity of musical populists at the time, see Zuck's excellent *A History* and also the introduction of Joseph Kerman's *Contemplating Musicology: Challenges to Musicology* (Cambridge, Mass.: Harvard University Press, 1985), which speaks extensively on Seeger's musicological (though not political) contributions.

25. Quoted in Zuck, *A History*, p. 95.

26. Copland, *The New Music, 1900–1960* (New York: Norton, 1968), pp. 161–62.

27. Leo Marx, *The Machine in the Garden: Technology and the Pastoral Ideal in America* (London: Oxford University Press, 1964).

28. Quoted in Samuel Lipman, *Music after Modernism* (New York: Basic Books, 1979), p. 167.

29. Quoted in Richard Taruskin, "The Pastness of the Present," in *Authenticity and Early Music*, ed., Nicholas Kenyon, (London: Oxford University Press, 1988), pp. 146–47.

30. See Taruskin, "The Pastness." My thanks to Susan McClary for referring me to this source.

31. Cavalcanti writes: "In style, the music of the cinema, by and large, represents a fixation at a stage of development which the art itself left behind about thirty years ago. It is music of the late romantic period: Tschaikovsky, Rachmaninoff, Sibelius, are the spiritual fathers of most cinema music." Quoted in Elisabeth Weis and John Belton, eds., *Film Sound: An Anthology* (New York: Columbia University Press, 1986), p. 106.

32. Shead, *Music in the 1920s*, p. 92.

33. Quoted in Alfred Einstein, *Music in the Romantic Era* (New York: Norton, 1947), p. 22.

34. Berg, *An Investigation*, p. 245.

35. Wilfred Mellers, *Romanticism and the Twentieth Century* (Fair Lawn, N.J.: Essential Books, 1957).

36. David C. Large and William Weber, eds. *Wagnerism in European Culture and Politics* (Ithaca, N.Y.: Cornell University Press, 1984), p. 284.

37. Susan Stewart, *On Longing: Narratives of the Miniature, the Gigantic, the Souvenir, the Collection* (Baltimore, Md.: Johns Hopkins University Press, 1984), pp. 79–80.

38. For interesting close analyses of these scores, see Claudia Gorbman, "The Drama's Melos: Max Steiner and *Mildred Peirce*," *Velvet Light Trap* no. 19 (1982): 35–39; and Louis Applebaum, "Hugo Friedhofer's Score to *The Best Years of Our Lives*," *Film Music Notes* 9, no. 5 (1947).

39. See chapter one, "Prejudices and Bad Habits," in Hanns Eisler, *Composing for the Films* (London: Dennis Dobson, 1947).

40. Theodor Adorno, *In Search of Wagner*, trans. Rodney Livingstone (London: New Left Books, 1981), p. 46.

41. Thomas Mann, "Reflections of a Non-political Man," in *Pro and Contra Wagner*, trans. Allan Blunden (Chicago: University of Chicago Press, 1985), p. 41.

42. Jacques Attali, *Noise: The Political Economy of Music*, trans. Brian Massumi (Minneapolis: University of Minnesota Press, 1985), p. 92.

43. Richard Wagner, "The Art-Work of the Future," in *Richard Wagner's Prose Works*, trans. William Ashton Ellis, 2d ed. (London: Kegan Paul, Trench, Trübner, and Co., 1895), vol. 1, p. 127.

44. Richard Wagner, "The Public in Time and Space," *Wagner's Prose Works*, trans. William Ashton Ellis (1897; reprint St. Clair Shores, Mich.: Scholarly Press, 1972), vol. 6, pp. 86, 89, 87. These comments call into question Wagner's promotion of a revived Teutonic culture and a specifically German *Gesamtkunstwerk*; in an 1863 letter, in fact, he writes of his nation and countrymen, "It is a miserable country, and a certain man named Ruge is right when he says, '*The German are vile*' " (quoted in Einstein, *Music in the Romantic Era*, p. 270).

45. Richard Wagner, "Public and Popularity," *Wagner's Prose Works*, vol. 6, p. 55.

46. Quoted in Evans, *Soundtrack*, p. 28. Importantly, Korngold goes on to say that this disinterest is not due to the fact that it is a film audience, for he states that, when he composes, he does not differentiate between cinematic and operatic audiences and situations. His concern, he says, rests solely with the formal development and variation in his music.

47. Antheil, "Hollywood Composer," pp. 160–61.

48. Attali, *Noise*, pp. 46–47. Wagner—especially the early Wagner—would probably not disagree with Attali on this point. In fact, the two theorists share a nostalgia for lost periods in which they believe music was consumed "properly" and in harmony with its culture.

49. Einstein, *Music in the Romantic Era*, p. 14.

50. Erich Leinsdorf, "Some Views on Film Music," *Music Publishers Journal* 3, no. 5 (September–October 1945): 53–54.

51. Gail Kubik, "Music in Documentary Films," *Music Publishers Journal* 3, no. 5 (September/October, 1945): 13.

52. Walter Benjamin, "The Work of Art in the Age of Mechanical Reproduction," in *Illuminations*, trans. Harry Zohn, ed. Hannah Arendt (New York: Schocken Books, 1969), pp. 217–51.

53. Nathan Levinson, "Recording and Re-recording," in *We Make the Movies*, ed. Nancy Naumberg (New York: Norton, 1937), p. 187.

54. Prendergast, *Film Music*, pp. 31, 38.

55. Rózsa also states:

We are now at the lowest abyss you can imagine. We play to the lowest common denominator. The dramatic, let alone the symphonic, score is gone. My generation tried to establish the serious motion picture score with a symphonic background. I personally believe in the form of motion picture music derived from Wagner's book "Opera and Drama." He discusses the *Gesamtkunstwerk*, an all-comprising art of drama, writing, and music. What could come closer to this description than motion pictures? I believed that music could play an important part in films. Nobody goes to the cinema to listen to music, they go to see a drama. But dramatic music can be an important factor. This is all finished now; all they want is to sell a song, play a cheap tune over and over, and sell records. The high ideal of the *Gesamtkunstwerk* has gone out the window.

Quoted in Evans, *Soundtrack*, p. 207.

56. Harry Sosnik, "Screen Musicals Killed Conductors and Replaced Them with Engineers," *Variety* (5 January 1977): 9.

57. Leonard Meyer, *Emotion and Meaning in Music* (Chicago: University of Chicago Press, 1956), p. 76.

58. Ken Sutak, *The Great Motion Picture Soundtrack Robbery* (Hamden, Conn.: Archon Books, 1976), p. xxxvi.

59. Law of 11 March 1857, quoted in Attali, *Noise*, p. 79.

60. Richard Shale, *Academy Awards*, 2d ed. (New York: Frederick Ungar Publishing, 1982), p. 161.

61. The significance of these allusions to male fertility will be examined in the following chapter.

62. Sutak, *Great Motion Picture Soundtrack*, p. xvii.

63. Leonard Zissu, "The Copyright Dilemma of the Screen Composer," *Hollywood Quarterly* 1, no. 3 (April 1946): 317.

64. Elmer Bernstein, "Film Composers vs. the Studios," *Film Music Notebook* 2, no. 1 (1976): 33.

65. Quoted in Manvell and Huntley, *Technique of Film Music*, p. 229.

66. See Eisler, *Composing for the Films*, pp. 13–14.

67. Gorbman, *Unheard Melodies*. For an elaboration of the categories of parallelism and counterpoint within the history of film music theory, see the chapter "Narratological Perspectives on Film Music." Here Gorbman rightly argues that the dichotomous conception of film music has curtailed scholars' understanding of its function within film narrative.

68. Leonard Quinto, "Some Questions for Music Educators on Film Music," *Music Publishers Journal* 3 no. 5 (September–October, 1945): 27.

69. Herbert Stothart, "Film Music Through the Years," *The New York Times Encyclopedia of Film 1941–1946*, ed. Gene Brown (New York: New York Times Books, 1984; reprinted from *New York Times*, 7 December 1941, A.

70. Max Steiner, "Scoring the Film," in Naumberg, *We Make the Movies*, p. 225. Sheer musical duration, however, was used to promote the sense of totality and synthesis to the Hollywood film before it was achieved through instrumentation (consider again Steiner's score for *Bird of Paradise*).

71. Quoted in Manvell and Huntley, *Technique of Film Music*, p. 225.

72. Quoted in François Porcile, *Présence de la musique à l'écran* (Paris: Editions du cerf, 1969), p. 272. The translation is mine.

73. Oscar Levant, *A Smattering of Ignorance* (New York: Doubleday, 1940), p. 90.

74. Quoted in *Pro Musica Sana* 9 no. 3 (Spring 1982): 22.

75. Miklós Rózsa, *Double Life: The Autobiography of Miklós Rózsa* (New York: Hippocrene Books, 1982), p. 66.

76. Steiner, "Scoring the Film," p. 225.

77. Ernest Lindgren, *The Art of the Film* (New York: Macmillan, 1963), pp. 139–40.

78. Quoted in an interview with Randall Larson in *CinemaScore* no. 10 (Fall 1982): 19.

79. Martin Williams, "Jazz at the Movies," in *Film Music: From Violins to Video*, ed. James L. Limbacher (Metuchen, N.J.: Scarecrow Press, 1974), p. 42.

80. Quoted by John Ellis, "Art, Culture and Quality: Terms for a Cinema in the 40s and 70s," *Screen* 19, no. 3 (1978): 26.

81. London, *Film Music*, p. 37.

82. Quoted in Randall Larson, *Musique Fantastique: A Survey of Film Music in the Fantastic Cinema* (Metuchen, N.J.: Scarecrow Press, 1985), pp. 47–48.

83. See chapter seven, "Suggestions and Conclusions," in Eisler, *Composing for the Films*.

84. Quoted in Manvell and Huntley, *Technique of Film Music*, p. 242.

85. Ibid.

86. London, *Film Music*, pp. 126, 144.

87. Ibid., p. 125.

88. Irwin Bazelon, *Knowing the Score: Notes on Film Music* (New York: Arco Publishing, 1975), pp. 7, 12.

89. See Cockshott, *Incidental Music*.

90. David Ewen, *Music Comes to America* (New York: Thomas Y. Crowell Company, 1942), p. 224.

91. Ibid., p. 223.

92. Quoted in Porcile, *Présence*, p. 54.

93. For another brief discussion of film music's compensatory function, see Gorbman, *Unheard Melodies*, pp. 39–41, 67.

94. Rick Altman, "Introduction," *Yale French Studies* 60, no. 1 (1980): 13.

95. David Cook, *A History of Narrative Film* (New York: Norton, 1981), pp. 247–48.

96. Rudolf Arnheim, "A New Laocoön: Artistic Composites and the Talking Film," in *Film as Art* (Berkeley: University of California Press, 1957), pp. 199–230.

97. For a fuller discussion of this idea and some of its theoretical ramifications see chapter one, "Lost Objects and Mistaken Subjects," in Kaja Silverman's *The Acoustic Mirror* (Bloomington: Indiana University Press, 1988).

98. Virgil Thomson, "Processed Music," *Music Publishers Journal* 3, no. 5 (September/October 1945): 33, 60.

99. Silverman has noted that this desire to gain verisimilitude—or to make up for its loss—is in fact a central preoccupation of film theory more generally. See her excellent discussion of the stakes for the female subject in this preoccupation in "Lost Objects."

100. See, respectively, Alan Williams, "The Musical Film and Recorded Popular Music" in *Genre: The Musical*, ed. Rick Altman (London: Routledge, Kegan Paul, 1981), pp. 147–58; Nancy Wood, "Towards a Semiotics of the Transition to Sound," *Screen* 25, no. 3 (1984): 16–24; and Doane, "Ideology and the Practice of Sound Editing and Mixing," pp. 47–56.

101. Wood, "Towards a Semiotics," p. 19.

102. Levinson, "Recording and Re-recording," p. 198.

103. Mortimer Browning, "Establishing Standards for the Evaluation of Film Music," *Music Publishers Journal* 3, no. 5 (September–October 1945): 23.

104. London, *Film Music*, p. 34.

105. Elsewhere, in an essay called "How to Write a Piece, or Functional Design in Music," Thomson refers to the "quiet tick-and-flicker of an unaccompanied film" as "soporific" and writes that music adds "emotional poignancy to the dangerously frigid spectacle of a series of photographs," in *A Virgil Thomson Reader* (New York: Dutton, 1981), p. 149.

106. Berg, *An Investigation*, p. 24.

107. Max Winkler, "The Origin of Film Music," in James Limbacher, ed. *Film Music*, p. 16.

108. Susan Stewart has gone on to argue more specifically that along with the idea of the individual, self-sufficient work of "art" that has been displaced by mass production, so too has the idea of internal coherence and the illusion of wholeness between form and content been lost. See her discussion "On Description and the Book," in *On Longing*, p. 34.

109. See Doane, "Ideology," p. 50. Important here are the gender roles that this "marriage" implies, with the sound track functioning as the feminine term and the image a masculine one. This assumption permeates a wide number of theoretical accounts of film music, and I will be returning to it in the following chapter.

110. James Naremore, from *Filmguide to Psycho*, quoted in Prendergast, *Film Music*, p. 144.

111. Quoted in Graham Bruce, *Bernard Herrmann: Film Music and Narrative* (Ann Arbor: University of Michigan Research Press, 1985), p. 216.

112. G. A. Lazarou, *Max Steiner and Film Music* (Athens, Greece: Max Steiner Music Society, 1971), p. 8.

113. Quoted in Manvell and Huntley, *Technique of Film Music*, p. 244.

114. Ibid., p. 65.

115. Tony Thomas, *Film Score: The View from the Podium* (New York: A. S. Barnes, 1979), p. 9.

116. Bazelon, *Knowing the Score*, p. 22.

117. See Mary Ann Doane, "The Voice in the Cinema: The Articulation of Body and Space," in *Narrative, Apparatus, Ideology: A Film Theory Reader*, ed. Philip Rosen (New York: Columbia University Press, 1986), pp. 335–48.

118. Helen Van Dongen, discussing her work for *Louisiana Story*, quoted in Karel Reisz and Gavin Millar, *The Technique of Film Editing* (New York: Hastings House, 1968), p. 155.

119. Among the few who have been exploring this in relation to film sound are Mary Ann Doane and Kaja Silverman. In their discussions of acoustic plenitude, both emphasize the concept of immersion and envelopment.

120. Bernard Herrmann, "Music in Motion Pictures: A Reply to Mr. Leinsdorf," *Music Publishers Journal* 3, no. 5. (September–October 1945): 17.

121. See chapter five, "Elements of Aesthetics," in Eisler, *Composing for the Films*.

122. Sergei Eisenstein, *Film Sense*, trans. and ed. Jay Leyda (New York: Harcourt Brace Jovanovich, 1942), part four.

123. Eisler, *Composing for the Films*, pp. 69, 70.

124. Jeffrey Embler, "The Structure of Film Music," in Limbacher, *Film Music*, p. 63.

125. Carl Dahlhaus, *Between Romanticism and Modernism*, trans. Mary Whittall (Berkeley: University of California Press, 1989), p. 5.

126. Even though Wagner located this cultural paragon in ancient Greece, his music dramas are dominated by themes of the middle ages, providing another rift between his theoretical and compositional work.

TWO

1. See Martin Jay, *Marxism and Totality* (Berkeley: University of California Press, 1985) for an extended discussion of the concept of totality. Although Jay makes his primary observations on the idea of totality in relation to twentieth-century Western Marxism, he contextualizes them within intellectual and aesthetic traditions that extend significantly beyond Marxist parameters.

2. Gorbman, *Unheard Melodies*, p. 61.

3. Quoted in Gérard Blanchard, *Images de la musique de cinéma* (Paris: Edilig, 1984), p. 95.

4. Denis Vasse develops this formulation in his influential *L'ombilic et la voix: deux enfants en analyse* (Paris: Editions du seuil, 1974).

5. See, for instance, the work of Anne-Marie Blanchard (as quoted in Gérard Blanchard, *Images*, pp. 101–2) and Denis Vasse.

6. Guy Rosolato, "Répétitions," *Musique-en-jeu* no. 9 (November 1972): 39.

7. See Guy Rosolato, "La voix: Entre corps et langage," *Révue française de psychanalyse* 38 (January 1974): 75–94.

8. Ibid., p. 81.

9. Ibid., p. 83. Jean-François Lyotard stresses this same connection, arguing that "tonal music belongs to the fantasmatic scene." See "Plusieurs silences," *Musique-en-jeu* no. 9 (November 1972): 64–76.

10. Rosolato, "Répétitions," p. 42.

11. Doane, "Voice," p. 34.

12. See chapter nine, "En souffrance de corps," in Michel Chion's *La voix au cinéma* (Paris: Editions de l'étoile, 1982).

13. See Silverman's "Dis-Embodying the Female Voice," *Re-Vision: Essays in Feminist Film Criticism*, ed. Mary Ann Doane, Patricia Mellencamp, and Linda Williams (Frederick, Md.: University Publications of America and the American Film Institute, 1984), pp. 131–49 and its sustained development in *The Acoustic Mirror*.

14. Quoted in Dominique Avron, "Notes pour introduire une métapsychologie de la musique," *Musique-en-jeu* no. 9 (November 1972): 102. The translation is mine.

15. Interviewed in "La musique utilitaire," *Musique-en-jeu* no. 24 (September 1976): 68–74.

16. Langer, *Feeling and Form*, p. 27.

17. Barthes, "The Third Meaning," reprinted in *The Responsibility of Forms: Critical Essays on Music, Art, and Representation*, trans. Richard Howard (New York: Hill and Wang, 1986), pp. 41–62.

18. It should be noted that for as much as Barthes might try to locate the "third meaning" *in* the text, it clearly emerges as a consequence of an attending subject (the peasant's scarf will surely not have the same effect—or perhaps none at all—on another viewer). Ultimately, Barthes's notion of the third meaning gives its most generous insight into its "author."

19. Barthes, "The Grain of the Voice," reprinted in *Responsibility of Forms*, pp. 267–77.

20. Ibid., p. 270.

21. Barthes and Kristeva are by no means alone in emphasizing music's relationship to the body. They are joined by as unlikely a colleague as rocker Little Richard, who in a *Rolling Stone* interview claims that music "regenerates the heart and makes the liver quiver, the bladder splatter, the knees freeze." Little Richard in *The Rolling Stone Interviews* (New York: Paperback Library, 1971), p. 377.

22. Barthes, "Rasch," reprinted in *Responsibility of Forms*, p. 308.

23. Gilles Deleuze and Félix Guattari, *A Thousand Plateaus: Capitalism and Schizophrenia*, trans. Brian Massumi (Minneapolis: University of Minnesota Press, 1987), p. 297.

24. Ibid., pp. 296–97.

25. Ibid., p. 293.

26. Ibid., pp. 291, 292.

27. See Alice Jardine's critique in *Gynesis: Configurations of Woman and Mod-*

ernity (Ithaca, N.Y.: Cornell University Press, 1985), especially chapter ten, "Becoming a Body without Organs: Gilles Deleuze and His Brothers."

28. For an excellent discussion of Barthes's use of femininity in this regard, see Naomi Schor, "Dreaming Dissymetry: Barthes, Foucault, and Sexual Difference," in Alice Jardine and Paul Smith, eds., *Men in Feminism* (New York: Methuen, 1987), pp. 98–110.

29. Julia Kristeva, *Desire in Language*, trans. Thomas Gora, Alice Jardine, and Leon S. Roudiez (New York: Columbia University Press, 1980), p. 133.

30. This idea has been observed by Jardine in "Spaces for Further Research" in *Gynesis*, as well as by Kaja Silverman in her work on the interiorization of the female voice in *The Acoustic Mirror*.

31. Julia Kristeva, *Revolution in Poetic Language*, trans. Margaret Walker (New York: Columbia University Press, 1984), p. 68.

32. Kristeva, *Desire in Language*, p. 136.

33. Ibid., p. 167.

34. The term is Catherine Clément's, from her book *Opera or the Undoing of Women*, trans. Betsy Wing (Minneapolis: University of Minnesota Press, 1988).

35. Barthes, "Music, Voice, Language," reprinted in *Responsibility of Forms*, pp. 278–85.

36. Ibid., p. 280.

37. Quoted in Leonard B. Meyer, *Style and Music: Theory, History, and Ideology* (Philadelphia: University of Pennsylvania Press, 1989), pp. 203–4.

38. Both quoted in Meyer, *Style and Music*, p. 204.

39. Barthes, "The Romantic Song," in *Responsibility of Forms*, pp. 286–92.

40. The tessitura is the general "lie" of a vocal part. Since it does not include extremely low or high pitches, the tessitura is not be confused with the "range" of a part. See *The Harvard Dictionary of Music*, ed. Willi Apel, 2d edition (Cambridge, Mass.: Belknap Press, 1972), p. 839.

41. Barthes, "The Romantic Song," p. 289.

42. Ibid., p. 289.

43. Barthes, "The Grain of the Voice," p. 270.

44. Ibid, p. 268.

45. Kristeva, *Desire in Language*, p. 286.

46. Kristeva, *Revolution in Poetic Language*, pp. 27–28.

47. Paul Smith, *Discerning the Subject* (Minneapolis: University of Minnesota Press, 1988), p. 129.

48. Kristeva develops this in the essays collected as *Powers of Horror: An Essay on Abjection*, trans. Leon S. Roudiez (New York: Columbia University Press, 1982).

49. For an extended feminist critique of Kristeva's theory of abjection, see Jennifer Stone, "The Horrors of Power: A Critique of 'Kristeva'," in *The Politics of Theory: Essex Conference on the Sociology of Literature*, ed. Francis Barker et al. (Colchester: University of Essex, 1983), pp. 38–48. Silverman's critique of Kristeva appears in her chapters on "The Fantasy of the Maternal Voice" in *The Acoustic Mirror*.

50. Kristeva, *Desire in Language*, p. 191.

51. Ibid., pp. 241–42.

52. This footnote accompanies Kristeva's discussion on "The Semiotic and the Symbolic" in *Revolution in Poetic Language* and may be found on p. 241. For English translations of Lacan's work on the maternal, consult *Feminine Sexuality*, trans. Jacqueline Rose, eds. Juliet Mitchell and Jacqueline Rose (New York: Norton, 1985), whose introduction by the editors offers insightful commentary on Lacan's reluctance to theorize the maternal body.

53. *Desire in Language*, p. 242. This same usurpation of the female voice by male artists is theorized in relation to popular rock music by Barbara Bradby and Brian Torode, "The Musical Inclusion, Exclusion, and Representation of Women" (Unpublished conference paper presented to the British Sociological Association conference on Gender and Society, University of Manchester, April 1982). Bradby and Torode combine sociological and Lacanian approaches in their analyses of several rock songs from the 1950s, focusing primarily on the "male buddy" mode of composition and performance in the work of, among others, Buddy Holly and Bo Diddley, in which they argue "the mother [may be constituted] as specifically absent by his repetition of her words, even though she may not be mentioned in those words" (p. 8). This in particular is strikingly reminiscent of Kristeva, although, unlike her, Bradby and Torode are at pains to interrogate this irony. My thanks to Mark Hustwitt for supplying me with a copy of this paper.

54. Wagner, "Art-Work of the Future," p. 73.

55. Ibid., p. 172.

56. Ibid., p. 167.

57. Wagner, "Opera and the Nature of Music," in *Richard Wagner's Prose Works*, vol. 2, p. 111.

58. Barthes, "Music, Voice, Language," p. 283.

59. Barthes, "Rasch," p. 304.

60. This notion has significant implications for Barthes's theory of authorship, bringing as it does the somewhat unsettling perspective to what was once a doing away of authorial mastery. In fact, feminists like Silverman have claimed that the vestiges of the author that remain in Barthes's writing rework themselves according to a *feminine* model.

61. I again refer the reader to Silverman's *The Acoustic Mirror* for a fuller discussion of this ambivalence. See her chapters on the maternal voice.

62. Avron, "Notes," p. 106.

63. See, for instance, Francis Hofstein, "Musique et drogue," *Musique-en-jeu* no. 9 (November 1972): 111–15.

64. Georg Groddeck, "Musique et inconscient," as reprinted in *Musique-en-jeu* no. 9 (November 1972): 3–6.

65. Vladimir Jankélévitch, *La musique et l'ineffable*, p. 10.

66. See Janice Doane and Devon Hodges, *Nostalgia and Sexual Difference: The Resistance to Contemporary Feminism* (New York: Methuen, 1987).

THREE

1. Lawrence Grossberg, "'I'd Rather Feel Bad than not Feel anything at All': Rock and Roll, Pleasure and Power," *enclitic* 8, nos. 1–2 (Spring–Fall 1984): 101. See also Lawrence Grossberg, "The Politics of Youth Culture: Some Observations on Rock and Roll in American Culture," *Social Text* no. 8 (Winter 1983): 104–26,

and Simon Frith, "The Sociology of Rock: Notes from Britain," in *Popular Music Perspectives: Papers from the First International Conference on Popular Music Research, Amsterdam, June 1981*, eds. David Horn and Philip Tagg (Goteborg, Sweden, and Exeter, England: International Association for the Study of Popular Music, 1982), and *Sound Effects: Youth, Leisure, and the Politics of Rock 'n Roll* (New York: Pantheon, 1981). Frith has significantly modified his earlier position and no longer claims that rock and roll has any immediate claim to the idea of subversion, revolt, or transgression. Still, the idea has tremendous force and staying power.

2. John Fiske, "MTV: Post-Structural Post-Modern," *Journal of Communication Inquiry* 10 no. 1 (Winter 1986): 75. See the "Afterword" to Simon Frith's recent *Music for Pleasure* (New York: Routledge, 1988) for an enjoyable response to Fiske.

3. Attali develops this idea in *Noise*.

4. Antoine Hennion, "Popular Music as Social Production," in Horn and Tagg, eds., *Popular Music Perspectives*, p. 40. See Dick Hebdige, *Subculture: The Meaning of Style* (London: Methuen, 1979) for his discussion of countercultural musical movements such as punk and reggae.

5. János Maróthy, *Music and the Bourgeois, Music and the Proletarian*, trans. Eva Róna (Budapest: Akadémiai Kiadó 1974), p. 521.

6. Maróthy, *Music and the Bourgeois*, p. 145.

7. In Jean-Louis Comolli and Jean Narboni's well-known categorization of films, they too fail to define the "classic" Hollywood model or account for variables such as distribution and exhibition practices that contribute to the meanings produced by different films. Just as Comolli and Narboni assign fixed properties to (film) texts—again, without concern for viewing situation or subjectivity—Adorno classifies (listening) subjects without considering the texts being consumed. See Comolli and Narboni, "Cinema/Ideology/Criticism," *Screen* 12, no. 1 (Spring 1971): 27–36, and, for an excellent critique that raises many of these issues, Barbara Klinger's " 'Cinema/Ideology/Criticism'—The Progressive Text," *Screen* 25, no. 1 (January–February 1984): 30–44, reprinted in slightly altered form in *Film Genre Reader*, ed. Barry Keith Grant (Austin: University of Texas Press, 1986), pp. 74–90.

8. See Theodor Adorno, *Introduction to the Sociology of Music*, trans. E. B. Ashton (New York: Seabury Press, 1976).

9. Christopher Ballantine, *Music and Its Social Meanings* (New York: Gordon and Breach, 1984), p. 119. Ballantine borrows the idea of music "jolting signification" from Adorno.

10. See Jay's *Marxism and Totality* for a thorough overview of this concept.

11. Donald M. Lowe, *The History of Bourgeois Perception* (Chicago: University of Chicago Press, 1982). See in particular his introduction.

12. This last point is taken from Michel de Certeau, *The Practice of Everyday Life*, trans. Steven Rendall (Berkeley: University of California Press, 1984).

13. Walter Ong, *The Presence of the Word* (Minneapolis: University of Minnesota Press, 1967), p. 111.

14. Eisler, *Composing for the Films*.

15. Quoted in Eisler, *Composing for the Films*, pp. 20–21.

16. See Kathryn Kalinak, "The Ear and the Eye: Cognition and Cultural Imperialism" (Presented at the 1989 Society for Cinema Studies Annual Conference, Iowa City, Iowa). Forthcoming in her book, *Settling the Score*.

17. Claude Lévi-Strauss, *Myth and Meaning* (New York: Schocken Books, 1979), p. 50.

18. See chapter four, "Charles Ives and the Meaning of Quotation in Music," in Ballantine, *Music and Its Social Meanings*.

19. Ibid., p. 36.

20. Ibid., p. 47.

21. Ibid., p. 92.

22. Ibid., p. 22.

23. Ibid.

24. See John Shepherd, "The Musical Coding of Ideologies," in *Whose Music? A Sociology of Musical Languages*, eds. John Shepherd, Phil Virden, Graham Vulliamy, and Trevor Wishart (London: Latimer, 1977), pp. 69–124.

25. Shepherd, "Media, Social Process and Music" in Shepherd et al., eds., *Whose Music?* p. 35.

26. Shepherd, "Musical Coding," p. 111.

27. Ibid.

28. Shepherd, "Musical Coding," p. 105.

29. Shepherd, "The 'Meaning' of Music," in Shepherd et al., eds., *Whose Music?* p. 60.

30. Shepherd, "Media, Social Process and Music," in Shepherd et al., eds., *Whose Music?* pp. 13–14.

31. Shepherd, "Musical Coding," p. 78.

32. Ibid., p. 75.

33. In a different context, Maróthy has critiqued this kind of fantasy. He argues that by romanticizing mass art into something that is authentic, aboriginal, or elemental, critics partake in a kind of cult of the noble savage. Criticism involves little more than a search for lost mass experience, a search for the "missing part." See Maróthy, *Music and the Bourgeois*, p. 133.

34. The authorship of this text is in question, with some arguing that Eisler wrote it alone, others arguing that it was a collaboration from which Adorno later withdrew his name. At any rate, it is clear that Eisler was deeply influenced by Adorno in writing *Composing for the Films*.

35. Gorbman briefly touches upon Adorno's nostalgic underpinnings in *Unheard Melodies*. See page 109.

36. Adorno, *Introduction*, p. 44.

37. Theodor Adorno, *Aesthetic Theory*, trans. C. Lenhardt (London: Routledge and Kegan Paul, 1984), p. 322.

38. Adorno, "Perennial Fashion—Jazz" in *Prisms*, trans. Samuel Weber and Shierry Weber (Cambridge, Mass.: MIT Press, 1981), p. 121.

39. Adorno, *Aesthetic Theory*, p. 212.

40. See Adorno, "On the Fetish-Character in Music and the Regression of Listening," in *The Essential Frankfurt School Reader*, eds. Andrew Arato and Eike Gebhardt (New York: Urizen, 1978), especially pp. 278, 286. The term *autonomous music*, as Clayton Steinman has observed, pertains less to the idea that music

exists beyond history or culture than to the notion it enjoys relative independence from the culture industry. Of course, only modernism—and only certain forms of modernism, like Schönberg but not Stravinsky—may be considered in Adorno's scheme. For an excellent treatment of Adorno and other early Frankfurt School members, see Clayton Steinman's 1979 dissertation, *Hollywood Dialectic: Force of Evil and the Frankfurt School's Critique of the Culture Industry*, New York University. My thanks to Dana Polan for bringing my attention to this thesis.

41. Adorno, "The Radio Symphony: An Experiment in Theory," in *Radio Research 1941*, eds. Paul Lazersfeld and Frank N. Stanton (New York: Duell, Sloane, and Pearce, 1941), pp. 110–39.

42. Ibid., p. 115.

43. Ibid., p. 119.

44. Adorno, "On the Fetish Character," p. 278.

45. Adorno maintains this line of thought in discussing the instrumentation of hit songs, referring to their being scored for "infantile" instruments (he cites the ukulele, guitar, banjo, and the accordion—all of whose proportions and status diminish in contrast to that of the more majestic piano). See "On the Fetish Character," p. 290.

46. This reading of Adorno has recently been attacked in print by Calvin Thomas, who attempts to defend Adorno against the critique of being nostalgic for lost totalities, particularly when it is psychoanalytically conceived, which for him produces "reductive" and "simplified charges of nostalgia." His is a solid, if subtle, disdain for psychoanalysis, whose aims, he argues, are at odds with political interpretation: "Whereas in the psychoanalytic logic the appeal of totality is read as a function of male lack, a nostalgia for lost mastery and a maternally overdetermined plenitude . . . we find Adorno arguing against a qualitatively different type of totality engendered by mercantile dynamics and their system of exchange value" (p. 160).

Although Thomas admirably cites Adorno's well-known interest in Schönberg as evidence of his desire to the eschew the facile totality of traditional tonal music, in a deeply puzzling move he goes on to argue that Adorno believes that negotiation, criticism, and choices are possible "not only within various modernisms, but within all forms of aesthetic and cultural practice" (p. 166). No evidence is given for this creative reading, and Thomas goes on to insist that Adorno's other critics have got him all wrong (even Martin Jay) by labeling him an elitist. He positions his own argument against virtually all of these other critics who have acknowledged in some form or another Adorno's preference for the aesthetic formal practices of high and elite art.

One needs to question the political motivation behind such an idiosyncratic reading, particularly in its contemptuous dismissal of psychoanalysis ("An appeal to the past does not necessarily conceal a 'craving' to return to the womb of timeless undifferentiation," p. 158) and its dubious handling of gender and subjectivity. For example, Thomas insists that "Adorno, *without specifically mentioning gender in his writings on music*, mobilizes a particular brand of nostalgia in a critique not only of capitalism but of patriarchy as well" (p. 156, emphasis added).

On this last point I am certain the author would appreciate German director Alexander Kluge's remarks on Adorno, whom the director knew personally: "He loved his mother [who was a professional singer] like a goddess and had strong reservations about his strict father. In his childhood, he took shelter behind his mother. For his mother nothing was enough for him, and she protected him from his father's cheapness. Adorno became a very sensitive man who knew music but couldn't ride alone on a streetcar. He led the impractical life of a very protected child" (p. 37). See Calvin Thomas, "A Knowledge That Would Not Be Power: Adorno, Nostalgia, and the Historicity of the Musical Subject," in *New German Critique* no. 48 (Fall 1989); 155–75; Stuart Liebman, "On New German Cinema, Art, Enlightenment, and the Public Sphere: An Interview with Alexander Kluge," *October* 46 (1988): 37–59, respectively.

47. Adorno, "On Popular Music," *Studies in Philosophy and Social Sciences* 9 (1941): 21, 19.

48. Adorno, *Aesthetic Theory*, p. 212.

49. Adorno, *In Search of Wagner*, p. 131.

50. Adorno, "Cultural Criticism and Society," in *Prisms*, p. 24.

51. For an interesting exploration of Adorno's work in relation to Beethoven (whose place in Adorno's writings is far from consistent), see Rose Rosengard Subotnik, "Adorno's Diagnosis of Beethoven's Late Style: Early Symptom of a Fatal Condition," *Journal of the American Musicological Society* 29 (1976): 242–75.

52. Adorno, *In Search of Wagner*, p. 99.

53. Ibid., p. 35.

54. Adorno, "The Radio Symphony," p. 115. Wagner demonstrates this xenophobia with even greater force in arguing that the true composer of music drama must be at one with his culture so that he may express its timeless natural truths and so on. The xenophobic element of this belief was, of course, rendered explicit in Wagner's anti-Semitism, since the "wandering Jew" has no homeland.

55. Andreas Huyssen, *After the Great Divide: Modernism, Mass Culture, Postmodernism* (Bloomington: Indiana University Press, 1986), p. 41.

56. Adorno, *In Search of Wagner*, p. 101.

57. See chapter seven, "Music Drama," in Adorno's *In Search of Wagner*.

58. Adorno, *In Search of Wagner*, p. 104.

59. It is unclear in the end whether the unified, plenitudinous condition Adorno theorizes rests ontologically alongside the idea of "art" itself or in the socioeconomic context in which art is circulated and consumed (his analyses of Beethoven's work suggest the former; his interest in the culture industry indicates the latter). To be sure, there are strains of both in his position, strains which can arguably be linked to his basic dialectical approach to art as both social and asocial phenomenon.

60. See Thompson, *The Making of the English Working Class* (New York: Random House, 1964). My thanks to Dan Cottom for his comments on this point.

61. Indeed Lowe's description of this electronic phase calls to mind many of postmodernism's tenets, particularly postmodernism's stress on surfaces, multiplicity, reproducability, collage, and so on. Michel de Certeau offers further insights into the visual epistemology of post-Enlightenment culture in his *Practice of Everyday Life*, especially part four, "Ways of Believing." Another argument that feeds nicely into Lowe's is Fredric Jameson's discussion of postmodernism. In his oft-cited essay, "Postmodernism, or the Cultural Logic of Late Capitalism," *New*

Left Review no. 146 (July–August 1984): 53–92, he argues persuasively that postmodernism operates as an aesthetic dominant that emerges from a larger context that is marked economically by late industrial capitalism and technologically by nuclear machinery and computers.

62. Maróthy argues that this transformation of mass cultural artifacts into something "aboriginal, natural and elemental" is to substitute and replace an element that is missing in bourgeois life. Rather harshly, Maróthy condemns this as a means of simultaneously upholding and justifying bourgeois ideology—a point that Shepherd's position clearly disputes (Maróthy, *Music and the Bourgeois*, p. 133).

63. Adorno conceives of history as a devolving process, one marked by increased fragmentation, alienation, and decay. As such the future can hold no utopian possibility. This is what requires him (in his critiques of romantic and contemporary popular music, for example) "regressively" to seek aesthetic and cultural paragons in the past. This position, however, was somewhat complicated by comments he later made regarding the possibility of partial utopian thought to exist (see note 65).

64. Adorno, "Resignation," trans. Wes Blomster, *Telos* 35 (Spring 1978): 168.

65. Quoted in Martin Jay, "Adorno and Kracauer: Notes on a Troubled Friendship," *Salmagundi* 40 (Winter 1978): 54. This article is an excellent source of information on the intellectual kindredship and differences over the years of these critics, and it devotes attention to the idea of utopia in both of their work.

FOUR

1. Jerome McGann's study, *The Romantic Ideology: A Critical Investigation* (Chicago: University of Chicago Press, 1983), explores how the scholarship on literary romanticism has also replicated the aesthetic ideology of the period.

2. Edward Said has recently offered a cogent critique of Adorno's belief that specific forms and styles of composition—like Schönberg's atonal music, or Wagner's use of the leitmotiv—articulate larger social patterns. Said notes how this idea (he includes Mann in *Doctor Faustus* as well) shows the ethnocentricity of Western thought since it "elevate[s] admittedly discernible patterns in Western society during the modern period to the level of the essential and the universal." Edward W. Said, *Musical Elaborations* (New York: Columbia University Press, 1991), p. 51.

3. De Certeau, *Practice of Everyday Life*, p. 32.

4. Elizabeth Cowie, "Fantasia," *m/f* no. 9 (1984): 73, 75.

5. See Fred Davis, *Yearning for Yesterday: A Sociology of Nostalgia* (New York: The Free Press, 1979), especially chapter one, "The Nostalgic Experience: Words and Meanings," for a fuller discussion on the etymology and development of this word.

6. Ibid., pp. 4–5n.

7. Susan McClary, "Sexual Politics in Classical Music" in *Feminine Endings: Music, Gender, and Sexuality* (Minneapolis: University of Minnesota Press, 1991). My reference to Carmen's "undoing" is once again indebted to Catherine Clément's recently translated work *Opera, or the Undoing of Women*, with a foreword by McClary.

8. Adorno, "On Popular Music," p. 42.

9. Maróthy, *Music and the Bourgeois*, p. 127.

10. Jack Zipes, "Bloch and the Obscenity of Hope," *New German Critique* no. 45 (1988): p. 7.

11. Quoted in Ernst Bloch, *Essays on the Philosophy of Music*, trans. Peter Palmer (Cambridge: Cambridge University Press, 1985), pp. 7–8.

12. Ibid., p. 7.

13. Ibid., p. 52.

14. In his notes concerning the problem of production, Marx writes, "The unequal development of material production and, e.g., that of art." This is followed by a very brief discussion. See his introduction in *A Contribution to the Critique of Political Economy* (New York: International Publishers, 1970), p. 215.

15. Jameson develops Bloch's dialectic at great length in *The Political Unconscious* (Ithaca, N.Y.: Cornell University Press, 1981), a work that is fundamentally indebted to Bloch's aesthetics and his philosophy.

16. Quoted in Fredric Jameson, *Marxism and Form* (Princeton, N.J.: Princeton University Press, 1971), p. 149.

17. Attali's position here clearly invokes Bloch's idea of nonsynchronous development between superstructural and economic phenomena. At the same time, however, he fails to consider fully the interrelationships of these two spheres. In the end, Attali embraces a kind of reflectionism in reverse by having the superstructural phenomenon of music illustrate the economic base—albeit one of a later period. See Attali, *Noise*, p. 10.

18. Attali, *Noise*, pp. 11, 9.

19. Timothy Leary, quoted in *Spy* (July 1989): A4 (advertising supplement).

20. Jameson, *Marxism and Form*, p. 142.

21. Ernst Bloch, "Art and Utopia," in *The Utopian Function of Art and Literature*, trans. Jack Zipes and Frank Mecklenburg (Cambridge, Mass.: MIT Press, 1988), p. 147.

22. Bloch, *Essays on the Philosophy of Music*, pp. 139, 138.

23. Ibid., pp. 119, 118.

24. Attali, *Noise*, p. 3.

25. See Jameson, *Marxism and Form*, pp. 121–22. In addition, see Zipes's introduction to *Utopian Function* for a useful discussion of these ideas.

26. Ernst Bloch, *The Principle of Hope*, trans. Neville Plaice, Stephen Plaice, and Paul Knight (Oxford: Basil Blackwell, 1986), vol. 1, pp. 407–8.

27. Richard Dyer, "Entertainment and Utopia," in Altman, ed. *Genre*, p. 177.

28. Attali, *Noise*, p. 6.

29. Quoted in Maynard Solomon, "Marx and Bloch: Reflections on Utopia and Art," *Telos* no. 3 (Fall 1972): 70.

30. In Bloch's "Art and Utopia," p. 126.

31. The oversight seems all the more remarkable since Bloch indirectly acknowledges the importance of subjectivity to utopia—not to mention utopia to subjectivity—in commenting that "to be human really means to have utopias." Quoted by his son, Jan Bloch, in "How Can We Understand the Bends in the Upright Gait?" *New German Critique* no. 45 (Fall 1988): p. 33.

32. Gerald M. Mayer, "American Motion Pictures in World Trade," *The Annals of the American Academy of Political and Social Science* 254 (November 1947): 34, quoted in Mary Ann Doane *The Desire to Desire: The Woman's Film of the 1940s* (Bloomington: Indiana University Press, 1987), p. 37.

33. Maynard Solomon, *Marxism and Art: Essays Classic and Contemporary* (New York: Vintage Books, 1974), p. 584.

34. I borrow the term *cock rock* from Angela McRobbie and Simon Frith. Although they were undoubtably not the first to coin it, theirs is one of the few solid critical efforts to address the term. See "Rock and Sexuality," *Screen Education* no. 29 (Winter 1978–79): 3–19.

35. Mark Roth, "Some Warners Musicals and the Spirit of the New Deal," in Altman, ed., *Genre*, pp. 41–56.

36. Lucy Fischer, "The Image of Woman as Image: The Optical Politics of *Dames*," in Altman, ed., *Genres*, pp. 70–84. The quote from Busby Berkeley appears on p. 74.

37. "When, as he occasionally does, Berkeley isolates chorus girls with the camera, or has their faces follow each other filling the screen, the dances are least effective and border on being foolish," Roth, "Some Warners Musicals," p. 55.

38. Jameson discusses this in *Marxism and Form*, pp. 126–27.

FIVE

1. About the film more generally, Dana Polan writes: "Romantic utopia exists only as a memory, subject to a rewriting of the present. Similarly, in *King's Row* the opening skinny-dipping scene of Parris Mitchell (Robert Cummings) and Cassandra Towers (Betty Field) becomes finally only a trace of a lost memory as Parris has to grow up and deal with the pains of maturity (including the death of Cassandra)." See Polan's *Power and Paranoia: History, Narrative, and the American Cinema, 1940–1950* (New York: Columbia University Press, 1986), p. 263.

2. During the title sequence, this is done to humorous effect as the male chorus is heard while we see herds of cows on the Chisholm Trail.

3. Rózsa, *Double Life*. See especially chapter eight, "The MGM Years."

4. Serafina Bathrick, "The Past as Future: Family and the American Home in *Meet Me in St. Louis*," *The Minnesota Review* no. 6 (Spring 1976): 132–39.

5. Meredith Wilson's *The Music Man* (1962) reprises this same idea in "Being in Love," sung by Marian the librarian when she explains her childhood crushes on (among others) a trolley car operator.

6. Jane Feuer, "The Self-reflexive Musical and the Myth of Entertainment," in Altman, ed., *Genre*, as well as her *The Hollywood Musical* (Bloomington: Indiana University Press, 1982), especially chapter five, "The History of the Hollywood Musical: Innovation as Conservation."

7. The association of song with virility is by no means exclusive to *Brigadoon*. Indeed, as Edward Turk's work on *New Moon* (1935) shows, Nelson Eddy and Jeanette MacDonald engage in a vocal competition of sorts, with the male versions showing off with long, sustained notes, "break[ing] out" periodically like uncontrolled physical eruptions. The song "Stout-Hearted Men" is particularly revealing

in this regard, sung as it is by an all-male group of outdoorsmen in animal-skin hats who make references to cockfights and refer to themselves as "fighting sons." For a close analysis, see Turk's "Song, Cinema and Psychoanalysis: The Case of Jeanette MacDonald" (Presented at the Society for Cinema Studies Annual Conference, April 1989, Iowa City, Iowa).

8. Clive Hirschhorn, *The Hollywood Musical* (New York: Crown Publishers, 1981), p. 326.

9. Rick Altman, *The American Film Musical* (Bloomington: Indiana University Press, 1987), p. 112. For a discussion on how the subgenre of the fairy tale musical is indebted to the ideas of nostalgia and a "fall from grace," see p. 170. For an indication of how "anti-musical" *The Country Girl* really is, consider Pauline Kael's reference to it as a "sado-masochist morass." Quoted in Leslie Halliwell, *Halliwell's Film Guide*, 6th ed. (New York: Scribner's, 1987), p. 218.

10. See Patrice Petro's excellent analysis "Rematerializing the Vanishing Lady: Feminism, Hitchcock, and Interpretation," in *A Hitchcock Reader*, eds. Leland Poague and Marshall Deutelbaum (Ames: Iowa State University Press, 1986), pp. 122–33.

11. Polan, *Power*, p. 303. For another insightful comparison of utopia in the melodrama and the musical, see Thomas Elsaesser's "Vincente Minnelli" in Altman, *Genre*, pp. 8–27.

12. For the purposes of the present argument I will be addressing both film groups as genres. This runs the risk of making generalizations to which individual films may or may not apply. In the case of film noir, for instance, there has been and continues to be considerable debate over its status and whether it is a genre at all. Many insist that it is not—that it is merely a style of filmmaking that crosses generic boundaries; others maintain that it is a film movement that came out of Hollywood in the 1940s and 1950s. The maternal melodrama is more accurately conceptualized as a subgenre of the woman's film, a subgenre of the melodramatic genre, popular in the 1930s and 1940s in Hollywood.

13. Michael Renov, *Hollywood's Wartime Woman: A Study of Historical/Ideological Determination* (Ann Arbor: University of Michigan Research Press, 1987).

14. Polan, *Power*, pp. 24, 31.

15. Maureen Turim, *Flashbacks in Film: Memory and History* (New York: Routledge, 1989). See chapter five, "Flashbacks and the Psyche in Melodrama and Film Noir."

16. See Comolli and Narboni's essay, "Cinema/Ideology/Criticism," pp. 27–36.

17. For exceptions to this, see Gorbman, "Drama's Melos," pp. 35–39; Kathryn Kalinak, "The Fallen Woman and the Virtuous Wife: Musical Stereotypes in *The Informer, Gone with the Wind,* and *Laura*," *Film Reader* no. 5 (1982): 76–82; J. P. Telotte, "Talk and Trouble: *Kiss Me Deadly*'s Apocalyptic Discourse," *Journal of Popular Film and Television* 13, no. 2 (Summer 1985): 69–79, and my own "Sound, Woman and the Bomb: Dismembering the 'Great Whatsit' in *Kiss Me Deadly*," *Wide Angle*, 8, nos. 3–4 (1986): 115–27.

18. Annette Kuhn writes of Val Lewton's contract as director of one of RKO's B units in 1942: "Lewton's contract stipulated that he was to produce only horror films, that budgets were not to exceed $150,000, that shooting schedules were not to exceed three weeks, and that running times were to average about seventy

minutes. Within these limits, however, Lewton had relative freedom: he was able to select and contract a stable core of creative personnel, functioning as an independent production unit in much the same way as the units producing prestige pictures in the Selznick era." See *The Cinema Book*, ed. Pam Cook (New York: Pantheon, 1986), p. 22. The argument about the ideological and aesthetic progressiveness of B pictures—and film noir in particular—is most explicitly laid out by Paul Kerr, "Out of What Past? Notes on the B Film," *Screen* 32–33 (Autumn–Winter 1979–80): 45–65. For a recent critique of this position and of Comolli and Narboni's, see Klinger, " 'Cinema/Ideology/Criticism' —The Progressive Text."

19. Todd McCarthy and Charles Flynn, "The Economic Imperative: Why was the B Movie Necessary?" in *Kings of the Bs*, eds. McCarthy and Flynn (New York: Dutton, 1975), p. 23.

20. Andrew Sarris, "Beatitudes of B Pictures," in McCarthy and Flynn, eds., *Kings*, p. 52.

21. For two notable exceptions see Tania Modleski, "Film Theory's Detour," *Screen* 23, no. 5 (November–December 1982): 72–79; and Michael Renov, "The Detour From Difference: The Structuring of Sexuality in a Post-War Text" (Paper presented at the Society for Cinema Studies Annual Conference, University of Pittsburgh, May 1983). My thanks to Michael Renov for sharing his manuscript with me.

22. Andrew Sarris, *The American Cinema* (New York: Dutton, 1968), p. 143.

23. Peter Bogdanovich, "Interview with Edgar G. Ulmer," in McCarthy and Flynn, eds. *Kings*, pp. 378, 377.

24. Myron Meisel, "Edgar G. Ulmer: The Primacy of the Visual," in McCarthy and Flynn, eds. *Kings*, p. 148.

25. Review of *Detour*, *Variety*, 23 January 1946. Pagination unknown.

26. Danny Peary, *Cult Movies* (New York: Delta Books, 1981), p. 68.

27. Sarris, *American Cinema*, p. 143.

28. Meisel, "Edgar G. Ulmer," p. 150.

29. Blake Lucas, entry on *Detour* in *Film Noir: An Encyclopedic Reference to the American Style*, eds. Alain Silver and Elizabeth Ward (Woodstock, N.Y.: Overlook Press, 1979), p. 90.

30. Quoted in Polan, *Power*, p. 271.

31. Although the passage is taken from Fredric Jameson in his discussion of Bloch in *Marxism and Form*, p. 131, "A Philosophical View of the Detective Novel" appears in its entirety in Zipes and Mecklenburg, trans. *Utopian Function of Art and Literature*, pp. 245–64.

32. Modleski, "Film Theory's Detour," p. 74.

33. Ibid.

34. Renov's psychoanalytic reading of the film argues that these projections work to fragment the ego of *Detour*'s protagonist, whom Renov considers in context of other weak males, "casualties" of the war that frequented films of this period. Stressing the parallels made between Al and Vera (not the least of which has Al looking into the mirror to see Vera's strangled body) and between Vera and Charles (their freakish deaths, their position as riders in the car, and so on), Renov argues that this loosens rather than rigidifies gender differentiation.

35. Curiously, and not insignificantly, the film never portrays the saxophonist who so irritates Roberts; he remains off frame on the street below the hotel window. So inconspicuous is he that Al has to point out that the horn playing on the soundtrack is in fact diegetic. Before this, the sax blends in perfectly with the strings that accompany the scene non-diegetically. It is as if the horn player does not exist and is only another projection of Al's dystopic fantasies.

36. Lucas, entry on *Detour*, in Silver and Ward, eds. *Film Noir*, p. 90.

37. Renov, "The *Detour* from Difference," pp. 4–5.

38. One is reminded here of the criminal Raven (Alan Ladd) in *This Gun for Hire*, whose hand had been permanently disfigured by a maternal aunt who had broken his wrist by putting a red-hot poker to it. We are asked to believe that this traumatizing incident precipitates the hero's descent into crime—by extension, we are asked to blame the "bad mother" for it as well. As we have already indicated, there are several other films noir that locate the source of their protagonists' criminality with a maternal figure, including *White Heat* and *The Strange Love of Martha Ivers* (1946).

39. Peary, *Cult Movies*, p. 70.

40. Ibid.

41. Tim Pulleine, "*Detour*," *Films and Filming* no. 335 (August 1983): 32.

42. Review of *Detour*, *Variety*.

43. David Coursen, "Closing Down the Open Road: *Detour*," *Movietone News* no. 48 (February 1976): 18. My thanks to Dana Benelli for making this source available to me.

44. Bogdanovich, "Interview with Ulmer," p. 403.

45. Ibid., p. 408.

46. Bill Krohn, "King of the B's," *Film Comment* 19, no. 4 (July–August 1983): 60.

47. Renov's essay elaborates the extent to which this notion of a fractured and disenfranchised male subjectivity is contingent upon postwar social and discursive exigencies; Modleski's essay addresses the extent to which this same condition is projected onto woman.

48. Robert Lang, *American Film Melodrama: Griffith, Vidor, Minnelli* (Princeton, N.J.: Princeton University Press, 1989), p. 230.

49. Thomas Elsaesser, "Tales of Sound and Fury: Observations on the Family Melodrama," *Monogram* no. 4 (1972): 2–15.

50. Geoffrey Nowell-Smith, "Dossier on Melodrama," *Screen* 18, no. 2 (Summer 1977): 113–18.

51. Peter Brooks, *The Melodramatic Imagination* (New Haven, Conn.: Yale University Press, 1976), p. 35.

52. Doane, *Desire to Desire*, p. 30.

53. Joanne Stang, "Stevens Relives Anne Frank's Story," *The New York Times*, 3 August 1958, sec. A.

54. Bosley Crowther, "Review," *The New York Times*, 23 May 1941, p. 25, col. 2.

55. Tania Modleski, *Loving with a Vengeance: Mass-Produced Fantasies for Women* (Hamden, Conn.: Archon Books, 1982), p. 21. This appears in a discussion where Modleski addresses herself to gothic films such as *Rebecca* and *Gaslight*,

texts that are particularly marked by a feminine "paranoia," a suspicion of masculinity that (most notably in *Gaslight*) turns out to be entirely founded.

56. Molly Haskell, *From Reverence to Rape: The Treatment of Women in the Movies* (New York: Penguin Books, 1974), p. 188.

57. Mary Ann Doane, *Desire to Desire*, p. 3.

58. Laura Mulvey, "Notes on Sirk and Melodrama," *Movie* no. 25 (Winter 1977–78): 54.

59. Pam Cook, "Melodrama and the Woman's Picture," *The Gainsborough Melodrama*, eds. Sue Aspinall and Sue Harper (London: British Film Institute, 1983), pp. 18–19.

60. Lang, *American Film Melodrama*, p. 229.

61. Linda Williams, "Something Else besides a Mother: *Stella Dallas* and the Maternal Melodrama," *Cinema Journal* 25 no. 1 (Fall 1984): 2–27.

62. She makes this argument on the basis of both film types containing "the same perverse figure," namely, the "male masochist whose fate is embodied by women," Turim, *Flashbacks*, p. 182.

63. For an especially thorough account, see Brooks, *Melodramatic Imagination*.

64. Martha Vicinus, " 'Helpless and Unfriended': Nineteenth-Century Domestic Melodrama," *New Literary History* 13, no. 1 (Autumn 1981): 131.

65. Ibid., p. 132.

66. My thanks to Holly Hughes for locating the music for me.

67. I am grateful to Sabina Gölz for sharing her comments on this with me.

68. Doane makes this observation in *Desire to Desire*. See in particular chapter two, "Clinical Eyes."

69. The phrase is taken from the title of Doane's study of the woman's film.

70. Polan, *Power*, p. 289.

71. Mary Ann Doane, *Desire to Desire*, p. 106.

72. Ibid., pp. 90–91.

73. Tania Modleski, "Time and Desire in the Woman's Film," *Cinema Journal* 23, no. 3 (Spring 1984): 19–30.

74. Sigmund Freud and Josef Breuer, *Studies on Hysteria*, trans. and eds. James Strachey and Alix Strachey (New York: Avon Books, 1966), p. 42.

75. Modleski, "Time and Desire," p. 28.

76. See Polan, *Power*, pp. 216, 289.

77. O'Pray goes on to note that the ensuing tortured, anxious style is a defense against a larger sense of guilt and loss (in a Kleinian sense) and speaks to the specifically masculine agency of the film's mise-en-scène and the sexual displacement behind it. O'Pray, "Movies, Mania and Masculinity," *Screen* 23 no. 5 (November–December 1982): 63–70.

78. Several critics have commented on this unusual handling of time, although, not surprisingly, they usually discuss it in terms of the director's personal stamp. *The New York Times* notes how long it takes Stevens to complete films in general; Andrew Sarris refers to the director's mastery of "the slow buildup" and states that "his dawdling direction of comedy is the slowest in the business." For the former, see Stang, "Stevens Relives"; for the latter, see Sarris, *American Cinema*, p. 110.

SIX

1. Simone Signoret, *Nostalgia Isn't What It Used to Be* (New York: Penguin Books, 1977).

2. For an extended analysis of this trend, see Tania Modleski's excellent "The Incredible Shrinking He(r)man: Male Regression, the Male Body, and Film," *Differences* 2, no. 2 (Summer 1990): 55–75. Reprinted in her *Feminism Without Women* (New York: Routledge, 1991).

3. Fredric Jameson, "Postmodernism and Consumer Society," in *The Anti-Aesthetic* ed. Hal Foster (Port Townsend, Wa.: Bay Press, 1983).

4. At the same time, the desire for coherence still runs strong. It is easily arguable, for instance, that, with the idea of subjectivity having been put more or less into permanent crisis by poststructuralism and postmodernism, the beleaguered male subject of film noir would be desirable in that there is at least an established subject to be put at risk.

5. I refer the reader to Edward Said's recent book, *Musical Elaborations* for a discussion of the ways in which the plenitude often affiliated with music is constructed retroactively. Said maintains that the ephemeral, singular nature of the musical performance encourages us to fulfill and renew it through recollection. (Wagner's notion of the leitmotiv should be recalled here, since he argues that the leitmotiv only became meaningful after repeated hearing.) See especially chapter three, "Melody, Solitude, and Affirmation" in Edward W. Said, *Musical Elaborations*.

BIBLIOGRAPHY

Adorno, Theodor. *Aesthetic Theory*. Translated by C. Lenhardt. London: Routledge and Kegan Paul, 1984.

———. *In Search of Wagner*. Translated by Rodney Livingstone. London: New Left Books, 1981.

———. *Introduction to the Sociology of Music*. Translated by E. B. Ashton. New York: Seabury Press, 1976.

———. "On Popular Music." *Studies in Philosophy and Social Sciences* 9 (1941): 17–48.

———. "On the Fetish-Character in Music and the Regression of Listening." *The Essential Frankfurt School Reader*. Edited by Andrew Arato and Eike Gebhardt. New York: Urizen, 1978.

———. "The Radio Symphony: An Experiment in Theory." *Radio Research 1941*. Edited by Paul Lazersfeld and Frank N. Stanton. New York: Duell, Sloane, and Pearce, 1941.

Adorno, Theodor, and Max Horkheimer. "The Culture Industry: Entertainment as Mass Deception." *Dialectic of Enlightenment*. Translated by John Cumming. New York: Continuum, 1986.

Antheil, George. "Hollywood Composer." *Atlantic Monthly* 165 (February 1940).

Attali, Jacques. *Noise: The Political Economy of Music*. Translated by Brian Massumi. Minneapolis: University of Minnesota Press, 1985.

Avron, Dominique. "Notes pour introduire une métapsychologie de la musique." *Musique-en-jeu* no. 9 (November 1972): 102–10.

Ballantine, Christopher. *Music and Its Social Meanings*. New York: Gordon and Breach, 1984.

Barthes, Roland. *Camera Lucida: Reflections on Photography*. Translated by Richard Howard. New York: Hill and Wang, 1981.

———. *The Responsibility of Forms: Critical Essays on Music, Art, and Representation*. Translated by Richard Howard. New York: Hill and Wang, 1986.

Bathrick, Serafina. "The Past as Future: Family and the American Home in *Meet Me in St. Louis*." *The Minnesota Review* no. 6 (Spring 1976): 132–39.

Bazelon, Irwin. *Knowing the Score: Notes on Film Music*. New York: Arco Publishing, 1975.

Benjamin, Walter. "The Work of Art in the Age of Mechanical Reproduction." *Illuminations*. Translated by Harry Zohn. Edited by Hannah Arendt. New York: Schocken Books, 1969.

Berg, Charles Merrell. *An Investigation of the Motives for and Realization of Music to Accompany the American Silent Film, 1896–1927*. New York: Arno Press, 1976.

Bernstein, Elmer. "Film Composers vs. the Studios." *Film Music Notebook* 2, no. 1 (1976): 33.

Blanchard, Gérard. *Images de la musique de cinéma*. Paris: Edilig, 1984.

Bloch, Ernst. *Essays on the Philosophy of Music*. Translated by Peter Palmer. Cambridge: Cambridge University Press, 1985.

———. *The Principle of Hope*. Translated by Neville Plaice, Stephen Plaice, and Paul Knight. Vol. 1. Oxford: Basil Blackwell, 1986.

Bordwell, David; Janet Staiger; and Kristin Thompson. *The Classical Hollywood Cinema: Film Style and Mode of Production to 1960*. New York: Columbia University Press, 1985.

Brooks, Peter. *The Melodramatic Imagination*. New Haven, Conn.: Yale University Press, 1976.

Brown, Royal S., "Herrmann, Hitchcock, and the Music of the Irrational," *Cinema Journal* 21, no. 2 (1982), pp. 14–49. Revised and reprinted in Mast and Cohen, eds., *Film Theory and Criticism* 3rd ed. (New York: Oxford University Press, 1985), pp. 618–49.

Bruce, Graham. *Bernard Herrmann: Film Music and Narrative*. Ann Arbor: University of Michigan Research Press, 1985.

Chion, Michel. *La voix au cinéma*. Paris: Editions de l'étoile, 1982.

Clément, Catherine. *Opera, or the Undoing of Women*. Translated by Betsy Wing. Minneapolis: University of Minnesota Press, 1988.

Comolli, Jean-Louis and Jean Narboni. "Cinema/Ideology/Criticism." *Screen* 12, no. 1 (Spring 1971): 27–36.

Cook, Pam, ed. *The Cinema Book*. New York: Pantheon, 1986.

———. "Melodrama and the Woman's Picture." *The Gainsborough Melodrama*. Edited by Sue Aspinall and Sue Harper. London: British Film Institute, 1983.

Corse, Sandra. *Opera and the Uses of Language: Mozart, Verdi, and Britten*. Cranbury, N.J.: Associated University Presses, 1987.

Dahlhaus, Carl. *Between Romanticism and Modernism*. Translated by Mary Whittal. Berkeley: University of California Press, 1989.

Davis, Fred. *Yearning for Yesterday: A Sociology of Nostalgia*. New York: The Free Press, 1979.

de Certeau, Michel. *The Practice of Everyday Life*. Translated by Steven Rendall. Berkeley: University of California Press, 1984.

Dickstein, Morris. "Time Bandits." *American Film* (October 1982): 39–43.

Doane, Mary Ann. *The Desire to Desire: The Woman's Film of the 1940s*. Bloomington: Indiana University Press, 1987.

———. "Ideology and the Practice of Sound Editing and Mixing." *Film Sound: Theory and Practice*. Edited by Elisabeth Weis and John Belton. New York: Columbia University Press, 1986.

———. "The Voice in the Cinema: The Articulation of Body and Space." *Yale French Studies* no. 60 (1980): 33–50; Reprint Philip Rosen, ed. *Narrative, Apparatus, Ideology: A Film Theory Reader*. New York: Columbia University Press, 1986.

Dyer, Richard. "Entertainment and Utopia." *Genre: The Musical*. Edited by Rick Altman. London: Routledge and Kegan Paul, 1981.

———. "The Sound of Music." *Movie* no. 23 (1976): 39–49.

Einstein, Alfred. *Music in the Romantic Era*. New York: Norton, 1947.

Eisenstein, Sergei. *Film Sense*. Translated and edited by Jay Leyda. New York: Harcourt Brace Jovanovich, 1942.

Eisler, Hanns. *Composing for the Films*. London: Dennis Dobson, 1947.

Elsaesser, Thomas. "Tales of Sound and Fury: Observations on the Family Melodrama." *Monogram* no. 4 (1972): 2–15.

Engels, Frederick. *Socialism: Utopian and Scientific*. Translated by Edward Aveling. New York: International Publishers, 1935.

Evans, Mark. *Soundtrack: The Music of the Movies*. New York: Da Capo, 1979.

Ewen, David. *Music Comes to America*. New York: Thomas Y. Crowell Company, 1942.

Faulkner, Robert. "Dilemmas in Commercial Work: Hollywood Film Composers and Their Clients." *Urban Life* 5, no. 1 (April 1976): 12.

Feuer, Jane. *The Hollywood Musical*. Bloomington: Indiana University Press, 1982.

Flinn, Carol. "The 'Problem' of Femininity in Theories of Film Music." *Screen* 27, no. 6 (November–December 1986): 56–72.

————. "Sound, Woman and the Bomb: Dismembering the 'Great Whatsit' in *Kiss Me Deadly*." *Wide Angle* 8, nos. 3–4 (1986): 115–27.

Freud, Sigmund, and Josef Breuer. *Studies on Hysteria*. Translated and edited by James Strachey and Alix Strachey. New York: Avon Books, 1966.

Frith, Simon. *Sound Effects: Youth, Leisure, and the Politics of Rock 'n' Roll*. New York: Pantheon, 1981.

Gledhill, Christine, ed. *Home Is Where the Heart Is: Studies in Melodrama and the Woman's Film*. London: British Film Institute, 1987.

Gorbman, Claudia. "The Drama's Melos: Max Steiner and *Mildred Pierce*." *Velvet Light Trap* no. 19 (1982): 35–39.

————. *Film Music: Narrative Functions in French Film*. Ph.D. dissertation. University of Washington, 1978.

————. *Unheard Melodies: Narrative Film Music*. Bloomington: Indiana University Press, 1987.

Groddeck, Georg. "Musique et inconscient." *Musique-en-jeu* no. 9 (November 1972): 3–6.

Grossberg, Larry. " 'I'd Rather Feel Bad Than Not Feel Anything at All': Rock and Roll, Pleasure and Power." *enclitic* 8, nos. 1–2 (Spring–Fall 1984): 94–110.

————. "The Politics of Youth Culture: Some Observations on Rock and Roll in American Culture." *Social Text*, no. 8 (Winter 1983), pp. 104–26.

Haskell, Molly. *From Reverence to Rape: The Treatment of Women in the Movies*. New York: Penguin, 1974.

Hebdige, Dick. *Subculture: The Meaning of Style*. London: Methuen, 1979.

Heninger, S. K., Jr. *Touches of Sweet Harmony: Pythagorean Cosmology and Renaissance Poetics*. San Marino, Calif.: Huntington Library, 1974.

Hofstein, François. "Musique et drogue." *Musique-en-jeu* no. 9 (November 1972): 111–15.

Horn, David and Philip Tagg, eds. *Popular Music Perspectives: Papers from the First International Conference on Popular Music Research, Amsterdam, June 1981*. Goteborg, Sweden, and Exeter, England: International Association for the Study of Popular Music, 1982.

Jameson, Fredric. *Marxism and Form*. Princeton, N.J.: Princeton University Press, 1971.

———. *The Political Unconscious*. Ithaca, N.Y.: Cornell University Press, 1981.

———. "Postmodernism, or the Cultural Logic of Late Capitalism." *New Left Review* no. 146 (July–August 1984): 53–92.

———. "Reification and Utopia in Mass Culture." *Social Text* 1, no. 1 (Winter 1979): 130–48.

Jankélévitch, Vladimir. *La musique et l'ineffable*. Paris: Editions du seuil, 1983.

Jardine, Alice. *Gynesis: Configurations of Woman and Modernity*. Ithaca, N.Y.: Cornell University Press, 1985.

Jay, Martin. *Marxism and Totality*. Berkeley: University of California Press, 1985.

Kalinak, Kathryn. "The Fallen Woman and the Virtuous Wife: Musical Stereotypes in *The Informer, Gone with the Wind*, and *Laura*. *Film Reader* no. 5 (1982): 76–82.

Kaplan, E. Ann, ed. *Women in Film Noir*. London: British Film Institute, 1980.

Kerr, Paul. "Out of What Past? Notes on the B Film." *Screen* 32, no. 33 (Autumn–Winter 1979–80): 45–65.

Kristeva, Julia. *Desire in Language*. Edited by Leon S. Roudiez. Translated by Thomas Gora, Alice Jardine, and Leon S. Roudiez. New York: Columbia University Press, 1980.

———. *Powers of Horror: An Essay on Abjection*. Translated by Leon S. Roudiez. New York: Columbia University Press, 1982.

———. *Revolution in Poetic Language*. Translated by Margaret Walker. New York: Columbia University Press, 1984.

———. *Tales of Love*. Translated by Leon Roudiez. New York: Columbia University Press, 1987.

Lacan, Jacques. *Feminine Sexuality*. Translated by Jacqueline Rose. Edited by Juliet Mitchell and Jacqueline Rose. New York: Norton, 1985.

Langer, Suzanne K. *Feeling and Form*. New York: Scribner's, 1953.

Large, David C., and William Weber, eds. *Wagnerism in European Culture and Politics* (Ithaca, N.Y.: Cornell University Press, 1984).

Leppert, Richard, and Susan McClary, eds. *Music and Society: The Politics of Composition, Performance, and Reception*. Cambridge: Cambridge University Press, 1987.

Levinson, Nathan. "Recording and Re-recording." *We Make the Movies*. Edited by Nancy Naumberg. New York: Norton, 1937.

Limbacher, James L. *Film Music: From Violins to Video*. Metuchen, N.J.: Scarecrow Press, 1974.

Lindgren, Ernest. *The Art of the Film*. New York: Macmillan, 1963.

London, Kurt. *Film Music*. Translated by Eric S. Bensinger. London: Faber and Faber, 1936.

Lowe, Donald M. *The History of Bourgeois Perception*. Chicago: University of Chicago Press, 1982.

Lyotard, Jean-François. "Plusieurs silences." *Musique-en-jeu* no. 9 (November 1972): 64–76.

McCarthy, Todd, and Charles Flynn, eds. *Kings of the Bs*. New York: Dutton, 1975.

McClary, Susan. *Feminine Endings: Music, Gender, and Sexuality*. Minneapolis: University of Minnesota Press, 1991.

Mann, Thomas. *Pro and Contra Wagner.* Translated by Allan Blunden. Chicago: University of Chicago Press, 1985.

Manvell, Roger, and John Huntley. *The Technique of Film Music.* 2d ed. Revised by Richard Arnell and Peter Day. New York: Focal Press, 1975.

Marks, Martin, "Film Music: The Material, Literature and Present State of Research," *Notes* (The Quarterly Journal of the Music Library Association) 36, no. 2 (December 1979): 282–325.

Maróthy, János. *Music and the Bourgeois, Music and the Proletarian.* Translated by Eva Róna. Budapest: Akadémiai Kiadó, 1974.

Meyer, Leonard B. *Emotion and Meaning in Music.* Chicago: University of Chicago Press, 1956.

———. *Style and Music: Theory, History, and Ideology.* Philadelphia: University of Pennsylvania Press, 1989.

Modleski, Tania. "Film Theory's Detour." *Screen* 23, no. 5 (November–December 1982): 72–79.

———. *Loving with a Vengeance: Mass-Produced Fantasies for Women.* Hamden, Conn.: Archon Books, 1982.

———. "Time and Desire in the Woman's Film." *Cinema Journal* 23, no. 3 (Spring 1984): pp. 19–30.

Mulvey, Laura. "Notes on Sirk and Melodrama." *Movie* no. 25 (Winter 1977–78): 53–56.

Neubauer, John. *The Emancipation of Music from Language: Departure from Mimesis in Eighteenth-Century Aesthetics.* New Haven, Conn.: Yale University Press, 1986.

Nietzsche, Fredrich. *The Birth of Tragedy and the Case of Wagner.* Translated by Walter Kaufmann. New York: Vintage Books, 1967.

Nowell-Smith, Geoffrey. "Dossier on Melodrama." *Screen* 18, no. 2 (Summer 1977): 113–18.

Peary, Danny. *Cult Movies.* New York: Delta Books, 1981.

Polan, Dana. *Power and Paranoia: History, Narrative, and the American Cinema, 1940–1950.* New York: Columbia University Press, 1986.

Porcile, Françoile. *Présence de la musique à l'écran.* Paris, Editions du cerf, 1969.

Prendergast, Roy M. *Film Music: A Neglected Art.* New York: Norton, 1977.

Pulleine, Tim. *"Detour."* *Films and Filming* no. 335 (August 1983): 32.

Reisz, Karel, and Gavin Millar. *The Technique of Film Editing.* New York: Hastings House, 1968.

Renov, Michael. "The *Detour* From Difference: The Structuring of Sexuality in a Post-War Text." Paper presented at the Society for Cinema Studies Annual Conference, University of Pittsburgh, May 1983.

———. 'From Fetish to Subject: The Containment of Sexual Difference in Hollywood's Wartime Cinema." *Wide Angle* 5, no. 1 (1982): 16–27.

Rosolato, Guy. "La voix: Entre corps et langage." *Revue Française de psychanalyse* 38, no. 1 (January 1974): 75–94.

———. "Répétitions." *Musique-en-jeu* no. 9 (November 1972): 39.

Rouget, Gilbert. *Music and Trance: A Theory of the Relations between Music and Possession.* Translated by Brunhilde Biebuyck and Gilbert Rouget. Chicago: University of Chicago Press, 1985.

Said, Edward W. *Musical Elaborations*. New York: Columbia University Press, 1991.

Shepherd, John, Phil Virden, Graham Vulliamy, and Trevor Wishart, eds. *Whose Music? A Sociology of Musical Languages*. London: Latimer, 1977.

Silverman, Kaja. *The Acoustic Mirror: The Female Voice in Psychoanalysis and Cinema*. Bloomington: Indiana University Press, 1988.

———. "Dis-Embodying the Female Voice." *Re-Vision: Essays in Feminist Film Criticism*. Edited by Mary Ann Doane, Patricia Mellencamp, and Linda Williams. Frederick, Md.: University Publications of America and the American Film Institute, 1984.

Solomon, Maynard. "Marx and Bloch: Reflections on Utopia and Art." *Telos* no. 3 (Fall 1972): 70.

Stewart, Susan. *On Longing: Narratives of the Miniature, the Gigantic, the Souvenir, the Collection*. Baltimore, Md.: Johns Hopkins University Press, 1984.

Stone, Jennifer. "The Horrors of Power: A Critique of 'Kristeva.' " *The Politics of Theory: Essex Conference on the Sociology of Literature*. Edited by Francis Barker et al. Colchester: University of Essex, 1983.

Sutak, Ken. *The Great Motion Picture Soundtrack Robbery*. Hamden, Conn.: Archon Books, 1976.

Telotte, J. P. "Talk and Trouble: *Kiss Me Deadly*'s Apocalyptic Discourse." *Journal of Popular Film and Televsion* 13, no. 2 (Summer 1985): 69–79.

———. *Voices in the Dark: The Narrative Patterns of Film Noir*. Urbana: University of Illinois Press, 1989.

Thomas, Tony. *Film Score: The View from the Podium*. New York: A. S. Barnes, 1979.

———. *Music for the Movies*. New York: A. S. Barnes, 1973.

Tischler, Barbara. *An American Music: The Search for an American Musical Identity*. New York: Oxford University Press, 1986.

Turim, Maureen. *Flashbacks in Film: Memory and History*. New York: Routledge, 1989.

Vasse, Denis. *L'ombilic et la voix: Deux enfants en analyse*. Paris: Editions du seuil, 1974.

Wagner, Richard. *Wagner's Prose Works*. Translated by William Ashton Ellis. St. Clair Shores, Mich.: Scholarly Press, 1972.

Weis, Elisabeth, and John Belton, eds. *Film Sound: An Anthology*. New York: Columbia University Press, 1986.

Williams, Linda. "Something Else besides a Mother: *Stella Dallas* and the Maternal Melodrama." *Cinema Journal* 25, no. 1 (Fall 1984).

Zissu, Leonard. "The Copyright Dilemma of the Screen Composer." *Hollywood Quarterly* 1, no. 3 (April 1946): 317.

Zuck, Barbara A. *A History of Musical Americanism*. Ann Arbor: University of Michigan Research Press, 1980.

INDEX